Canyon Gardens

Other Titles by These Authors

V. B. Price

Anasazi Architecture and American Design
(with Baker H. Morrow)

Proceedings of the Mesa Verde Symposium on Anasazi Architecture and American Design
(with Baker H. Morrow)

Albuquerque: A City at the End of the World

Chaco Body (with Kirk Gittings)

Chaco Trilogy

The Oddity: A Novel

Baker H. Morrow, FASLA

Anasazi Architecture and American Design
(with V. B. Price)

Proceedings of the Mesa Verde Symposium on Anasazi Architecture and American Design
(with V. B. Price)

A Harvest of Reluctant Souls: The Memorial of Fray Alonso de Benavides, 1630
(University Press of Colorado)

Best Plants for New Mexico Gardens and Landscapes

Horses like the Wind and Other Stories of Africa
(University Press of Colorado)

A Dictionary of Landscape Architecture

A Tropical Place Like That: Stories of Mexico

CANYON GARDENS

The Ancient Pueblo Landscapes of the American Southwest

EDITED BY

V.B. Price

AND

Baker H. Morrow

University of New Mexico Press

ALBUQUERQUE

Printed in the United States of America

First paperbound printing, 2008
Paperbound ISBN: 978-0-8263-3860-0

21 20 19 18 17 16 2 3 4 5 6 7

Library of Congress Cataloging-in-Publication Data

Canyon gardens : the ancient Pueblo landscapes of the American Southwest / edited by V.B. Price and Baker H. Morrow.
p. cm.
Includes bibliographical references and index.
ISBN-13: 978-0-8263-3859-4 (cloth : alk. paper)
ISBN-10: 0-8263-3859-3 (cloth : alk. paper)
1. Pueblo Indians—Ethnobotany. 2. Landscape architecture—Southwest, New. 3. Sustainable architecture—Southwest, New. 4. Landscape archaeology—Southwest, New. 5. Southwest, New—Environmental conditions. I. Price, V. B. (Vincent Barrett) II. Morrow, Baker H., 1946–
E99.P9C26 2006
712.089'974—dc22
2006029799

Front and back cover image courtesy of Mary Beath

Book design and composition by Damien Shay
Body type is Minion 10/14
Display is Colonial Dame and Papyrus

For our wonderful families.

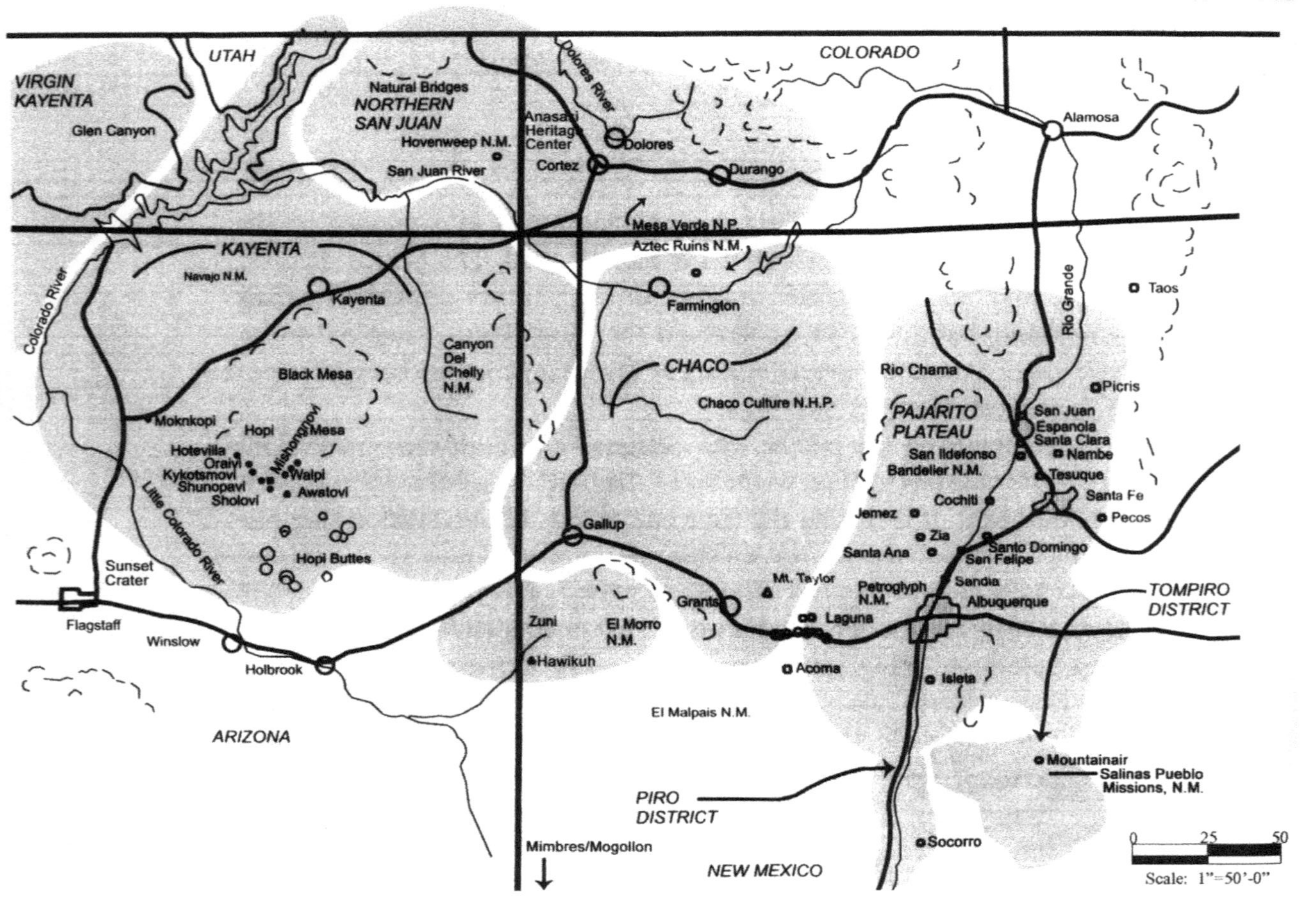

The Puebloan tradition: Ancient settlement areas and modern Pueblos.

Contents

LIST OF ILLUSTRATIONS ix

ACKNOWLEDGMENTS xiii

PROLOGUE xv
by V. B. Price

PART ONE:
Landscape and Garden in the
Land of the Ancestral Puebloans

CHAPTER ONE 1
Europe, the New World, and Buildings Without History
by Stephen H. Lekson

CHAPTER TWO 17
The Berry Gardens of Quarai and the Pocket Terraces of Abó
by Baker H. Morrow

CHAPTER THREE 33
Reading the Ancestral Puebloan Landscape:
A Paleoethnobotanist's Text of Seeds and Wood
by Carol B. Brandt

CHAPTER FOUR 45
A Durable Legacy: Construction and Spatial Analysis
at Sand Canyon Pueblo in the Mesa Verde Country
by Bruce A. Bradley

CHAPTER FIVE 57
Tewa Fields, Tewa Traditions
by Kurt F. Anschuetz

CHAPTER SIX 75
The Estancia: The New Mexican Hacienda
by James E. Ivey

PART TWO:
The Influence of the Ancestral Puebloan Landscape in Our Own Time

CHAPTER SEVEN 87
Zuni Maize
by Mary Beath

CHAPTER EIGHT 113
The Narrative Construction of Landscape: Hopi, 1879–94
by Louis A. Hieb

CHAPTER NINE 125
Conflicting Landscape Values:
The Santa Clara Pueblo and Day School
by Rina Swentzell

CHAPTER TEN 133
Mary Jane Colter and the Ancestral Puebloan Tradition
by Kenneth A. Romig

CHAPTER ELEVEN 145
AMREP and the Pueblos: River's Edge and La Luz
by Anthony Anella

CHAPTER TWELVE 169
Landscape and Survival: Thoughts on New Urbanism and Ancestral Puebloan/Pueblo Strategies for Designing Pragmatic Desert Built Environments
by V. B. Price

CHAPTER THIRTEEN 189
The Chaco Ancestral Puebloans: Lessons Learned
by David E. Stuart

EPILOGUE 205
by Baker H. Morrow

CONTRIBUTORS 209

INDEX 211

List of Illustrations

Fig. 1.1	Casa Grande, near Coolidge, Arizona.	3
Fig. 1.2	A warrior from a Mimbres bowl.	7
Fig. 1.3	Chetro Ketl, one of the largest great houses at Chaco Canyon, northwestern New Mexico.	9
Fig. 1.4	Pueblo Bonito, in Chaco Canyon.	10
Fig. 1.5	Paquimé (also called Casas Grandes), in northern Chihuahua, Mexico.	12
Fig. 2.1	Map of Abó and Quarai.	18
Fig. 2.2	Abó/Tenabó, Tompiro period, typical jacal reconstruction.	19
Fig. 2.3	Petroglyphs at Abó.	21
Fig. 2.4	Water at Abó.	23
Fig. 2.5	View of fields and berry gardens, Quarai.	24
Fig. 2.6	Currants and sand plums, Quarai.	25
Fig. 2.7	Priest's garden with wolfberry and buffalo gourd, Quarai.	26
Fig. 2.8	Shrine at Abó.	28
Fig. 3.1	The archaeologists are removing burnt roofing material from the Great Pit structure at LA 61955.	36
Fig. 3.2	Charred roofing timbers are obvious in the center of the pit structure.	37
Fig. 3.3	A ceramic pipe found on the pit structure bench.	39
Fig. 3.4	Seeds like this heirloom bean (*Phaseolus vulgaris*) are still used in the Night Dances at Zuni Pueblo.	42
Fig. 3.5	Timing of traditional ceremonies is signaled at the Zuni Pueblo according to cosmological cycles.	43
Fig. 4.1	Location of Sand Canyon Pueblo.	46

Fig. 4.2	Sand Canyon Pueblo plan map.	47
Fig. 4.3	Excavated architectural suites at Sand Canyon Pueblo.	48
Fig. 4.4	Construction sequence of Kiva Suite 1206.	49
Fig. 4.5	Examples of differences in kiva suite accesses.	50
Fig. 4.6	Construction sequence of Kiva Suite 501.	51
Fig. 4.7	a) Initial construction and b) pioneer kiva suites.	53
Fig. 4.8	Cliff Palace Community on Mesa Verde.	54
Fig. 5.1	Stone-lined squares, forming garden "grids."	62
Fig. 5.2	Stone implements such as these were commonly used in stone-lined gardens.	63
Fig. 5.3	Stone terraces channel and contain water in sandy soils, even on steep slopes.	64
Fig. 5.4	Grid gardens were often laid out in piñon-juniper woodlands.	65
Fig. 6.1	Las Majadas site, LA 591.	77
Fig. 6.2	Sanchez site, LA 20,000.	78
Fig. 6.3	Pecos Mission estancia.	79
Fig. 6.4	Upper reach—seventeenth-century priests' garden at Pecos.	80
Fig. 6.5	Site of seventeenth-century priests' garden at Pecos.	81
Fig. 7.1	Zuni cornfield.	93
Fig. 7.2	Zuni corn showing multiple "imperfect" ears.	96
Fig. 7.3	South Dakota corn palace.	97
Fig. 7.4	Relationship between areas of cultivated akchin fields and the areas of the watersheds that supply them with water.	101
Fig. 7.5	Old peach orchard.	105
Fig. 7.6	Reviving peach tree.	106
Fig. 8.1	Eagle Cage.	116
Fig. 8.2	Moki Indian.	117
Fig. 9.1	Santa Clara Pueblo.	129
Fig. 10.1	Hopi artisans on the rooftop terrace of Hopi House.	137
Fig. 10.2	Lookout Studio view north.	138
Fig. 10.3	Mary Jane Colter looking out a door of Twin Towers Ruin, Hovenweep National Monument.	139
Fig. 10.4	The Round Tower in Cliff Palace, Mesa Verde National Park.	140
Fig. 10.5	Desert View Watchtower, 2001.	141
Fig. 11.1	River's Edge.	147

Fig. 11.2	Aerial photo of La Luz.	148
Fig. 11.3	Cliff Palace at Mesa Verde.	152
Fig. 11.4	Pueblo Bonito at Chaco Canyon.	153
Fig. 11.5	Non-buildable Peaks.	157
Fig. 11.6	Historic and Archaeological Sites.	158
Fig. 11.7	Prime Agricultural Land.	158
Fig. 11.8	Water Bodies and Drainage.	159
Fig. 11.9	Wildlife Habitat.	160
Fig. 11.10	Steep Slopes.	160
Fig. 11.11	Public Viewshed.	161
Fig. 11.12	Conservation Areas.	162
Fig. 11.13	Buildable Land.	162
Fig. 11.14	House Sites Relative to Buildable Land.	163
Fig. 11.15	Conservation Development.	164
Fig. 11.16	Conventional Development.	165
Fig. 12.1	Ritual played a key role in Ancestral Puebloan life east of the Rio Grande.	171
Fig. 12.2	Swallows' nests with pictographs, Tompiro country.	172
Fig. 12.3	Southwest juniper woodland—classic Ancestral Puebloan settlement area.	174
Fig. 12.4	Franciscan priests created a cloistered environment of their own in the desert within the *conventos* of the seventeenth century.	176
Fig. 12.5	Ancient Puebloan stone masonry was adapted in the early seventeenth century for use in Franciscan mission complexes.	177
Fig. 12.6	Gardens in the ancient Southwest often follow the flow of nearby water.	180
Fig. 13.1	Pueblo Bonito, Chaco Canyon.	191
Fig. 13.2	Chetro Ketl great house, Chaco Canyon.	194
Fig. 13.3	Pueblo Bonito plaza and great house, Chaco Canyon.	195

Acknowledgments

We would like to thank our essayists for their insights, patience, and goodwill.

We would also like to thank Mr. Luther Wilson, director of the University of New Mexico Press, for his unflagging enthusiasm for this project.

We very much appreciate the efforts of Ms. Rosine McConnell, Ms. Amanda Duckert, and Mr. Robert Loftis of Morrow Reardon Wilkinson Miller, Ltd., Landscape Architects, in the preparation of this manuscript. The assistance of Mr. John Folkner with photographs was invaluable.

The wonderful cover painting is by our essayist Mary Beath, to whom we owe a debt of gratitude.

As a special note, the extraordinary work of Dr. James Judge and his colleagues at Chaco has been an ongoing source of inspiration for the editors and for a new generation of students of the Southwest landscape.

Prologue

by V. B. Price

When one thinks of landscape the first images that might come to mind are natural vistas, or household gardens and golf courses that have been "beautifully landscaped" and "manicured." It seems strange in that context to associate landscape with Ancestral Puebloans, an ancient people who inhabited an arid and often inhospitable environment in Arizona and New Mexico more than a millennium ago. The title of this anthology, however, reflects a broader idea of landscape than that normally associated with ornamental gardening. This is not a study of Southwestern archaeology, either, though many references are made to recent theories and studies in this field. This anthology focuses on the man-made or cultural landscape of Ancestral Puebloan urban cultures that have survived into the present as contemporary Pueblo peoples. This is a broad view that is perhaps best represented by the discipline of landscape architecture, a field rarely applied to the analysis of ancient sites.

In this anthology, however, we are more interested in the future than the past, emphasizing the relevance of ancient landscape design and horticultural practices for contemporary American builders and architects, and their clients. The study of this amalgam of exterior spaces with various functions derives to a considerable extent from the interests and observational acumen of the late cultural geographer J. B. Jackson and his magazine *Landscape*, which began in the 1950s. Jackson was among the first to popularize the exploration of utilitarian and social forms and symbols in the built environment other than formal architecture. His interest in vernacular, or popular, landscape patterns and objects is a major inspiration for this endeavor. The authors in this collection have extended Jackson's range beyond his fascination with the modern vernacular to examine the still largely unexplored cultural landscape of Ancestral Puebloans, one of the most heavily studied peoples in the New World.

The idea of cultural landscape in this volume is based on the definition proposed by Baker Morrow in his *A Dictionary of Landscape Architecture*. Cultural landscape is "manipulated, artificially created landscape..., including farms, ranches, estates, roads, cities, gardens, parks, pastures and other areas. Man-made landscape is always an expression of society, culture, and local geography.... [It] may also be the larger, regional landscape in which a society traditionally finds its home, develops its myths, and imagines its future." Landscape architecture, as a field of study and as a design profession, is a practical application of the insights of those who study cultural geography and its human landscape.

Just as J. B. Jackson wrote about everything from invisible international borders, trailers, garages, and billboards to courthouses, hot rods, roadside eateries, and country stores, so the authors of this anthology have explored the particulars of how the Ancestral Puebloans altered, designed, and filled their general landscape with cultural forms and meanings. Not only did Ancestral Puebloan builders and their Pueblo heirs construct great cities and urban precincts, they also engineered complex road systems, astronomical observation points, irrigation systems, shrines, and elaborate horticultural and agricultural microenvironments sufficient to feed and sustain virtually countless generations of their people. Ancestral Puebloan landscape features also include plazas, small patios, horticultural terraces, check dams, shade structures, stairs cut into cliffs, canals, cisterns, stone benches, and a fascinating array of protected fields and mulches suited to the needs of various crops. Still in the early stages of investigation, Ancestral Puebloan landscapes give clues about their inhabitants' skills and strategies for everyday survival amid the quixotic weather patterns, extreme temperature fluctuations, and aridity of the desert Southwest. Long neglected by many scholars, these "commonplace aspects" of the human landscape "teach us a great deal... about ourselves and how we related to the world. It's a matter of learning how to see" (Jackson 1984:ix).

The authors in this anthology see landscape in Jackson's terms as a "formula" in which landscape becomes "a composition of man-made spaces on the land." A landscape, Jackson observes, is not a natural feature of the environment but a synthetic space, a man-made system of spaces superimposed on the face of the land and evolving not according to natural laws but to serve a community" (Jackson 1984:7–8).

Another theme undergirds this anthology, that of applying what ancient cultures in the Southwest can teach us about surviving in a region that's been climatologically pretty much the same across more than a millennium, a high desert surrounded by timbered mountains, hot and dry in the summer and extremely cold in the winter. The editors and authors have taken the approach that Puebloan peoples have a vast storehouse of practical knowledge about how to work the land and build on it, knowledge that has made their pre-urban and urban cultures not only "sustainable" over perhaps the last two thousand years, but also adaptable to changing natural and historic circumstances. Insofar as Puebloan peoples still exist with their culture intact throughout New Mexico and in parts of Arizona, many of them inhabiting sites that have been continuously occupied for as long as nine hundred or more years, we believe contemporary designers and urban planners have important things to learn from these masters of survival.

Their lessons for us far transcend the matters of style and cosmetic design that have preoccupied the image builders of Santa Fe and other resort settings in New Mexico and the West. We believe that in times of global climate change, water scarcities, and upheavals in energy sources and technologies, an observant sensitivity as to how the natural environment works and a mastery of its demands could prove to be immensely useful in designing and retrofitting urban environments in the future.

Perhaps the chief lesson Ancestral Puebloan builders have to teach us is that it's possible to "design with nature," as landscape architect and planner Ian McHarg has famously argued, while at the same time altering natural flows and engineering landscapes to better serve human needs. Ancestral Puebloans were not "primitives" nor "environmentalists" in that romantic sense we have come to associate with those words. They were pragmatists, in a life and death struggle with natural forces, who experimented with and refined an array of agricultural and ceremonial forms that allowed them to survive and culturally flourish.

Designing with nature, in the McHargian sense, means treating the land with the respect it deserves. "Let us ask the land where are the best sites. Let us establish criteria for many different types of excellence responding to a wide range of choice." This is precisely the pragmatic approach that Ancestral Puebloan builders took, and perhaps the chief reason why they survived for two millennia in their drought-ridden landscape.

McHarg puts that pragmatism eloquently when he writes, "In the quest for survival, success, and fulfillment, the ecological view offers an invaluable insight. It shows the way for the man who would be the enzyme of the biosphere—its steward, enhancing the creative fit of man–environment, realizing man's design with nature" (McHarg 1971:197).

But even the Ancestral Puebloans made mistakes, as Southwest archaeologist David Stuart has observed (see Stuart, chapter 13). The massive architectural and landscape engineering projects of the "capital" of Ancestral Puebloans in Chaco Canyon in northwest New Mexico were a sign, Stuart contends, of a hierarchical and rigid will to power that overrode the requirements of sustainable efficiency and savvy environmental flexibility in arid climates.

Chaco was abandoned in the mid-1200s A.D. as much because of an early form of sprawl and uncontrolled growth as a drastic change in weather patterns. Ancestral Puebloans and their Pueblo descendants never made that mistake again.

Modern Americans, however, continue to make that mistake even to this day (see Anella, chapter 11). When one explores booming sprawl development on the West Mesa in Albuquerque, New Mexico, for instance, and then compares normal American suburban tract housing with a unique desert-suited cluster development like the award-winning condominiums of La Luz, designed thirty-five years ago by Antoine Predock, power and efficiency are made as plain as bulldozer swaths on the mesa. Predock is a pioneer in what he has called portable regionalism, adapting a building's design to the cultural context and natural constraints of its surroundings. Albuquerque architect Anthony Anella has taken McHarg's dictum of designing with nature and applied it to the preservation of open space on New Mexico's ranchlands by employing a mapping concept of "conservation planning" for ranchers who wish to subdivide small portions of their holdings and continue raising cattle on the rest. Known as "sieve mapping," because it strains out all the sites that shouldn't be built on, the mapping process isolates the most ecologically desirable building locations, which, quite often in New Mexico, are associated with Ancestral Puebloan ruins. Those ancient builders knew the tricks of the landscape a millennium before it even occurred to us to pay attention to the idiosyncrasies of landforms, sun, and weather.

Creating a new urban agenda for the Southwest from Ancestral Puebloan landscape and design principles seems tailor-made for adoption by alternative planners who work with the microecologies of local landscapes. National Park Service designer and architect Mary Colter, for instance, pioneered the idea of taking the work of Ancestral Puebloan builders seriously by not only building structures at the Grand Canyon that mirror Ancestral Puebloan styles, but also by doing extensive fieldwork near the turn of the last century. She visited Ancestral Puebloan sites and examined how they were built and where they were placed in the landscape (see Romig, chapter 10). What Colter did to influence an enlightened federal bureaucracy, moving it toward indigenous forms and site strategies, is a model approach for all other public buildings and their campus landscapes in the Southwest.

Ancestral Puebloan landscape patterns are virtually self-evident in modern pueblos, where they both express and enforce cultural values and pragmatic survival tactics. Compare, for instance, the humane clustered housing landscape of Santa Clara Pueblo with its militaristic Bureau of Indian Affairs–designed day school nearby (see Swentzell, chapter 9). The social and cultural values reflected in how these two spaces are designed show clearly the cooperative and communitarian attitudes of the Pueblos in conflict with the imposed colonial building patterns of the paternalistic BIA. The basic contrast is between people who consider their full landscape to be embodied with human meaning and spiritual import and people who consider place to be utilitarian and replaceable (see Hieb, chapter 8). As J. B. Jackson would have it, both landscapes, with their "commonplace" details, have much to teach us about the cultures and worldviews of those who built them.

The same is true of Zuni Pueblo, to the far southwest of Santa Clara. After years of legal wrangling, Zuni recently won its case against the federal government claiming years of gross, imposed environmental degradation on its lands and cultural landscape (see Beath, chapter 7). The Zuni used part of the settlement to create the Zuni Sustainable Agriculture Project, creating a relationship between scientific agronomists and Zuni farmers and their traditional maize, a relationship that is uncovering, in part, why Pueblos and their Ancestral Puebloan forebears have been able to create landscapes that allowed to them survive for thousands of years. The basic lesson here is that the Zuni designed their horticulture with the nature of their land, modifying it in minor ways, but never treating it like an obstacle to be radically and disrespectfully altered in such a way that disastrous unintended consequences undermine their survival enterprise.

One can see the connection between the Pueblos' use of landscape and that of their Ancestral Puebloan forebears in the understanding of sustainable, indigenous landscape design that comes from the recent analyses of Ancestral Puebloan sites in south-central New Mexico at the Salinas Pueblo Missions National Monument ruins of Abó and its not too distant neighbor, Quarai (see Morrow, chapter 2). Both were agricultural communities, and yet both inhabited radically different physical landscapes. The elaborate local differences in horticultural techniques and crops between these two ancient pueblos show us the principle of designing, and growing, with nature at work, rather than forcing nature to conform to human convention.

This designing and growing with nature as practiced by Ancestral Puebloans is not merely a byproduct of technical deficiency. Even without wheeled vehicles, or anything other than human labor using wood and stone tools, Ancestral Puebloans could radically alter their natural landscape by sheer force of will, as the gigantic sites of the Chaco phenomenon show us so clearly. The examination of ancient "ecofacts," such as charred seeds and other microscopic plant remains (see Brandt, chapter 3), also allows us to make inferences about the lifeways, importation and domestication of crops, growing practices, and population size in Ancestral Puebloan communities. These techniques give archaeologists the kind of evidence they need to see how earning a living in the Pueblo landscape involved not only agricultural and irrigation techniques, but a cyclical movement through the whole cultivated and cultured landscape in which fields were never completely abandoned, even if left fallow for years (see Anschuetz, chapter 5).

On a regional scale, macroanalysis shows that Ancestral Puebloan builders were capable of sustaining, over generations, great efforts at monumental landscape engineering (see Lekson, chapter 1) that resulted in the construction of roads of exacting accuracy that, for instance, could stretch from Aztec Ruins in northern New Mexico all the way south, some five hundred miles, to Casas Grandes in the Mexican state of Chihuahua. Prehistoric Pueblo people were highly mobile and moved around their vast landscape with periodic regularity, responding to cyclical weather patterns, political upheavals, and social decline.

Cultural landscape studies have, over the last thirty years or so, exploded the conventional view that the most meaningful elements to study in the built environment are the histories of invention and of aesthetic and social theories embodied in formal architecture. In fact, such a common term as "built environment" itself didn't become popular until the 1970s. Archaeology today is breaking away from similar preoccupations with monumental buildings to explore the meanings of the entire built environment of sites (see Bradley, chapter 4), including transitional landscapes such as those created by Pueblo peoples and their Hispanic conquerors that appear when early modern Pueblo peoples operated hacienda-like farms and ranches under the supervision of mission friars before the Pueblo Revolt of 1680 (see Ivey, chapter 6).

Examining ancient vernacular landscapes in the Southwest, and their continuity in contemporary Pueblo communities, gives us a chance to see more clearly than ever, perhaps, how profoundly human beings change their environment to make it more fit for their survival. Chacoan and pre-Columbian Pueblo peoples constructed huge buildings of timber, mud, and stone, requiring vast amounts of human labor; built thousands of miles of roads, some of them straight as an arrow; cultivated every suitable place in their immediate environment; and mastered the intricacies of mulching, flood farming, and the construction of water weirs and check dams. They were so successful at making over their surroundings to serve their needs, and so socially and culturally resilient and responsive to change, that they are the only North American Native peoples to survive European contact virtually intact.

What modern designers, planners, and builders see when they study the immense sophistication of the Ancestral Puebloan landscape is that while Puebloan peoples modified their surroundings, they did so for the most part in ways that were extremely sensitive to how climate, landforms, and their survival needs interacted. Puebloan peoples in Chaco Canyon did, it seems clear now, fall prey to what Lewis Mumford once called "mindless giantism," a kind of early form of sprawl that attempted to dominate the landscape rather than cooperate with it and modestly channel its great powers to serve human needs. The Chacoan experiment failed, but Ancestral Puebloans and their Pueblo descendants did not. The unprecedented flourishing of the Pueblos' culture into the twenty-first century is bound up, I believe, in their relationship to the land and the way they work with it and not design against it. As cultural landscape studies in the Southwest evolve over this century, a more detailed account of the startling success and sophistication of Pueblo survival techniques may well be revealed. In the water-scarce world of the future, it will be up to modern builders and designers, then, to take their clues from the past to construct more sustaining and resource-efficient contemporary desert landscapes.

References Cited

Jackson, J. B.

1984 *Discovering the Vernacular Landscape*. New Haven, CT: Yale University Press.

McHarg, Ian

1971 *Design with Nature*. New York: Doubleday/Natural History Press.

PART ONE

Landscape and Garden in the Land of the Ancestral Puebloans

Chapter One

Europe, the New World, and Buildings Without History

by Stephen H. Lekson

Ancestral Puebloan sites and land use patterns disclose that although pre-Pueblo people had a very different view of architecture than we do, their view of cultural landscape was surprisingly similar to our own, dominated as it was by high mobility and something approaching superhighways. Ancestral Puebloan-built environments were not bulwarks against change and monuments to permanence. Their landscape architecture was geared for a Pueblo worldview that was animated by histories of migration, fluidity of movement, and a sense of space and distance that was not limited to specific sites. In archaeologist Stephen Lekson's view, Ancestral Puebloans occupied whole regions rather than single sites, moving and changing to meet their needs. The whole Southwest itself can be examined as a gigantic cultural landscape, full of human artifacts. Ancestral Puebloan/Pueblo culture was "far more dynamic and transitory than we used to believe," he writes. Ancestral Puebloans both inhabited huge landscape spaces and modified those spaces. As an example, Lekson describes the massive "landscape monument of the Great North Road" linking Chaco Canyon and Aztec in the thirteenth century A.D. *Road building, waterworks of many kinds, agricultural spaces, sacred precincts, patios, and middens are some of the Ancestral Puebloan artifacts studied by landscape historians.*

"Pueblo culture . . . has a long homogeneous history behind it, and we have special need of knowledge of it because the cultural life of these peoples is so at variance with that of the rest of North America" (Benedict [1934] 1989:59).

Ruth Benedict's *Patterns of Culture*, from which this (slightly abbreviated) quote comes, was and remains one of the most influential anthropology books in American libraries. First published in 1934, it has gone into dozens of editions, translations, and reprints. It was not the first, but it is certainly the most eloquent and influential popular declaration of "cultural relativism"—the diversity, plasticity, and intrinsic worth of the astonishing variety of human societies. It is cited today, in fields far beyond anthropology, as a classic introduction of anthropological insights into American intellectual life.

Benedict studied Zuni. Her detailed accounts of Pueblos in *Patterns of Culture* were particularly influential. It is from Benedict and generations of her readers/interpreters that we receive an idealized vision of Pueblos as happy, peaceful, harmonious, egalitarian, and permanent. Each of these terms is freighted with meanings—what's "happy"?—but my focus here is on the last, and lasting, term: "permanent." Puebloan and Ancestral Puebloan ("Anasazi") architecture is solid, enduring, permanent. At Chaco Canyon, the walls are a thousand years old: solid. At Mesa Verde, cliff dwellings (we are told) look just as they left them, at A.D. 1300: enduring. At Casa Grande, in Arizona, an adobe tower rises four stories tall, five centuries after abandonment: permanent (figure 1.1).

These great ruins came to the public attention just before the turn of the nineteenth century through exposition exhibits, illustrated weeklies, and lantern-slide lectures. Their antiquity and permanence appealed to the United States, a nation of immigrants keenly conscious of its intellectual and political adolescence. A century later, that same quality appeals to our present rootlessness: we move too much and are comforted that someone lived here before us, someone who *stayed in place*. The ruins today are empty, but contemporary visitors—illogically, but powerfully—experience continuity, deep history, and permanence. That depth-in-place is carefully nurtured by the town fathers and tourism promoters at pueblos such as Acoma and Oraibi, both of which lay claim to be the oldest continuously occupied settlements in the United States. At both, there is evidence of settlement as far back as A.D. 1100. We find that impressive; no U.S. cities are that old nor could they be, unless Vikings did more than we know. But wait a minute: every major European city, back in Europe, is that old and most are far older. Euro-Americans come from historical and architectural traditions in which a thousand years is yesterday. Rome rules still, in the academy and its awards.

Is it only in contrast to the upstart United States that Puebloan permanence seems remarkable? Well, no: it is remarkable to many Pueblo people as well. For many Pueblo towns, it wasn't planned this way. They have long, detailed histories of migrations and movements, seeking a center place. Some clans and towns found that center place, the right place. Many others have not; they were arrested in their search by a change of environment: the arrival of conquistadores. The

Fig. 1.1 Casa Grande, near Coolidge, Arizona. This "great house" was built about A.D. 1250 to 1300 by the Hohokam. Pima legends identify Casa Grande as the house of an overlord who was slain in a revolt by the people against their oppressors. Photo by Stephen H. Lekson.

King of Spain granted Pueblo towns their lands, four leagues square, homelands in which they were expected to live. In effect, those grants pinned the Pueblos down, like butterflies on a mounting board. When the United States conquered northern Mexico in 1848, we promised by treaty to honor those grants and perpetuate those homelands. We honored them mainly in the breach. But, failing to dispossess the Pueblos entirely, we came to terms with their territories and reserved Pueblo places for Pueblo peoples—or so we thought. We will return to the misfit between cadastral lands and mythic landscapes, below.

Many Pueblos were caught, their movement arrested. I have spoken with people from Rio Grande pueblos who say, in effect, "If you people weren't here, we'd be in Mexico by now." Their migrations are incomplete, stopped by Euro-American incursions. The last five hundred years may be an aberration, a pause in larger cycles of movement. Who knows? In the unknown future, that enforced interruption may end and the clan movements begin again.

Historical continuity is not inconsistent with mobility. Pueblo towns and clans have long histories that cover lots of territory. According to one clan's story, the people originated in central Mexico and moved north in a series of stops and starts to end at Hopi (Washburn 1995). Another history begins in the Grand Canyon, covers most of the Southwest, and ends at Zuni (Ferguson and Hart 1985). Each history is different, but all are stories of movement over vast distances.

Or, rather, distances we today consider vast. We think nothing of hopping on a plane in L.A. and landing in New York a few oxygen-deprived, foully fed hours later. While the flight itself is unpleasant, the distance is nothing on a jet. People do it every day. If, however, we walked that same distance, we'd expect a page in *National Geographic* and fifteen minutes of fame on the Discovery Channel. Distances deceive. Our own ancestors walked much farther and so, certainly, did Native Americans. Ancient worlds were not small (another topic to which we will return, below). We judge the marches of ancient peoples by our own tender feet: a hundred miles is phenomenal, a thousand miles impossible. Traditional histories and archaeology tell us that distances of a hundred or a thousand miles were not unusual; they were typical.

Begin at the beginning: the peopling of the New World. Archaeology and Native history tell different tales. Archaeology says the many millions of New World peoples came, originally, from the Old World, primarily from northeastern Asia. The routes and timings are matters for research, and additional Old World sources may yet emerge, but science is united in the understanding that the first Native Americans came from other continents. Those are astonishingly long distances—jet plane distances—when the societies involved had profoundly simple means of transport. Compared to the later civilizations of Mexico and Peru, the first immigrants were technologically primitive people. Yet science has no problem with (and no alternative to) their transcontinental migrations, movements on scales correctly called vast.

Native histories start closer to home: Pueblo peoples emerged from earlier worlds out onto the continent they now occupy, the world Euro-Americans call "New." Indian writers and thinkers are almost all united in their rejection of the "Bering Strait" theory (Deloria 1995). Many Pueblo peoples emerged somewhere in or near the Southwest; other Pueblo peoples emerged elsewhere and walked to the Southwest.

Curiously, archaeology admits transcontinental migrations but balks at intraregional movements. Pueblo migration stories are culturally secure, restricted in their distribution. Anthropologists, nevertheless, learned and published many such stories in the late nineteenth and early twentieth centuries. These histories are not obscure and early archaeologists used them. Modern archaeology (for reasons that made sense at the time but which need not detain us here) rejected migration as a valid area of inquiry. An influential textbook of the 1970s, when baby boomer archaeologists trained, dismissed migration as "an old, stale, overworked concept" and "a nonprinciple" (Martin and Plog 1973:337). Most Southwestern archaeologists agreed. Migration took a hike and all but disappeared from professional discourse, and with it went the concept of an extended cultural landscape.

Archaeological thinking discouraged migration, but some movement was allowed. "Mobility" is archaeological jargon for movement, and specifically for movement of people to and from resources. Seasonal mobility centered on the search for harvestable plants or fattening game, or the outflux of farmers from a central town to villages nearer their fields. Longer term mobility might take whole settlements from one valley farmed to exhaustion to another valley fresh for agriculture (Nelson and Anyon 1996).

An astonishing study by Michael Berry, published in 1982, pushed this kind of mobility to (and perhaps beyond) its limits. Berry compiled graphs of all the tree-ring dates from the Pueblo regions of the Colorado Plateau and then compiled a similar graph of all the carbon-14 dates from the Hohokam areas of the southern Arizona deserts (where trees for tree-ring dating were few and far between). The two graphs were strikingly complementary—that is, a decade for which there were many tree rings on the Colorado Plateau seemed to be a decade with very few carbon-14 dates in the desert and, conversely, where there were many carbon-14 dates from the desert, there were comparatively few tree-ring dates from the Colorado Plateau. There were many technical problems with Berry's study but the overall pattern was remarkable. Based on the number of dates, it appeared that population "peaks" on the plateau were population "valleys" in the desert, and vice versa. Berry suggested mobility on a huge scale. When the environment was sour on the Colorado Plateau, the people archaeologists call "Ancestral Puebloan" went south to the very different environment of the deserts and became the people archaeologists call "Hohokam." They changed places, changed clothes, changed pottery, and changed architecture. This was too much for most archaeologists. The geographic scale was far larger than we envisioned for economic mobility. And, worse yet, the idea that people might change their archaeological appearance ran absolutely counter to long-held conventions that pottery styles, architectural details, and other material items identified social units; that is, pots equaled people. Berry suggested that the relationship of past peoples to pots, buildings, and other artifacts was more complex and plastic. His book was torched in the reviews and its ideas anathematized.

The acceptable scales of archaeological mobility were much smaller than Berry's interregional movements. Berry's daring scales were much smaller than the migrations described in Pueblo traditional histories. Mobility, as archaeologists envisioned it, was small, tidy, and contained; it was not on the scale of hypothetical migrations. It took a court case, or series of court cases, to shake the firm faith that Pueblo people moved only within small, well-defined districts, if at all. *The Zuni Atlas* by T. J. Ferguson and E. Richard Hart appeared in 1985, and it was in large part a product of a lawsuit by Zuni against the U.S. government for loss of their traditional lands. The Pueblo of Zuni, at the turn of the nineteenth century, was a dense, almost urban town. A few smaller villages were scattered about the small valley around the principal town, but the total area of built Zuni was small. The Zuni had a grant from the King of Spain, but even that area was not enough for Zuni life. The Zuni world was big. *The Zuni Atlas* established an "area of Zuni Sovereignty" at 1846 (a date significant for legal considerations) by mapping various aspects of traditional Zuni land use in the mid-nineteenth century: agriculture, grazing, hunting, wild plant collection, mineral collection, and religious use. Taken together, the area necessary for sustained land use was enormous: 250 miles east-to-west and 150 miles north-to-south with Zuni itself near the middle. The regions necessary for some aspects of Zuni life—religious use, in particular—were much, much larger. But the court did not accept religious use as a basis for damages.

The map of Zuni migrations, "general direction of Zuni origin and migration" (Ferguson and Hart 1985:20), was not, apparently, admissible. Zuni migrations ranged over enormous areas, from the Colorado River to the Rio Grande and back again, with some clans disappearing off the map entirely to the south, to the "land of everlasting sunshine." Like the courts, archaeologists regarded this map as a curiosity—a cartographic representation of myth that was of great interest but little practical application. Migration histories were relegated to ritual: important, powerful, but largely or entirely symbolic. Similarly, migration itself was still, for most archaeologists, a "nonprinciple." (But not all archaeologists: Jefferson Reid and his colleagues maintained a measured interest in migration through the 1970s and '80s as the most sensible way to understand ruins in the mountains of southern Arizona.)

With the inevitability of a pendulum, migration has returned to archaeology. Why? Data, perhaps, triumphed over doctrine. The high-profile research of Crow Canyon Archaeological Center near Mesa Verde, Colorado, focused on the thirteenth-century abandonment of that famous district (Varien et al. 1996). Abandonment is the reverse of the coin of migration, and Crow Canyon's research led to a renewed interest in the old chestnut question "Where did they go?" (Cameron 1995). Dam construction spurred a huge archaeological project in the Tonto Basin of Arizona—one of the largest field projects ever. In the Tonto Basin, migration emerged as the best framework for understanding the bewildering variety of pottery and architecture that was discovered (Clark 2001). Migration is back, and it's hot.

Recall Ruth Benedict's characterization of Pueblo peoples in *Patterns of Culture*. The smallness and containment of Pueblo life as depicted by Benedict and generations of interpreters influenced by *Patterns of Culture* was unrealistic; the Zunis proved it in court and archaeologists recognized it in the field. Pueblo life and Pueblo prehistory played out not within towns, but over vast geographic regions. Migrations were followed by complicated sequences of smaller buildings, abandonments, and reestablishments of villages within the small Zuni River valley and its uplands (Ferguson and Hart 1985; Kintigh 1985). After the Spanish arrived, separate Zuni villages coalesced into a single town for defense. Whole

Fig. 1.2 A warrior from a Mimbres bowl. The Mimbres of southwestern New Mexico were contemporaries of Chaco Canyon, about A.D. 1020 to 1130. Their villages were quite large but constructed of materials that did not leave impressive ruins. Mimbres art, in contrast, is well represented in museums around the world. Photo by Stephen H. Lekson.

towns were rebuilt on high defensible mesas or built again on valley bottoms nearer farm fields, consistent with perceived threats.

What about the other elements of the Benedictine vision: happy, peaceful, egalitarian? We cannot fruitfully explore happiness here: we can wish that it is so, and pass on to peace. Peaceful the Zunis are today, but not so in the past. In their histories, Zunis tell of an epic three-day-long battle with the Black People, who happened to occupy lands the Zunis wanted (Wright 1988). The first serious encounter with the Spanish was a battle, too, and it was not the last. In the past, when necessary, Zunis waged war and they chronicle their battles in their histories. They were not the exception: recent work by Steven LeBlanc (1999) demonstrates the pervasiveness of violence and warfare in the archaeological past throughout the Southwest (figure 1.2). The Pueblo Southwest was not a peaceful place; its peoples fussed and fought like human beings all over the world, all through history. The intensity of violence varied from raiding to full-scale war, with a remarkable interval of peace from A.D. 900 to 1250—to which we will return.

War, not peace. What remains of Benedict's Zuni? Egalitarianism: the absence of leaders and personal aggrandizement: "Personal authority is perhaps the most vigorously disparaged trait in Zuni. A man who thirsts for power or knowledge, who wishes to be as they scornfully phrase it 'a leader of his people' receives nothing but censure," says Benedict ([1934] 1989:99). But Benedict notes that Zuni war chiefs have executive authority and political power. Today their functions are only a pale reflection of the office's past duties. War requires leaders, and the traditional Zuni histories feature Warriors of the Bow, Bow Priests, and Twin War Gods who lead the fighting and who figure prominently in Zuni history and Zuni life. Benedict's Zuni was far removed from the precolonial situation of Chaco and Mesa Verde. In the past, there were leaders, political power, and many of those traits that Zuni has learned to avoid. In my reconstruction of Zuni political structure at mid-nineteenth century, a hereditary council—more priests than kings—ruled the town and the people through a proto-bureaucracy of appointed officials; the ruling council was supported by taxes and lived in a special building at the exact center of the world (Lekson 1999). An attenuated version of this political structure survives at Zuni (and other pueblos) today, and I think that a far stronger hierarchy, with real kings wielding real power, existed in the more distant Pueblo past, yet another topic to which we will soon return.

Not much is left of Benedict's Zuni. It inspired a great many coffee-table book essays and architectural histories, which perpetuate her Edenic—but mistaken—version of Pueblo life. Permanent, peaceful, egalitarian? For architecture, the key point is that nothing lasts forever. The Pueblo sense of place is wonderfully centered; but the Pueblo past was dynamic, active, and mobile. The Pueblos may be in their middle places today, but getting there was much more than half the fun. The ruined pueblos of the Colorado Plateau were *meant* to be impermanent.

Zuni architecture—and Pueblo architecture—were far more dynamic, more transitory than we are accustomed to believe. The prehistoric towns of Zuni (and the other pueblos) were not built for the ages. They typically lasted about a generation (or even less) before the towns were abandoned, relocated, and rebuilt (Kintigh 1985; Varien et al. 1996). That pattern seems typical for the entire Pueblo region. The famous cliff dwellings of Mesa Verde were short lived, although they were sometimes built atop the ruins of earlier ages. Archaeological sites may have considerable "depth"—that is, they may show occupations spanning several centuries—but those occupations are almost always discontinuous. A pit house occupied in the seventh century lies beneath a pueblo of the tenth century, which was reoccupied or rebuilt in the thirteenth century. Prehistoric sites with long continuous occupations—like Acoma and Oraibi—are rare indeed. Impermanence was the norm.

There were, of course, exceptions. A handful of the thousands of large pueblo ruins that dot the Colorado Plateau had longer continuous histories, which we would call permanence. Most notable of these were the "great houses" of Chaco

Fig. 1.3 Chetro Ketl, one of the largest great houses at Chaco Canyon, northwestern New Mexico. Constructed between A.D. 1020 and 1125, this huge edifice required the procurement of over twenty-five thousand large timbers, from forests fifty miles away. Photo by Stephen H. Lekson.

Canyon and its region (figure 1.3). These magnificent tenth- through twelfth-century buildings were remarkable for their longevity. Pueblo Bonito, perhaps the largest great house, was begun in the mid-ninth century and completed in the early twelfth century. All the evidence points to continuous occupation and to a nearly continuous series of building events at Pueblo Bonito (figure 1.4).

What were great houses? They were not pueblos. They were not the short-lived farming villages represented by the other 95 percent of the archaeological sites of Chaco's era. Nor were they the longer-lived towns we see today at Acoma, Oraibi, and Zuni. The great houses, in my opinion, were palaces—monumentally proportioned buildings that combined and encompassed elite residences, warehouses, central governmental and religious facilities, and settings for public events. They were seats of government. There are Native American histories saying just that: the great houses of Chaco Canyon were the palaces of kings. Both the Native stories and the archaeological arguments are far too long to repeat here (see Lekson 1999). The key point is this: the Pueblo past was rather different from our visions of the Pueblo present, and markedly unlike Ruth Benedict's stereotypic view of Zuni as a town full of happy, peaceful egalitarians.

Things happened in the ancient Southwest. There was history, with the full sweep of human history everywhere. Somehow, Southwestern archaeology lost history. Adolph Bandelier, the great pioneer Southwestern archaeologist, concluded his monumental *Final Report of Investigations among the Indians of the*

Fig. 1.4 Pueblo Bonito, in Chaco Canyon. The largest and most important of the Chaco great houses, Pueblo Bonito fell into ruin after construction ceased about A.D. 1125. It remained an important place: the great kivas of Pueblo Bonito were maintained (refloored, reroofed) into the thirteenth century. Photo by Stephen H. Lekson.

Southwestern United States with: "The picture which can be dimly traced of this past is a very modest and unpretending one. No great cataclysms of nature, no waves of destruction on a large scale, either natural or human, appear to have interrupted the slow and tedious development of the people" (Bandelier 1892:590). They were, in Eric Wolf's words, "people without history." Bandelier did not credit the Pueblo traditional histories, nor did he recognize the archaeology of power, war, and events. He was wrong, but his view of a pallid, colorless, boring Southwest pervades the textbooks and thinking of all the generations of archaeologists who followed him.

A new Southwest is emerging, with governments, cities, wars, peace, cataclysms, and—in short—history. Treating archaeological information on the larger geographic scales of the Pueblo traditional histories suggests a very different Southwest than we are accustomed to see in coffee-table books, national parks, and Discovery Channel specials. Like any scholarly or scientific endeavor, we do not have the story "right" in every detail, and we probably never will; but the vast difference in tone and genre of the new histories signals a shift in our understanding of the ancient Southwest that, for staid archaeology, is revolutionary.

One version (my version) of the ancient Southwest has capitals and kings, starting at Chaco Canyon (A.D. 850–1125) and moving to Aztec Ruins (A.D. 1110–1280). Early capitals often moved; Rome was the exception and I am suggesting nothing like Rome in the ancient Southwest. Rather, the political structure of Chaco and Aztec was probably much like thousands of Mesoamerican kingdoms and Mississippian chiefdoms. Indeed, the term "chiefdom" can be usefully replaced by "kingdom" as long as we recognize we are talking about Bronze-Age Irish kings, not Louis XIV.

Chaco and Aztec were cities, comparable in size and population to cities in many early political systems. That is to say, they were small: five thousand people at most and more likely half that size. Their architecture was modestly monumental and cosmologically symbolic; again, characteristics of many early capitals. They were short lived: a few centuries for Chaco, a century and a half for Aztec. Many early capitals were evanescent. David Anderson describes Mississippian chiefdoms as "cycling"—a bubbling stew of short-lived capitals that boom and bust in rapid succession. So, too, in Mesoamerica.

I do not claim that Chaco and Aztec rivaled Tula in Mexico or Cahokia in the Mississippi valley. Indeed, I claim only that the political structure of the ancient Southwest was an attenuated version of political power as it was expressed, prehistorically, across all the agricultural regions of North America. The Mississippian chiefdoms are gone; Tula and the myriad of smaller Mesoamerican capitals are gone; so, too, is Southwestern political complexity.

Where did it go? When people get power, and power becomes institutionalized in kingship and monumentalized in cities, power tends to perpetuate itself until natural or human cataclysm puts it out. I argue that the political capital of the Pueblo Southwest shifted, about A.D. 1275, to the amazing site of Paquimé at Casas Grandes, Chihuahua, Mexico (figure 1.5). This ruin is far less known than Mesa Verde, but it dwarfs every other Southwestern ruin in its architectural complexity, wealth, and trappings of power. The leaders of Chaco and Aztec appealed to the architecture and symbolism of Mesoamerica to legitimize their power. Paquimé cemented the Southwest's distant connections to the south. Great I-shaped ball courts, colonnades, small pyramids, and other Mexican forms were the architectural expression. Heavily charged artifacts and objects were also deployed in the service of the leaders: copper bells in astonishing quantity and quality, ocean shell by the ton, and tropical birds kept for their plumage. In pre-Columbian societies, feathers were not fluff: they were used on regalia as enormously important symbols of prestige and power. For Aztecs, certain feathers were far more valuable than gold. Chaco imported tropical birds over a thousand miles of mountains and wastelands. Paquimé imported the birds and the specialized knowledge it took to raise them and bred macaws on almost commercial scales.

I believe that the rulers of Chaco, Aztec, and Paquimé were closely related, genetically or symbolically. Each capital referenced the preceding capital through architectural continuities and directional symbolism. There are many examples, but the most dramatic was siting: Aztec was due north of Chaco and Paquimé

Fig. 1.5 Paquimé (also called Casas Grandes), in northern Chihuahua, Mexico. This great city rose about A.D. 1250 and ended (perhaps in violence) by A.D. 1450. Paquimé was the most cosmopolitan Southwestern center, with huge quantities of imported luxury goods and monumental forms borrowed from the architecture of Mesoamerica, far to the south. Photo by Stephen H. Lekson.

was due south of both Chaco and Aztec. We know this was not a fluke or coincidence because Aztec was linked back to Chaco in a massive landscape monument we call the Great North Road. Ancient Pueblo roads were monuments in the cultural landscape, symbolizing the connection of distant places to centers, or past places to present places. The Great North Road was the most elaborate and most important example of the latter, a "road through time" (Fowler and Stein 1992) linking the first capital, Chaco, to its successor, Aztec. I believe that the same directional symbolism—much like the Islamic *qibla* that orients all mosques to Mecca—sited Paquimé due south of Chaco.

The rulers of Chaco, Aztec, and Paquimé are remembered in Pueblo traditional histories, but not kindly. Chaco and Aztec are collapsed, historically, into a place called (by some Pueblos) White House: an astonishing city of wealth and prosperity, where gods lived among the people until the people themselves sought power and fought with the holy spirits. The assumption of power had two results: the gods left to become the kachinas of modern Pueblo cosmology, and the people themselves departed, due south, to raise parrots. (This is my slant on a compilation of pueblo histories [Lekson 1999].) Colleagues and acquaintances from the Rio Grande pueblos have told me: "We remember Chaco, but we don't talk about it because bad things happened there"—things that were highly inappropriate to modern Pueblo life, like political power.

And other things, too: the political power of Chaco and Aztec was enforced. The reign of Chaco and the early history of Aztec were times of unprecedented peace, a fact established by Steven LeBlanc (1999). Before Chaco, there was endemic and escalating raiding—small in scale but sufficient to cause aggregation into the large, defensible settlements of the eighth and ninth centuries. Widespread, low-level violence ends with the ascendancy of Chaco, but another form of violence appears: the mass execution and mutilation of groups of people ranging from six to sixty or more in number. Christy Turner (Turner and Turner 1999) identified this pattern of violence during a time otherwise remarkable for its real peace. We know there was peace because the tightly aggregated villages of the eighth and ninth centuries deconstructed into single-family houses that were scattered in undefended farmsteads across the Colorado Plateau. Population was increasing but, except for the capital, urbanization decreased. The brutal events Turner described took place in that bucolic setting of farmsteads. We know of only a few-score such events, in several thousands of farmsteads, but we can be sure that when these people were executed and mutilated, the event was widely known. I think that Turner's events were directed by Chaco, enforcing the political system that created and kept the peace. Things happened at White House that were bad.

Around 1275, it ends. The political power of Chaco and Aztec vanishes from the Colorado Plateau, and full-scale warfare begins. Village on village, and alliances of several villages, fought, and the sites we see are burned and sacked (LeBlanc 1999). Warfare continued until the arrival of the Spanish.

This is history: kings, governments, wars, and even (perhaps) rebellions, all recalled in traditional accounts. There were also natural cataclysms and catastrophes. In the early eleventh century, a volcano erupted northeast of modern Flagstaff. With the exception of the Grants malpais in New Mexico, no eruptions had occurred in the Southwest for thousands of years. The volcano was not large, but its plume was enormously tall and charged with nonstop lightning and thunder. It could be seen from Chaco and from most of the Pueblo Southwest. We do not know how long this event lasted, perhaps until 1250. The effect was profound: monumental structures were built at the base of this towering pillar of smoke and lightning. Indeed, at Wupatki, there is a combination of Chaco-style great houses, great kivas, and Hohokam ball courts (oval ball courts characteristic of ancient non-Pueblo peoples of southern Arizona). The volcano was a magnet for esoteric and religious architecture from across the wide Southwest, and in the great house at Wupatki, archaeologists found more tropical birds than at Chaco.

What other signs and portents influenced political and religious decision making we do not know, but we are finding out. Full and partial eclipses were particularly frequent in the era of Ancestral Puebloan abandonments, compared to earlier centuries. Larger natural disasters shaped history, too. The Great Drought of 1275–1300 coincides exactly with the demise of Aztec Ruins, the rise of Paquimé, and the onset of warfare among Pueblo peoples of the northern Southwest. Great floods destroyed the Hohokam civilization about 1360, with historic ripples and repercussions that we are only beginning to understand.

I do not attempt to present, here, a full history of the ancient Southwest. I offer these anecdotes and examples to assert that there *was* real history, comparable to the histories of Mesoamerican and Mississippian kingdoms, comparable to early Old World sites and states. For over a century since Bandelier, we recognize no "great cataclysms ... [that] interrupted the slow and tedious development of the people." The Pueblos, for us, had (in Benedict's words) "a long homogeneous" past. If I were a Pueblo person, I think I would resent those views. Things happened: good things, bad things, and—occasionally—ugly things. The story of the Pueblos was as complicated and complex as any other people's history.

What are the implications of this new Southwest for our understanding and appreciation of its built environment? Instead of visiting Mesa Verde and seeing farming villages of happy, peaceful people living in harmony with nature, think instead of Cliff Palace as the last gasp of the frontier citizens of a crumbling empire, as Aztec's power wanes and warfare erupts. Instead of viewing Chaco as a spiritual center worthy of a Harmonic Convergence, see instead an authoritarian capital with warriors ready to make brutal examples of families who broke the rules. Conventional interpretations could still be true—Chaco could have been a spiritual center, and the villagers of Mesa Verde almost certainly tried to be happy, peaceful, and harmonious—but the larger sweep of history, good and bad, should also color our reading of the Pueblo past. Government and religion are not exclusive, but peasants live one life, kings another. This history is remembered in Native traditions; as students of Pueblo architecture and landscape architecture, we should remember that history as well. We have made the Pueblos "people without history," and our appreciation of their buildings and their landscapes is poorer for it. Southwestern ruins are historical monuments, memorials to dynamic, active history.

References Cited

Bandelier, Adolf F.

1892 *Final Report of Investigations among the Indians of the Southwestern United States, Carried on Mainly in the Years from 1880 to 1885, Part II.* Papers of the Archaeological Institute of America. Cambridge, MA: J. Wilson and Son.

Benedict, Ruth

[1934] 1989 *Patterns of Culture*. Boston: Houghton Mifflin.

Berry, Michael S.

1982 *Time, Space, and Transition in Anasazi Prehistory*. Salt Lake City: University of Utah Press.

Cameron, Catherine M., ed.
1995 Migration and the Movement of Southwestern Peoples. *Journal of Anthropological Archaeology* 14 (2): 104–24.
Clark, Jeffrey J.
2001 *Tracking Prehistoric Migrations: Pueblo Settlers among the Tonto Basin Hohokam*. Tucson: University of Arizona Press.
Deloria, Vine, Jr.
1995 *Red Earth, White Lies: Native Americans and the Myth of Scientific Fact*. New York: Scribner.
Ferguson, T. J., and E. Richard Hart
1985 *A Zuni Atlas*. Norman: University of Oklahoma Press.
Fowler, Andrew P., and John R. Stein
1992 The Anasazi Great House in Space, Time, and Paradigm. In *Anasazi Regional Organization and the Chaco System*, ed. David E. Doyel, 101–22. Papers of the Maxwell Museum of Anthropology 5. Albuquerque: Maxwell Museum of Anthropology, University of New Mexico.
Kintigh, Keith W.
1985 *Settlement, Subsistence and Society in Late Zuni Prehistory*. Tucson: University of Arizona Press.
LeBlanc, Steven A.
1999 *Prehistoric Warfare in the American Southwest*. Salt Lake City: University of Utah Press.
Lekson, Stephen H.
1999 *Chaco Meridian: Centers of Political Power in the Ancient Southwest*. Walnut Creek, CA: Altamira Press.
Martin, Paul S., and Fred Plog
1973 *The Archaeology of Arizona*. Garden City, NJ: Doubleday/Natural History Press.
Nelson, Ben A., and Roger Anyon
1996 Fallow Valleys: Asynchronous Occupations in Southwestern New Mexico. *Kiva* 61 (3): 275–94.
Turner, Christie G., II, and Jacqueline A. Turner
1999 *Man Corn*. Salt Lake City: University of Utah Press.
Varien, Mark D., William D. Lipe, Michael A. Adler, Ian M. Thompson, and Bruce A. Bradley
1996 Southwestern Colorado and Southeastern Utah Settlement Patterns: A.D. 1100 to 1300. In *The Prehistoric Pueblo World, A.D. 1150–1350*, ed. Michael A. Adler, 86–113. Tucson: University of Arizona Press.
Washburn, Dorothy K.
1995 *Living in Balance: The Universe of the Hopi, Zuni, Navajo, and Apache*. Philadelphia: University of Pennsylvania Museum of Archaeology and Anthropology.
Wright, Barton, ed.
1988 *The Mythic World of the Zuni, as Written by Frank Hamilton Cushing*. Albuquerque: University of New Mexico Press.

Chapter Two

The Berry Gardens of Quarai and the Pocket Terraces of Abó

by Baker H. Morrow

The Tompiro people who built the great pueblo at Abó and their Tiwa-speaking neighbors at Quarai, both part of the Salinas Pueblo Missions National Monument in New Mexico, engaged in such a wide range of horticultural methods and landscape management techniques that they virtually ensured themselves enough redundancy to survive the ever-shifting and unpredictable climate of New Mexico. Though these pueblos were located only fourteen miles apart, Baker H. Morrow, FASLA, observes that each town's farming and gardening strategies were so deeply rooted in the uniqueness of its landscape that they give modern researchers a detailed view of the possibilities for landscape development practiced and experienced by ancient Puebloan peoples.

The Southwestern landscape history to be found at Abó and Quarai is, perhaps, unusually vivid because of the author's long acquaintance with these towns as a field researcher. In his analysis of connected features in a larger countryside, Morrow suggests that much of the original landscape remains to teach us about the lives of the ancient people who created it.

Zapato Creek. Espinoso Creek. Quarai. Abó.

By the fourteenth century A.D., there was a thriving collection of Pueblo towns and hamlets a little east and a little south of the Manzano range in central New Mexico. Some of these settlements, which were built by Tiwa-speaking and

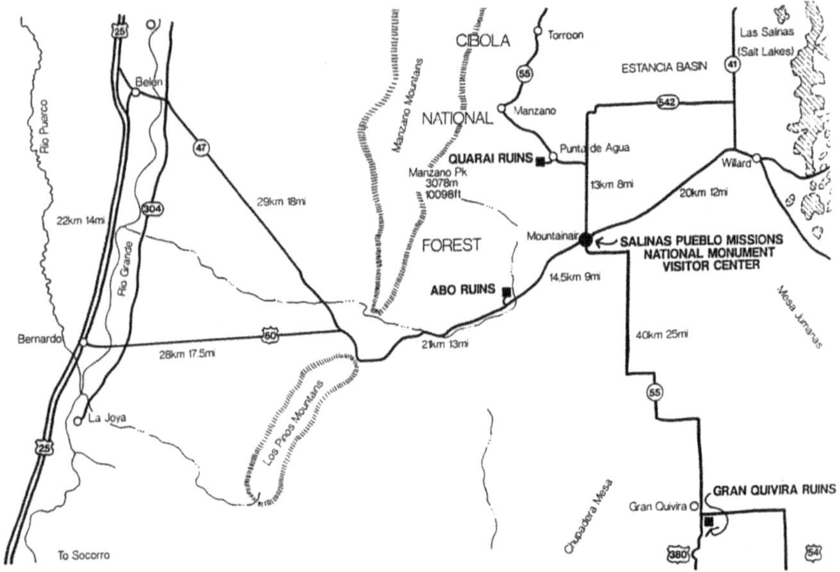

Fig. 2.1 Map of Abó and Quarai by MRWM Landscape Architects.

Tompiro-speaking people, had wells, and many had seeps. Today we know them by picturesque names like Tabirá, Pueblo Pardo, Chililí, Montezuma, or Pueblo Seco. But only two, Quarai and Abó, had little streams plus an altitude that was low enough, in this generally high country, to consistently allow four months or so in which skillful gardeners might grow corn, the core of existence, year after year. These two towns lay on the flanks of the mountains, not quite *in* them. The people of Quarai and Abó could hunt or forage or find timber and firewood in the Manzanos anytime they wished, but the little cities themselves were not built too high: they were foothills towns, with foothills gardens (figure 2.1).

That was a stroke of good planning. Tiny Zapato (or "Shoe") Creek rose in a wide, fan-shaped marsh and trickled eastward through the beautiful valley of Quarai and out into the dry bed of ancient Lake Estancia. Ten or twelve thousand years ago, in the late Pleistocene, this little stream was larger and full of fat trout, with bears splashing after them as the fish swam up the valley to spawn.

When the Tiwas first came to settle, probably in the thirteenth century A.D., the days of Lake Estancia and the trout and the roaring stream were long past. But the water, though diminished, was still substantial, the soil was quite fertile, and there was plenty of wood. The place itself was cold, as this was the time of the Little Ice Age; but Quarai had a forgiving eastern aspect and it could sustain a healthy population over a long time.

The Tompiro people had begun to build pit house hamlets at Abó earlier, perhaps in the eleventh century A.D. Stone was plentiful along Espinoso (Spiny)

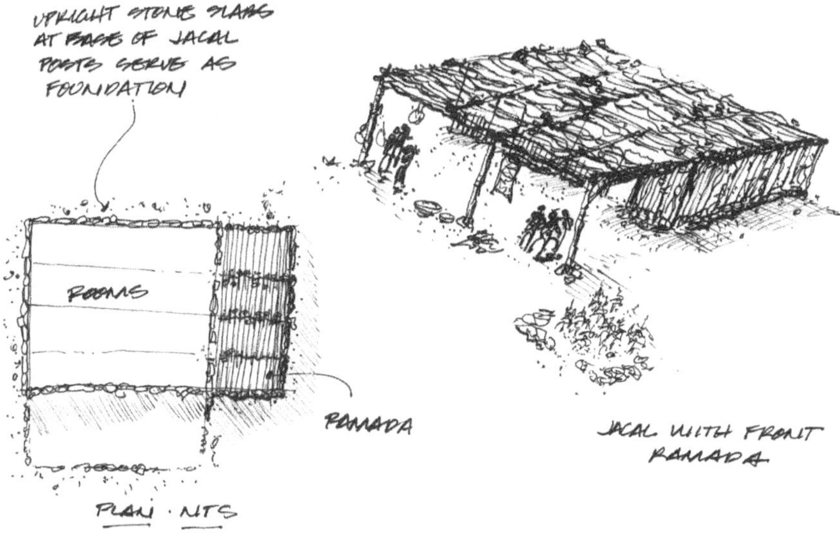

Fig. 2.2 Abó/Tenabó, Tompiro period, typical jacal reconstruction. Illustration by Baker H. Morrow.

Creek and its nearby draws, and the first settlers here erected jacal (or trimmed juniper wood) structures with overhead trellises for shade (figure 2.2). They used flagstones and slabs of irregular sandstone for foundations, placing them on edge, and they laid out their gardens in small plots beside the stream and on the terraces and hillsides above the valley. We can still see their outlines today, especially near sunup or sundown, traced out in squares and rectangles by dropseed and *Muhlenbergia* grasses waving in the breeze.

In later years, the plentiful red sandstone of Abó, naturally tabular and easily quarried, would be used to build a substantial pueblo of perhaps a thousand or so inhabitants. The Tiwas of Quarai would use much the same material to create their roomblocks on the north hillside next to Zapato Creek, and their own population would eventually reach about eight hundred souls.

In the sixteenth century, the newly arrived Spaniards would construct with impressive Indian skill and assistance two of their most memorable missions at the edges of these towns, having seen in their practical Iberian way a couple of prosperous farming and trading communities that they could make over into ecclesiastical haciendas. But that is another story.

Abó and Quarai, neighboring towns some thirteen or fourteen miles apart, one Tompiro speaking and the other Tiwa speaking, grew and flourished for a time and left an intriguing history of landscape planning and open-space design. Here are a few of the landscape features that made these places so exceptional in their day and so important in the history of Southwestern landscape architecture.

Abō, Its Pocket Gardens, and the Case of the Mute Stone Bench

Abó feels like the South. The southern Southwest, that is. Espinoso Creek flows quietly through the place, winding down a canyon lined with deep red sandstone cliffs and joining Abó Creek (in the pass of the same name) a mile or so below the pueblo itself. It is very warm here, and stony, though it can be bone-chilling in the winter. The winds buffet the hills of Abó from every direction.

On the flat sides and tops of boulders and under ledges at Abó, the curious visitor may come across a parrot or macaw scratched out in lively, yellowish lines. These tropical birds, which originate in south-central Mexico, may be mixed with the figures of warriors carrying shields and feathered spears. Or the visitor may find a quiet dancer, painted on the stone in vivid greens and reds and yellows, still poised to take part in a dance of the kachinas (figure 2.3).

Abó and Tenabó pueblos, along with the southeastern hamlet today known as LA 503, make up the larger community of Abó. Remarkably, all three are sited on headlands or peninsulas, and each of them lies at the confluence of two stream courses.

In Abó Pass, the macaws and other birds on the stones are sometimes next to plumed serpents, drawn frequently in pairs, or the outlines of hands, bear paws, or young corn plants emerging from the earth. Migration spirals are never far away. These figures and forms are, of course, the Tompiros telling us about themselves and the lives they led five or six centuries ago.

Parrots and macaws: the South, in Pueblo thinking. In the 1300s and 1400s, Paquimé or Casas Grandes, a town the Acoma (Keres) people call Kuyapukauwak in what is presently the Mexican state of Chihuahua, was the greatest of Southwestern cities, and the source of parrots and macaws (which are themselves very large, noisy, brightly colored members of the parrot tribe) for virtually all of the pueblos of New Mexico and Arizona. This was a heady time for large Southwestern pueblos, and there were perhaps a hundred of them scattered across the region. Traders from Paquimé, sometimes referred to as *pochtecas*, carried the birds or sometimes simply their feathers for hundreds of miles to reach places like Abó and Tenabó. The stones in Abó Pass and elsewhere along the central Rio Grande say clearly that the birds were very popular indeed.

Kachina and other ceremonial dancing required good, flat, well-laid-out plazas, the most conspicuous of the landscape features of these towns, with kivas nearby and plenty of flat roofs for ease of viewing. By the fourteenth century, the great rectangular plaza of Abó (located just south of the spectacular ruin of the church of San Gregorio, built about 1627) was probably the best place in the Tompiro country to watch dances of any kind. The apartment blocks surrounding the plaza on all sides rose up above the nearby landscape for two or three

Fig. 2.3 Petroglyphs at Abó. Illustration by Baker H. Morrow.

stories, with covered, shady trellises (later called *corredores* by the Spaniards) on the roofs to ease the intolerable glare and heat of the sun. These trellises were also found in the plazas and courtyards of the pueblo at ground level, where the Spaniards knew them as ramadas.

The visiting Mexican traders needed salt and piñon nuts and good pots, and Abó was well provisioned with these. Or they may have wanted the exquisite chalcedony arrow points, small knives, and scrapers that the Tompiros of Abó produced. In addition to the great birds and their feathers, the *paquimeños* likely brought along shells from the Sea of Cortés, small copper bells, a bit of turquoise traded from the Rio Grande pueblos, and other very valuable but light goods. We don't know this yet as a certainty: extensive excavations of Tompiro structures have not yet been undertaken at Abó, Tenabó, or LA 503.

But the traders would have noticed and understood the strong north–south orientation of Abó's great plaza and its smaller adjoining *plazuela*. Paquimé itself was constructed on the cardinal directions, and in that remarkable city north was also the "heart of the sky" (see Lekson 1999). And the pochtecas may have witnessed a dance or two conducted on the enormous sandstone plates of the Middle Creek just west of the great plaza. Here a massive stone bench, set up and balanced neatly with props at one side of the creek-bottom bedrock, still waits for the reedy notes of a bone flute and the thumping of cottonwood drums to sound again.

In Tenabó, the plazas and the long western walls of the town are also oriented to the north, to the heart of the sky. Manzano Peak is Tenabó's prominent marker of direction, some fifteen miles or so due north of the plazas. And here, as at Abó, the people planted gardens in little pockets of soil along the wetter bottoms of arroyos, on benches beside the streams or the arroyos, on natural terraces above the valley floors, and on mesas and ridgetops. In some of these planting beds, the soil is still soft and friable and fertile three and a half centuries or more after the Tompiros last depended on its bounty.

The ritual landscape in and near Abó and Tenabó is rich with pecked circles (similar to Tewa "earth navels") in the sedimentary outcrops, arranged circles of stone on upper benches, and boulder fields perhaps used for women's rites near the water. The outlines of kivas (some of them square in the old Mimbres style) are also present at Abó and Tenabó.

But the plant variety at these two places is today a little sparse. These are hotter locales than Quarai, and a little lower. Corn, beans, and squash—the three staples of life in the Southwest—are subtropical or tropical plants imported from Mexico in the ancient past. They need a good deal of tending, and at least four months of warm weather to come to harvest. They were cultivated in "pocket" gardens of good soil along the Tompiro valleys. It is very likely that the Tompiros also grew or encouraged amaranth and goosefoot species (*quelites*) in their plots, as well as intense crops of Indian ricegrass and sand dropseed, all good bets for the table because of their delicious seeds or leaves. These species are still found here today.

The Tompiros foraged and hunted heavily in the woodlands surrounding their towns. Cholla fruit, the seeds of fourwing saltbush, the berries of the juniper tree and the algerita, the fruit and fiber of the yucca, the nuts of the piñon, and watercress could all be gathered and cultivated locally. In the thirteenth and fourteenth centuries, it is likely that at least two or three acres per year had to be farmed or foraged to a considerable degree to feed each person in a Pueblo settlement. At Abó, with its thousand or so residents, this might mean two to three thousand acres or more in small gardens and "cultivated" or systematically rummaged piñon-juniper woodland.[1] Thus, Abó itself might well have sat in the center of a garden area extending over some four or five square miles. There were growing plots virtually everywhere, with small, seasonal field houses used by the people who tended them. The cultivated garden area around Tenabó might have amounted to one thousand acres, or nearly two square miles; and around LA 503 it may have been four hundred acres, or two-thirds of a square mile.

Abó Pass is today a colorful but rather desolate place, deeply eroded where the creek flows. But the pass in the fourteenth and fifteenth centuries would have had a much different look. Abó, Tenabó, and LA 503 sat near the north, southwest, and southeast corners, respectively, of a communal complex of gardens and building clusters that dominated the western edges of the Tompiro country. This small city may have supported some sixteen to eighteen hundred people (400–500 at Tenabó, 150–250 at LA 503, and 1,000 at Abó itself) in its heyday, and

Fig. 2.4 Water at Abó. Photo by Baker H. Morrow.

it would have appeared to visitors as a string of pocket, terrace, and streamside garden plots with small outbuildings scattered among them. There were well-worn trails or perhaps roads connecting the gardens and the three substantial building clusters (the pueblos themselves) at the north, east, and west edges.

Traces of an ancient irrigation ditch, outlined in algerita, may still be found along the uphill edge of the lower crescent field at Abó today,[2] and it is possible that the Tompiros built more ditches around the town—especially along the flat open spaces lining Abó Creek just downstream. Canals and other irrigation works were very common among the Jornada Mogollon (post-Mimbres) people to the south and west of the Manzanos, and they were also found among the Ancestral Puebloans of the Four Corners. But there are no traces of Tewa-style grid gardens here, no stone-mulch gardens found to date, and no cairns or check dams. The Tompiro preferred to plant in little pockets of workable soil, on terraces, along small, flat ridges, at the mouths of small gullies, and in garden beds alongside their modest streams (figure 2.4).

Modest gardens. Small valleys moistened by reliable creeks. And to keep heaven and earth in good order, colorful rituals to be observed in the right space, open to the sky: the great central plaza.

The later Spanish, Mexican, and Anglo centuries at Abó brought complicated social and material change, with many new and fascinating landscape elements that would leave their mark. But the Tompiro times reached their zenith around A.D. 1600 and then faded fast.

Fig. 2.5 View of fields and berry gardens, Quarai. Photo by Baker H. Morrow.

Quitatác nasaul. "Our Father who art in heaven." Quiále mahimnague yo sé mahi kaná rrohoi. "Give us this day our daily bread."[3]

There is no more piki bread cooking deliciously on the flat hearthstones at Abó, and we know only the slimmest fragments of the old Piro language. The people and their words are simply gone. The antique gardens, a few stretches of mounded stone walls around their open courts, a yellowing copy of the Paternoster, and the dancers' faces and raucous birds on the stones are what is left to tell us a story of Abó.

The Berry Gardens of Quarai

Quarai was a fair-sized town at the edge of the plains a little northeast of Abó.

Perhaps Mina-Coya, the Old Salt Woman of Jemez country legend, came here from the valley of the Jemez River to trade for salt (Sando 1992). Many other Jemez Valley people did just that over the centuries, and the trip may have taken a week or two to complete. Turquoises and handsome pots and perhaps a bit of cotton yarn or dyestuffs (as well as alum, used to set dyes, collected in the Navajo country west of Jemez Canyon) would have been popular with the Tiwa people on the eastern side of the Manzano range.

In return, the rare and indispensable salt (collected at the Estancia salt lakes a few miles east and south of the pueblo) bartered by the Tiwas and the other Manzano people was much prized by the Towas of Jemez and their neighbors from the Keres-speaking towns of the lower Jemez Valley.

Fig. 2.6 Currants and sand plums, Quarai. Photo by Baker H. Morrow.

But the people of Quarai may have had something more to trade. There is nothing quite like the fruit and berry gardens that they established in their little valley anywhere else in the Pueblo world of the A.D. 1300s and 1400s (figure 2.5). At least, nothing like the sheer quantity and diversity of species of the fruit- and berry-producing plants that a visitor may find there today. There are currants, chokecherries, wolfberries, and sand plums growing abundantly, and cholla cactus with its pomegranate-like fruit is scattered widely over the ruins (figure 2.6). Algerita, with its berries, serviceberry, and Woods' rose, with its tart hips, are scattered along the hollows of the place. A sharp-eyed visitor can still find tomatillos or ground cherries, amaranth, and quelites (salad greens, from the goosefoot family) in the old planting terraces and garden plots. All these garden plants and more are still growing strongly with little or no human assistance at Quarai today, in open spaces set against the surrounding evergreen woodlands. Here there are singleseed junipers with their tart berries and masses of piñon pines with their delicious nuts. Boxelder (*Acer negundo*), which is a maple, grows in the valley as well, and a skillful tapper can coax maple syrup out of it that is as good, some say, as that of the eastern sugar maple (*Acer saccharum*).

With such abundance, the *quarenses* may have traded fresh fruits like plums and chokecherries; dried fruits and berries such as rose hips and currants; the seeds of tomatillos, amaranth, and Indian ricegrass; and other relatively rare, locally produced fruit and berry products with their neighbors near and far.

Fig. 2.7 Priest's garden with wolfberry and buffalo gourd, Quarai. Photo by Baker H. Morrow.

The Spaniards also found this place to be fertile. They first began to cultivate it in the late 1620s, when the Franciscans planted their gardens of cabbage, onions, lettuce, carrots, thistles (possibly artichokes), lentils, and lima beans (figure 2.7). Fray Alonso de Benavides, the third custodian of missions in New Mexico, also states in *A Harvest of Reluctant Souls*, his Memorial of 1630, that orchards of peaches, apricots, walnuts, and mulberries grew well throughout the province. Modern orchard remnants at Quarai produce excellent apples, too, and these have been a regular feature of the towns scattered along the eastern slopes of the Manzanos since the 1600s.

At the Estancia Zalazar, a Spanish hacienda established at the site of the modern village of Manzano (some four or five miles to the north of Quarai) in the 1620s, the hacendados planted apples in groves alongside the flowing water of the Ojo Gigante. The ancient orchards that a visitor sees there today are among the oldest in North America. Birds, travelers, and settlers over a four-hundred-year period have combined to spread these beneficent trees throughout the canyons and valleys of the eastern Manzano country, making late summer and early autumn visits to the area a special delight. And it is from these trees that the modern name of the mountain range is derived (Ivey 1991).

The Tiwas certainly grew corn (probably the early Mexican *chapalote* strain), squash, and beans up and down their valley and on its hillslopes. If their current presence is any indication, Indian ricegrass, dropseed, and amaranth were cultivated as well. On the south side of Zapato Creek, it is still possible to find fertile soil in pockets, free of stones, that are lined with berry- or fruit-producing plants. These remarkable small plots, now called "shrub-hollow" gardens, are not found at Abó. They lie in clearings in the woodland on the south hillslopes and along the south edge of Zapato Creek. The hillside itself is quite stony, and it is here that the Tiwa gardeners fashioned their cultivating tools. Tri-faced digging points and bi-faced flat hoes or shovels, attached to shafts, are the most common of these implements. Modern researchers looking into the landscape and site design history of Quarai have often found scrapers or small knives alongside these garden tools. The Tiwas used them to fashion and finish shafts and handles for their gardening tools and to trim cord or sinew to bind the tool parts together.

Remarkably, these tools are only found south of the stream. The land on the north side of Zapato Creek, certainly part of an ancient series of Tiwa planting terraces, has been much more thoroughly cultivated by the Spaniards, the Mexican-period pioneers, and the U.S. Territorial-period settlers of Quarai. The padres of Quarai from 1622 to 1676 introduced wheat here—a grain that is much more cold tolerant than Mesoamerican corn. They probably cultivated grapes as well. Today, only the native grape, *Vitis arizonica*, grows at Quarai or nearby, but in the 1600s the padres, who were good horticulturists, likely used this vine as a rootstock onto which they grafted their European wine-grape varieties.

Vines grow well at Quarai. In addition to the native grape, woodbine (*Parthenocissus inserta*) and western virgin's bower (*Clematis ligusticifolia*) are also common in the vicinity. The relatively abundant water in the valley flows quite close to the surface in many places, and berry- or fruit-producing shrubs and trees as well as vines establish themselves quickly and stay healthy for decades, or even centuries.

Quarai in the twenty-first century consists of several mounds scattered across a hill and down into a little valley. Ruinous apartment blocks that are poorly known and barely excavated surround two or three open plazas. There appears to be an associated small Tiwa settlement two or three miles to the north, in the spreading valley just to the east of Manzano town, but its history is even more benighted. By contrast, the easternmost, or European, structures of Quarai have been exhaustively excavated and repeatedly stabilized. A cloister with a kiva in it, probably planted as a physic garden by the Franciscans, terrace gardens enclosed by sandstone walls, and an *estanque* or "pond," with built-up masonry walls and irrigation channels, are outstanding landscape features next to the church. A Spanish courtyard, part of an *encomendero*'s compound just across the old Abó-Quarai-Manzano road to the west of the church, is also an important landscape space.[4]

But in contrast to Abó there are very few petroglyphs (figure 2.8). The red sandstone of Quarai was quarried from the twelfth or thirteenth century through the seventeenth century at outcrops that lie a little southeast of the town proper. There are no faces on the stones here, no plumed serpents, no kachina dancers, no turkeys or macaws or migration spirals. The occasional outline of a foot or

Fig. 2.8 Shrine at Abó. Photo by Baker H. Morrow.

hand on a rock face and a puzzling large ring of stones flanked by a marching east–west line of boulders (the "Spanish Corral") on the south hill are key features in the landscape. The sharp-eyed visitor may also spot an occasional small check dam still holding back runoff in a tiny wash or two. Big green collared lizards scamper across the stones on the south hill and rush off into the woods.

There is little else. The extraordinary stone gardening tools, the small plazas—more like affable courtyards amidst residential blocks—the berries and the fruits, the good soil, and the many springs are the greater elements of the old Tiwa landscape. The marks of ritual on the landscape are very restrained. The visible preoccupation with ceremony and the strong connections to the south that distinguish Abó and its landscape are not found here.

The priests' gardens and fields, the old *atrio* or forecourt of La Purísima Concepción de Quarai, the ponds and dams and long acequias, and great quantities of European produce and livestock changed the landscape character of the town after 1627 and in many ways added substantially to the features of the open space that we see there today. But these are later overlays made to an ancient, and still apparent, Tiwa base.

For its bucolic setting, for its water and fertile soil, and as a place to find fruit and berry gardens impressively expanding the traditional corn-beans-squash plots of the classic Pueblo diet, Quarai was an exceptional Southwestern town for a good two or three centuries. The venerable plants here provide quite a show for anyone who wants to see them even now, and they can still be experienced by taste as well as sight. It is the Tiwas' meticulous arrangement of open space and the success of their long-lived gardens at Quarai that give us perhaps the clearest picture of how life was lived in this little valley at the edge of a dried-up lake over half a millennium ago.

This essay is substantially based on field research for the National Park Service conducted at Quarai and Abó by BDA Architects, Cherry. See Architects, Baker H. Morrow and Morrow and Company, Ltd., Landscape Architects, between 1993 and 2002.

Notes

1. Conversations with Dr. Kurt Anschuetz and personal reconnaissance.
2. This ditch was likely embellished or renovated by Hispanic settlers at the site in the seventeenth, nineteenth, and twentieth centuries.
3. (Tom-) Piro manuscript by Pimentel, Colección de la Sociedad de Geografía, Mexico, ca. 1836, supplied by Dr. Elizabeth Brandt.
4. Encomendero: a local commissioner chartered by the king or the viceroy of New Spain.

References Cited

Brandt, Elizabeth A.

1996 Draft Cultural Affiliation Study, Salinas Missions National Monument, 1996. Unpublished report submitted to the National Park Service by E. A. Brandt.

Cordell, Linda S., ed.

1980 *Tijeras Canyon: Analyses of the Past*. Albuquerque: University of New Mexico Press.

Dunmire, William W., and Gail Tierney

1995 *Wild Plants of the Pueblo Province*. Santa Fe: Museum of New Mexico Press.

1997 *Wild Plants and Native Peoples of the Four Corners*. Santa Fe: Museum of New Mexico Press.

Frazier, Kendrick

1986 *People of Chaco*. New York: W. W. Norton.

Ivey, James E.

1991 *In the Midst of a Loneliness: The Architectural History of the Salinas Missions*. Santa Fe, NM: Southwest Cultural Resources Center, National Park Service.

Kubler, George

1990 *The Religious Architecture of New Mexico*. Albuquerque: University of New Mexico Press.

Lekson, Stephen H.
1999 *The Chaco Meridian: Centers of Political Power in the Ancient Southwest.* Walnut Creek, CA: Altamira Press.

Morrow, Baker H.
1995 *Best Plants for New Mexico Gardens and Landscapes.* Albuquerque: University of New Mexico Press.

———, ed. and trans.
1996 *A Harvest of Reluctant Souls: The Memorial of Fray Alonso de Benavides, 1630.* Boulder: University Press of Colorado.

———, and Suzanne Mortier
1998 *Cultural Landscape Inventory for Abo Unit, Salinas Pueblo Missions National Monument, National Park Service.* Albuquerque, NM: Morrow and Company, Ltd., Landscape Architects.

———, and V. B. Price, eds.
1997 *Anasazi Architecture and American Design.* Albuquerque: University of New Mexico Press.

———, and Kenneth Romig
2000 *Cultural Landscape Inventory for Quarai Unit, Salinas Pueblo Missions National Monument, National Park Service.* Albuquerque, NM: Morrow Reardon Wilkinson, Ltd., Landscape Architects.

Riley, Carroll L.
1987 *The Frontier People: The Greater Southwest in the Protohistoric Period.* Albuquerque: University of New Mexico Press.
1999 *Rio del Norte: People of the Upper Rio Grande from Earliest Times to the Pueblo Revolt.* Salt Lake City: University of Utah Press.

Sanchez, Joseph
1996 *The Rio Abajo Frontier, 1540–1692.* 2nd ed. Albuquerque, NM: Albuquerque Museum.

Sando, Joe S.
1992 *Pueblo Nations: Eight Centuries of Pueblo Indian History.* Santa Fe, NM: Clear Light Publishers.

Scully, Vincent
1991 *Architecture: The Natural and the Man-Made.* London: HarperCollins/Harvill.

Smith, Bruce D.
1995 *The Emergence of Agriculture.* New York: Scientific American Library.

Stuart, David E.
2000 *Anasazi America.* Albuquerque: University of New Mexico Press.

Tainter, Joseph A. and Frances Levine
1987 *Cultural Resources Overview: Central New Mexico.* Santa Fe, NM: U.S. Forest Service.

Toll, H. Wolcott, ed.
1995 *Soil, Water, Biology, and Belief in Prehistoric and Traditional Southwestern Agriculture.* Albuquerque: New Mexico Archaeological Council.

Toulouse, Joseph H.
1949 *The Mission of San Gregorio de Abó: A Report on the Excavation and Repair of a Seventeenth-Century New Mexico Mission.* Albuquerque: University of New Mexico Press.

Vivian, Gordon, and Sallie van Valkenburgh

1979 *Gran Quivira: Excavations in a 17th-Century Jumano Pueblo.* Washington, DC: National Park Service.

Wills, W. H.

1988 *Early Prehistoric Agriculture in the American Southwest.* Santa Fe, NM: School of American Research Press.

Chapter Three

Reading the Ancestral Puebloan Landscape

A Paleoethnobotanist's Text of Seeds and Wood

by Carol B. Brandt

The nature of ancient landscapes might seem to nonspecialists impossible to verify, much less model and describe. In this chapter, however, paleoethnobotanist Carol Brandt answers the question, "What kind of literacy do we use to read the landscape of the past?" The answer is the detailed analysis of minute "ecofacts" in the form of charred seeds, cob fragments, kernels, stems, and other bio-debris at ancient sites. One archaeologist calls this data the kitchen "crumbs" of prehistoric life. From these tiny scraps, along with pollen analysis, it is possible to reconstruct and describe with remarkable thoroughness the natural and horticultural landscape of a site at a specific point in time.

Each of us in the archaeological profession has experienced it: that moment when the crew arrives and an odd assemblage of screens, wheelbarrows, and crates are heaved from the back of dented and scratched pickup trucks. The first task is to set up the transit and plant the datum, the main reference point upon which our grid and all our records depend. Deep in thought, the field director walks back and forth, scanning the stone rubble protruding through the red clay, and notes the rise and fall of the ground. Standing atop the sandstone, one can see the roomblock extending more than six meters and the scatter of pottery to the southwest must be the midden, but where are the pit structures and just how many can we expect? While the archaeologists contemplate the landscape, the still air is scented with sagebrush. Turkey vultures spin above our heads on an invisible uplift.

As we consider this canyon, the eroded slopes uphill and arroyo just a hundred meters below us, our eyes are searching for subtleties: a nearly imperceptible dip in the soil just southeast of the rubble that might be a buried kiva; a few scraggly branches of *Lycium* or wolfberry, a plant that has an affinity for buried walls and rubble; and streaks of gray ash or charcoal from ancient fire pits that seem hidden among the black cryptogamic soil crusts. Our eyes seem to be focused on what is *not there*, attempting to peer into another world, a different time, and a distant landscape. How do we read this landscape? What literacy do we use? How do we arrive at understanding the Ancestral Puebloan landscape from the pottery sherds, architectural maps, or charred maize kernels?

One field director with whom I worked in southwestern Colorado had uncanny abilities to "sniff out" an archaeological site. Somehow he was always able to predict the location of buried features and was able to read the soils to understand that another, earlier house was buried beneath the floor. He grasped the gestalt of the archaeological site and how it rested upon the landscape; the way soil, rock, and vegetation came together was an open book for him. Each draw of his trowel across the excavation floor produced a curl of clay, another page in the text of landscape.

For myself, that attention to nuance, detail, and subtlety carries into the laboratory when labeled bags of dirt are delivered from the field. My work as a paleoethnobotanist is to locate clues in the form of burned seeds, charred fragments of twigs and wood, rind from squash, or fibers from twine. From these minute ecofacts, I attempt to gain some sense of the prehistoric landscape and its relationship with its inhabitants.

To arrive at any understanding or vision of the past, the intimacy of knobs, hooks, and wavy reticulations on seed coats are my world through the binocular dissecting scope. As I survey the hills and valleys of each seed surface, I come closer to knowing the vegetation in this ancient environment. Each sample might take anywhere from an hour to a day to sort. Methodically moving my needlenose tweezers through the charcoal, an unexplained series of mental recognition patterns allow me to pick out fragments for naming. I am surrounded by dozens of labeled plastic film vials containing a comparative collection of seeds, stems, leaves, fruits, twigs, and wood from modern specimens. For example, a seed whose surface is punctuated with rounded, raised bumps is hauntingly familiar, and something about it pulls me to the Cactaceae, the cactus family. Looking through the modern specimens, I try to find some definitive landmark that can help me identify the mystery seed. With a paintbrush that has been trimmed to several hairs, I roll the seed fragment back and forth, contemplating morphology. I move between the charred seed and specimens in the comparative collection until I convince myself that I must be looking at a seed of the hedgehog cactus, *Echinocereus*.

My colleagues in paleoethnobotany would agree that our work is obsessed with the details of identification. But now and again, we change our standpoint and ask a larger question: how do we read the "text" of this charred seed to construct a narrative of a people and their landscape? Moving through extremes of scale, from seed to regional landscape, is a daunting task. Mollie Toll, whose archaeobotanical research has helped us to understand the prehistoric economy of Chaco Canyon, talks about her work as looking at "crumbs" of prehistoric life. She says, "You know that place in your kitchen where there is a gap between the stove and the refrigerator? Every kitchen has a place where crumbs of food lodge, and because it's never cleaned you have this evidence." Indigenous people in the ancient past had these places in their homes, too: the bottom of storage pits, the gap between a metate and the pit structure wall, or in the sand that accumulates in the corners of floors.

Our work in paleoethnobotany is made easier when a structure has been burned, either accidentally or intentionally, when it was abandoned. When a structure burned and the roof collapsed to smother the fire, the plant remains are captured in time as charred fragments, impervious to decay. For reasons unknown to archaeologists, Basketmaker III and Pueblo I pit structures in the northern Southwest have a higher rate of burning upon abandonment. In these pit structures, it is not unusual to find the roofing timbers intact, along with worn-out yucca sandals that were used to fill holes in the ceiling, fragments of matting on floors, pieces of wooden tools or weaving looms, and seeds scattered around the hearth.

The Great Pit Structure at LA 61955

In the ten years that I conducted archaeobotanical research, one archaeological site stands out as being "encyclopedic" in its botanical assemblage, one that offered me a new reading of the Ancestral Puebloan landscape. At the southern end of the Chuska Mountains in north-central New Mexico is site LA 61955 (Damp 1999). This site is dominated by a Great Pit structure (figure 3.1), oval in shape and measuring 11.4 m in length with an earthen bench that encircles three-quarters of the structure. The pit structure was excavated a meter and a half into the soil and had a roof of grass thatch and cribbed logs, covered with earth. It included an antechamber, a small underground room connected to the main chamber by a tunnel. Tree-ring cutting dates for this structure ranged from A.D. 644 to 696 (figure 3.2), suggesting it was occupied for at least one generation, if not two, during the Basketmaker III period.

Within the first days of testing the structure, the field director, Mark Sant, realized the immensity of the structure and the quality of preservation it offered. Mark

Fig. 3.1 The archaeologists are removing burnt roofing material from the Great Pit structure at LA 61955 and have not yet uncovered the pit structure floor. Note the charred walls and the amount of charcoal uncovered by the excavation. Photo by Carol Brandt.

adjusted the excavation plan to maximize the botanical information we could recover; we developed an intensive botanical sampling strategy for the floor and bench and consulted a conservator about the basketry fragments we were finding.

Nearly three times the size of a typical pit structure from that time period, the Great Pit structure at LA 61955 burned with a hot fire that started near the wing walls, an area where the grinding stones and baskets were stored. The fire was so hot there that the metates fractured into pieces and an obsidian projectile point (arrowhead) melted and warped. But just as quickly, the fire was extinguished when the wooden supports collapsed, spilling tons of earth from the roof and smothering the flames. The depth of the roofing materials kept oxygen from reaching the fire and prevented plant materials from burning to ash. Upon excavation we found that the floor was remodeled twice with more than 243 features (pits, storage cysts, ashpits, hearth, postholes, and storage bins).

Along with its size and the wide earthen bench, other features suggest a communal use for the Great Pit structure. In the center of the structure was a hearth a meter in diameter and a half a meter deep. A floor vault next to the hearth was covered with planks of ponderosa pine (*Pinus ponderosa*) and constructed in much the same way that "foot drums" are in contemporary kivas.

The unique circumstances of the burning of the Great Pit structure provide us with a snapshot of the Basketmaker III landscape and the plant resources selected by this community. While the storage bins in the antechamber and main

Fig. 3.2 Charred roofing timbers are obvious in the center of the pit structure and provided valuable tree-ring data on the year these timbers were harvested for the pit structure construction. Photo by Carol Brandt.

structure were empty, those places that catch "crumbs," as Mollie Toll mentioned, were full of wild seeds, nutshells, and maize cob and kernel fragments. The diversity of plant species used for food, basketry, fuel, and construction betrays the extensive amount of plant collecting and cultivating that characterized the inhabitants' lives (table 3.1).

Table 3.1
Plant Species Recovered from the Great Pit Structure at LA 61955, a Basketmaker III Community

Common Name	Genus/Species	Plant Part
Amaranth	*Amaranthus* sp.	Seed, flower, inflorescence
Ash	*Fraxinus* sp.	Wood
Beeweed	*Cleome serrulata*	Seed
Blazingstar	*Mentzelia* sp.	Seed
Bugseed	*Corispermum* sp.	Seed
Cliffrose	*Cowania neomexicana*	Wood
Common reedgrass	*Phragmites communis*	Stem
Dogbane	*Apocynum* sp.	Fibers
Domestic bean	*Phaseolus vulgaris*	Seed
Domestic squash	*Cucurbita pepo*	Seed

Common Name	Genus/Species	Plant Part
Dropseed grass	*Sporobolus* sp.	Seed
Gaura	*Gaura* sp.	Seed
Globemallow	*Sphaeralcea* sp.	Flower
Goosefoot	*Chenopodium* sp.	Seed, flower
Groundcherry	*Physalis* sp.	Seed
Indian ricegrass	*Oryzopsis hymenoides*	Seed
Jimsonweed	*Datura meteloides*	Seed
Juniper	*Juniperus* sp.	Bark, twig, seed
Knotweed	*Polygonum* sp.	Seed
Maize	*Zea mays*	Kernel, cob, stem, leaf
Mint family	Lamiaceae	Seed
Oak	*Quercus* sp.	Wood
Piñon	*Pinus edulis*	Seed, cone, needle
Ponderosa pine	*Pinus ponderosa*	Wood
Prickly pear cactus	*Opuntia* sp.	Seed
Purslane	*Portulaca* sp.	Seed
Rabbitbrush	*Chrysothamnus* sp.	Wood
Rush family	Juncaceae	Seed
Saltbush	*Atriplex* sp.	Seed
Sunflower	*Helianthus* sp.	Seed, flower, inflorescence
Tobacco	*Nicotiana attenuata*	Seed
Willow	*Salix* sp.	Wood
Winged pigweed	*Cycloloma atriplicifolium*	Seed
Yucca	*Yucca* sp.	Seed, fiber, leaf

Adapted from Brandt 1999:tables 13.8 and 13.24.

The Great Pit structure also affords us the rare opportunity to go beyond the typical discussions of economy to talk about human culture and plants that might have been used for cultural, religious, or medicinal purposes. Archaeologists found fragments of a wooden flute on the bench and recovered "cigarettes" made from the stems of common reedgrass (*Phragmites communis*), as well as clay pipes from the sandy floor along with hundreds of tobacco (*Nicotiana attenuata*) seeds (figure 3.3). The seeds of the hallucinogenic jimsonweed (*Datura meteloides*) were clustered on the bench and floor. We found seeds of gaura (*Gaura*), a small perennial in the evening primrose family, scattered on the Great Pit structure floor. This plant has no nutritional value, but it has a long-standing heritage of medicinal use by indigenous people in the Southwest.

With kernels and cob fragments found in every context at site LA 61955, maize agriculture was undoubtedly at the center of the economy of this community. Nevertheless, the wild seeds of sunflower (*Helianthus*), amaranth (*Amaranthus*),

Fig. 3.3 A ceramic pipe found on the pit structure bench. Large amounts of charred tobacco (*Nicotiana attenuata*) seed were also recovered from the pit structure floor, features, and bench. Photo by Carol Brandt.

goosefoot (*Chenopodium*), winged pigweed (*Cycloloma atriplicifolium*), and bugseed (*Corispermum*) suggest that weedy annual plants were intensively harvested and perhaps encouraged in field or garden systems. Tantalizing data suggest that intensification of weedy plants was an important element in the prehistoric economy. For example, sunflower seeds (6.57 mm + 0.69 in length [Brandt 1999:481]) from the Great Pit structure measured in the range of domesticated sunflower (Crites 1993).

The botanical materials from our site, LA 61955, compel me to reconsider notions of resource intensification that have been generated by archaeologists. Despite their dependence upon agriculture, Basketmaker III communities (dating from A.D. 400 to 700) are thought to be somewhat transient, shifting across the landscape. As I look at the range of plants recovered from site LA 61955, I wonder how this prehistoric community divided its time among collecting wild plants, tending gardens, and cultivating agricultural fields. At this site we have evidence of the dominant role that weedy annuals and agricultural crops played in the community's subsistence, a pattern we typically associate with the later time periods of Ancestral Puebloan occupation, Pueblo II or III.[1] In the later occupations of Ancestral Puebloans, agriculture supported the construction of villages where large surpluses of cultivated crops were common. And yet, the range of wild plants at LA 61955 suggests that people were moving extensively across the landscape for collecting. While the inhabitants of site LA 61955 obviously had invested much time and energy in maintaining their communal structure and three other pit structures, how far did these people move across their landscape? Did these tasks of cultivating and gathering plant resources mean being tethered to one or several localities? How does this site compare to other Basketmaker III communities?

To answer some of these questions, we need to look at larger assemblages of botanical data that unfortunately are largely tucked away in the "gray" literature of archaeological excavation reports. The distribution of these reports is restricted to tribal, state, or federal agencies, and rarely do these analyses find their way into synthetic studies.

What I find so confusing about the archaeobotanical data from Ancestral Puebloan sites is often how similar assemblages can look across vast periods of time and across geographically different locations. While some species might change, the results from most Basketmaker III through Pueblo III botanical analyses are dominated by maize agriculture, a suite of weedy plants, and augmented with collected wild perennials. With such consistency, how does one see intensification? How do we begin to read the data in a different way to understand how a community responds to the pressures of higher population and more competition for resources?

Ancestral Puebloan Communities: From Center to Margins

One person who has helped me think about the Ancestral Puebloan landscape is Mark Varien (1999) whose synthesis of archaeological research addresses the issues of sedentism, mobility, and regional movements among prehistoric populations in southwestern Colorado. Varien enumerates those paradigmatic biases (prejudices about boundaries) that obscure the generation of new models in archaeology. Many archaeological studies assume that agriculture necessitates a certain degree of sedentism, and that we tend to judge mobility and sedentism on an either/or basis. If a primary residence appears to be maintained over several generations, as is the case with the Great Pit structure at site LA 61955, what portion of the community actually remains year-round at the site? Similarly, what portion of the community is moving among temporary sites to gather wild plants or tend crops from distant fields? Is the resource intensification centralized or dispersed across the landscape?

In the 1980s, most of the models generated by archaeologists were dependent upon ecological data. The environment was seen as the prime mover in decisions related to site abandonment and relocation. Rethinking this paradigm, Varien (1999) argues that residential mobility should not only consider environmental limitations—that it is a social process both "enabled and constrained" (9) by existing social structures. Variation in community movement and relocation must be deciphered through the changing social context in the region.

For example, concepts of ownership, inheritance, and property can also determine how residence is established or abandoned.

Pulling together results from archaeological surveys, excavations, and geographical information systems, Varien (1999) constructs a mosaic of community centers in the Mesa Verde region. In his model, the communities at the center of the Mesa Verde region had more overlapping catchment areas in the Pueblo II and III periods. That meant the land resource base was shared and negotiated between groups, resulting in more formal land tenure systems, shorter moves, and more persistent communities. Life at the margins, however, was more chaotic and involved more extensive moving and, at times, more conflict.

As I read Varien's (1999) writing, I realized that I had analyzed botanical materials from a series of sites in the Ancestral Puebloan margins. At the southern end of Sleeping Ute Mountain, southwest of Mesa Verde, are a series of archaeological sites whose inhabitants farmed the washes that seasonally flowed from the upper elevations. The archaeobotanical analysis from early occupations revealed an extensive use of the desert lowlands and higher elevations in the Sleeping Ute Mountain above (Brandt 1993). But sometime around A.D. 1150, the inhabitants of sites 5MT10206 and 5MT10207 met a disastrous finish: human remains were found smashed and scattered on the pit structure floors. The archaeobotanical assemblage from this time period, too, suggests a bleak life for these people. Only in one context did I find maize at each site (a single cob fragment in both cases); charred prickly pear cactus spines (*Opuntia*) and the seeds of weedy plants dominated the charred plant assemblage. Billman, Lambert, and Banks (2000) document similar findings in their excavation of an early Pueblo III site in Cowboy Wash six kilometers west of 5MT10206 and 5MT10207. Again, the shattered, disarticulated human bones indicate warfare or conflict that signaled a tragic ending for the community.

Seeds as a Text in Reading the Landscape

When I review the writing I have done in the past decade, I am unsatisfied with my dry reading of archaeobotanical data. I would like to imagine how I could bring more human culture into my reading of the Ancestral Puebloan landscape and arrive at a better understanding of how these people related to their natural world. Vorsila Bohrer, whose archaeobotanical work spans four decades, provides a model for rereading the data I have recovered from archaeological sites. Throughout her career she composed portraits of plant husbandry from archaeobotanical data by listening to contemporary indigenous people in the Southwest. Bohrer (1986) says that ethnographic analogies help us build hypotheses and to discard those models that are unworkable. Varien (1999), too, began his research by noticing how traditional agriculturalists established land ownership, tenure, and residence. Both researchers remind me that behind the charred

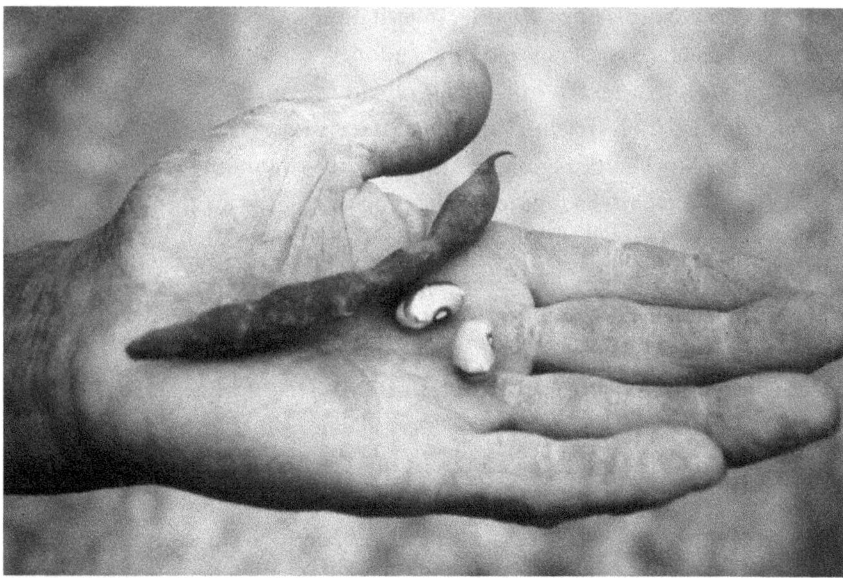

Fig. 3.4 Seeds like this heirloom bean (*Phaseolus vulgaris*) are still used in the Night Dances at Zuni Pueblo and continue to play an important role in traditional ceremonies. Photo by Carol Brandt.

seeds and woods are narratives of cultures, rich with ritual, rules, and proscriptions that guided their plant use.

Contemporary ethnographies remind us how to keep our vision focused on the landscape. For example, seeds carried by ceremonial dancers at Zuni have a special significance (figure 3.4). Ruth Bunzel (1932:714) says: "Every masked dancer carries a package of seeds in his belt. It is his 'heart.' At the close of any dance the priest who thanks the dancers takes some of the seeds to plant." In Bunzel's translation of Zuni ritual poetry, "Sayataca's Night Chant," the dancer enumerates no less than fifty-seven different seeds in a poem. These seeds are tied into a pouch at his belt: seeds of the different colors of maize and beans; seeds of wetland plants, grasses, and cacti; and seeds from the shrubs on the mesas. Each seed was deliberately chosen to record and remind a community of their long-held relationship with the landscape, a way to honor their ancestors from the Ancestral Puebloan landscape. And, in a sense, each seed is part of a text, a reading of this landscape. Each seed embodies rules that govern its cultivation and gathering, as well as myths and stories about its origin.

My own reading of this text emerges from an intimacy with the morphology of seeds, the vessels and fibers in wood, the hairs on leaves, and the ligules of grasses. I am certain that there were people in prehistory as familiar with the seeds and twigs as I am, but perhaps knowledgeable in different ways and for different purposes. Their intimacy was born out of survival, for developing a

Fig. 3.5 Timing of traditional ceremonies is signaled at Zuni Pueblo according to cosmological cycles and involves interplay between features of the landscape, such as Dowa Yallane mesa and the night sky or the position of the rising and setting sun. Photo by Carol Brandt.

relationship with the Southwest landscape that is difficult for me to fathom as I sit in my heated laboratory. The hue of a flower, the texture of a leaf, the taste or smell of a crushed stem told them where to look and when to harvest, and how to look at the land. But I imagine a reading of the landscape that extends beyond the plants growing there (figure 3.5).

What is the Ancestral Puebloan landscape? Do we simply mean the lay of the land? Or do we consider it to embrace the stars and the rising sun and moon that signaled planting or guided paths to distant places? What I know about landscape is terribly constrained by my microscope, textbooks, and plant keys. I suspect that landscape for Ancestral Puebloans embodied more than soil and rock, arroyos, and mesas. Reading the landscape might have included the querulous call of the piñon jay in the fall that signaled times to pack baskets for the harvest. A literacy of landscape suggests reading even the delicate tracks of deer mice in the sand to know where ricegrass grew in abundance and when the seeds were perfect for roasting. And perhaps by deciphering the patterns of insects caught on the sticky, glandular leaves, they knew which tobacco was pungent and would carry their prayers to the ancestors.

Rather than black symbols printed on a white page, I see a story of seeds and wood that speak to us of landscape. I imagine a ceremony in the Great Pit structure of LA 61955 where tobacco is smoked and the sounds of flute and foot drums accompany a narrative. In this poem, the seeds from the plants are named and the story of how they emerged from the underworld with the first people is told—those same plants that I found in my analysis.

Note

1. Ending ca. A.D. 1300.

References Cited

Billman, Brian R., Patricia M. Lambert, and Leonard Banks

2000 Cannibalism, Warfare, and Drought in the Mesa Verde Region during the Twelfth Century A.D. *American Antiquity* 65 (1): 145–78.

Bohrer, Vorsila

1986 Guideposts in Ethnobotany. *Journal of Ethnobiology* 6 (1): 27–43.

Brandt, Carol B.

1993 Prehistoric Plant Utilization in Anasazi Communities near Towaoc, Southwestern Colorado. In *Towaoc Canal Reach III Project*, ed. Nancy Hammack. Cortez, CO: Complete Archaeological Services Association.

1999 Analysis of Plant Macro-Remains. In *Chuska Chronologies, Houses, and Hogans: Archaeological and Ethnographic Inquiry along N30–31 between Mexican Springs and Navajo, McKinley County, New Mexico. Volume III—Part* 2, ed. Jonathan E. Damp, 441–92. Zuni, NM: Zuni Cultural Resource Enterprise.

Bunzel, Ruth

1932 *Zuni Ritual Poetry*. Forty-Seventh Annual Report of the Bureau of American Ethnology, 1929–1932. Washington, DC: Smithsonian Institution.

Crites, Gary D.

1993 Domesticated Sunflower in the Fifth Millennium B.P. Temporal Context: New Evidence from Middle Tennessee. *American Antiquity* 58 (1): 146–48.

Damp, Jonathan, ed.

1999 *Chuska Chronologies, Houses, and Hogans: Archaeological and Ethnographic Inquiry along N30–N31 between Mexican Springs and Navajo, McKinley County, New Mexico*. 4 Vols. Zuni, NM: Zuni Cultural Resources Enterprise.

Varien, Mark D.

1999 *Sedentism and Mobility in a Social Landscape: Mesa Verde and Beyond*. Tucson: University of Arizona Press.

Chapter Four

A Durable Legacy

Construction and Spatial Analysis at Sand Canyon Pueblo in the Mesa Verde Country

by Bruce A. Bradley

The landscape architecture of an Ancestral Puebloan settlement often consists of a refined set of open spaces that, together with their buildings, create a strong pattern. The Ancestral Puebloan "landscape" was as distinctive and useful to its inhabitants and creators as the more familiar Italian Renaissance piazza or the patio complexes of Moorish Spain were to theirs.

Archaeologist Bruce Bradley compares the diverse landscape and architectural features of the southern Colorado Ancestral Puebloan sites of Sand Canyon and Mesa Verde in his comments on the social organization expressed in these built environments. He shows that Ancestral Puebloan people who built these communities did so in a logical and systematic way. At Sand Canyon Pueblo, "courtyard suites" form the core of residential development, while great kivas, multiwall structures, and other large features are aspects of "public-area" site development. A surprising and remarkably consistent pattern language is the result.

Ancestral Puebloan architecture as an expression of social organization has been a topic of discussion in archaeological as well as popular literature for over a century. Many advances in analytical methodology have been made in the past two decades (for example, see Hillier and Hanson 1984), but few have been applied to the large late thirteenth-century sites that are known

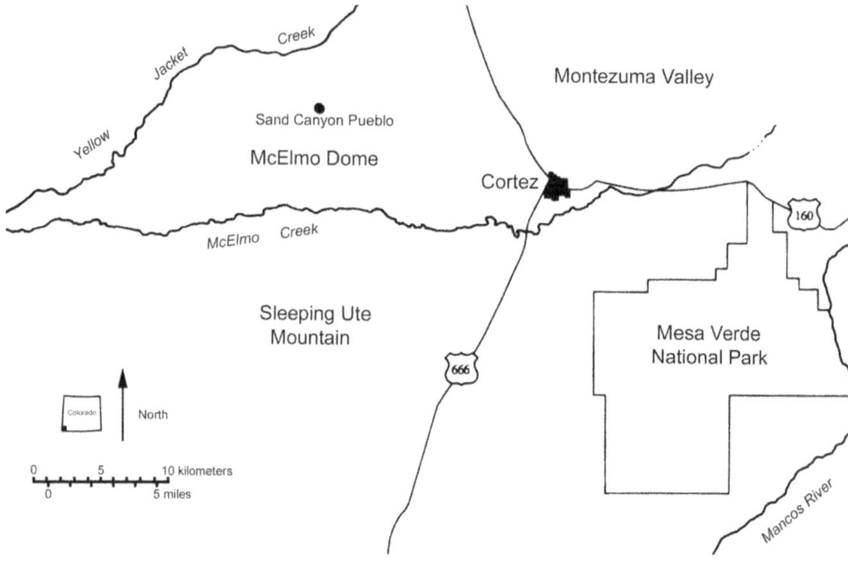

Fig. 4.1 Location of Sand Canyon Pueblo. Map by Bruce A. Bradley.

in southwestern Colorado. Most published research has focused on the large cliff dwellings on Mesa Verde (Rohn 1971; Cattanach 1980), even though the majority of the large sites lie in the adjacent Montezuma Valley. More recent research has focused on interpretation of social organization in a late thirteenth-century Ancestral Puebloan community in the McElmo Dome area west of Cortez, Colorado (Adler 1990; Bradley 1992, 1993; Lipe and Bradley 1988; Huber 1993) (figure 4.1).

Between 1985 and 1996, I conducted research at one of these large pueblo sites. Sand Canyon Pueblo (5MT765) is a massive open-air ruin located at the head of a canyon, and it includes about 100 kivas, 420 rooms, 14 towers, a central plaza, a D-shaped bi-wall structure, a great kiva, and other architectural and landscape architectural features and open spaces (figure 4.2). My research was designed to investigate the architectural diversity within the site as well as site history, use, function, and abandonment. Excavations included six complete kiva suites, one-half of the D-shaped bi-wall building, and testing in an additional eleven kivas, the great kiva, and areas outside of the architecture.

Generally speaking, open-air Pueblo II and Pueblo III (A.D. 900–1300) household architecture is fairly standardized with a basic unit consisting of a roomblock of from eight to twelve rooms, a subterranean kiva, and a midden area. These units are usually aligned on a north–south axis with the rooms on the north and the midden to the south. T. Mitchell Prudden (1903) dubbed this form a "unit type" pueblo, interpreted as representing households whose membership was a single family of five to ten people.

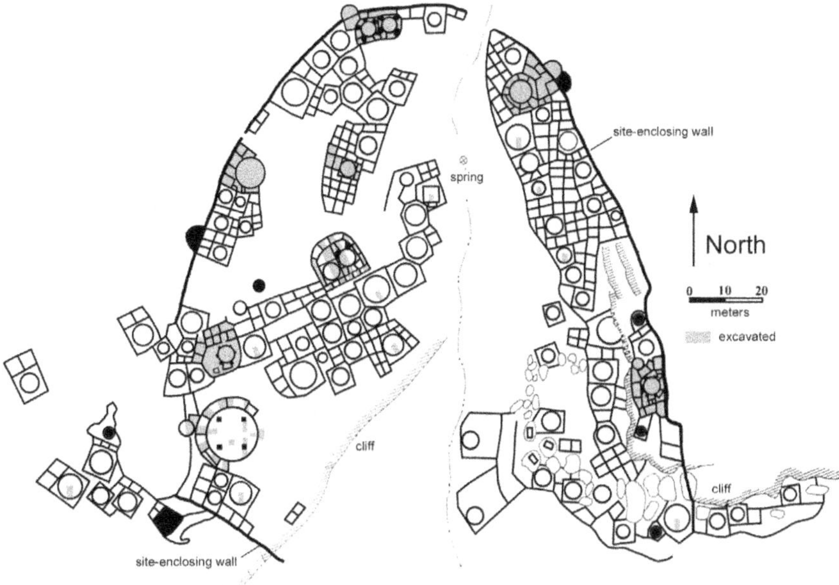

Fig. 4.2 Sand Canyon Pueblo plan. Map by Bruce A. Bradley.

Arthur Rohn (1971:37–39) has identified another form of late Ancestral Puebloan architecture in some of the thirteenth-century cliff dwellings on Mesa Verde. These units incorporate two or more suites of rooms adjacent to a courtyard, associated with a single subterranean kiva. These units are thought to represent multiple households of related families, which shared a kiva. In addition to habitations, public architecture in the form of great kivas, great houses, multiwall structures, and enclosed plazas has also been identified and described at many of the larger sites. The plaza, like the courtyard, is an important element of the landscape architecture of these sites. It is believed that these structures served special functions for large segments of or even entire communities.

Several forms of architectural units have been identified at Sand Canyon Pueblo. The basic unit is a kiva suite consisting of a kiva and associated architecture. The makeup of these suites is highly variable and there is probably a range of social units and activities represented by them. Kiva suites are organized into clusters known as architectural blocks. These in turn are spatially organized into a two-part site plan with east and west components separated by a drainage containing a spring.

Excavations in architectural units have disclosed kiva suites that consist of from ten rooms and a kiva to four rooms and a kiva (figure 4.3). Additional information about unit planning, construction, and function has been acquired and analyzed to interpret architectural unit function and to interpret the social groups that may have planned, built, and used them.

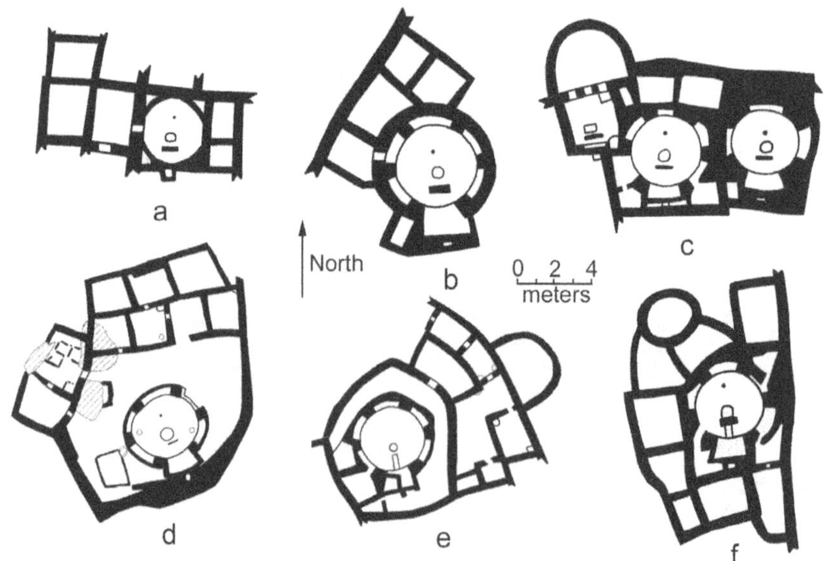

Fig. 4.3 Excavated architectural suites at Sand Canyon Pueblo: a) Block 300; b) Kiva Suite 208; c) Kiva Suites 102, 107, and 108; d) Kiva Suite 501; e) Kiva Suite 1004; and f) Kiva Suite 1206. Illustration by Bruce A. Bradley.

Determination of construction sequences of the units is critical in interpreting their degree of planning and use-histories. Analysis of construction sequences using wall ties and abutments, stratigraphy, and superposition has allowed the identification of core architectural units and subsequent additions to the core units. In one case, it has been possible to determine not only the relative construction sequence but also the time intervals between the building stages of the core unit. The core unit of Kiva Suite 1206 was completed in four stages beginning in A.D. 1260 with the construction of a two-story room (figure 4.4a), continued in A.D. 1261 with the addition of four rooms (figure 4.4b), and completed in A.D. 1262 with the addition of the kiva (figure 4.4c). Additional rooms were added as the unit was used (figure 4.4d).

I have calculated relative labor investment through the construction history of architectural units by a formula that determines person hours (ph) per cubic meter of masonry construction (37.5 ph) plus estimates of roofing effort by structure type. This formula was derived through experimental building and ruin stabilization records. The amount of labor investment expended in a given amount of time on the construction of a kiva suite should help determine the size of the social unit that could have undertaken the effort. The intensity of labor investment has been determined by the amount of labor expended on an architectural unit divided by the area covered by the unit. I believe there may be a difference in intended function and symbolic value

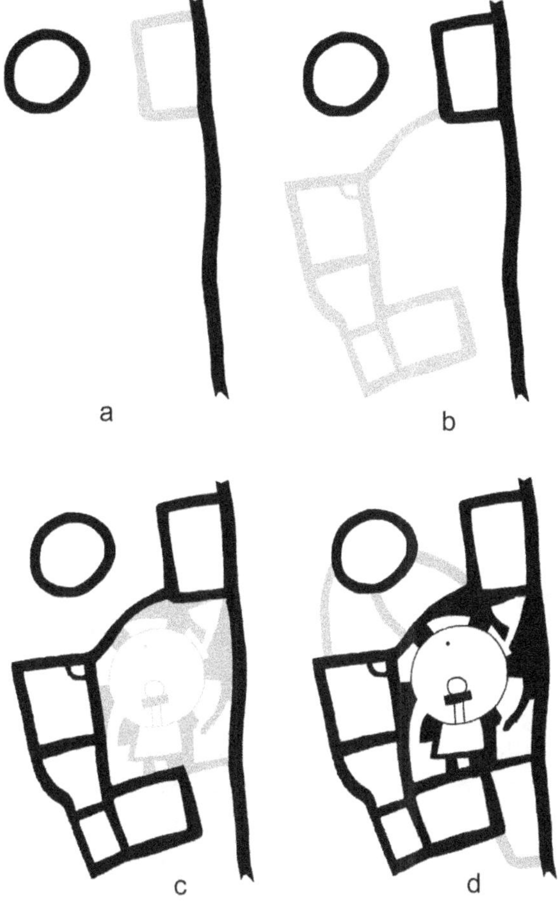

Fig. 4.4 Construction sequence of Kiva Suite 1206: a) first building stage; b) second building stage; c) third building stage; and d) additions to core unit. Illustration by Bruce A. Bradley.

expressed by the relative intensity of labor expended on an architectural unit. The greater the intensity (lower usable floor space per person hour of labor), the greater the probability of specialized function of the unit (for example, as seen in most monumental architecture).

Structure accessibility, through doorways and hatchways, expresses a measure of integration of structures within architectural units and is assumed to reflect unit function. The greater the degree of control of access, the greater the probability of specialized function for the structure and unit. A measure of integration (Bradley 1996) has been derived for each of the structures at Sand Canyon Pueblo, and differences between kiva suites have been noted (figure 4.5). Kiva suites with few rooms are poorly integrated, internally and with the adjacent open space, and may have served a special function, in this case ritual. Kiva suites that conform to the standard Ancestral Puebloan room-to-kiva ratio of around 10:1 are well integrated and were probably primarily habitations.

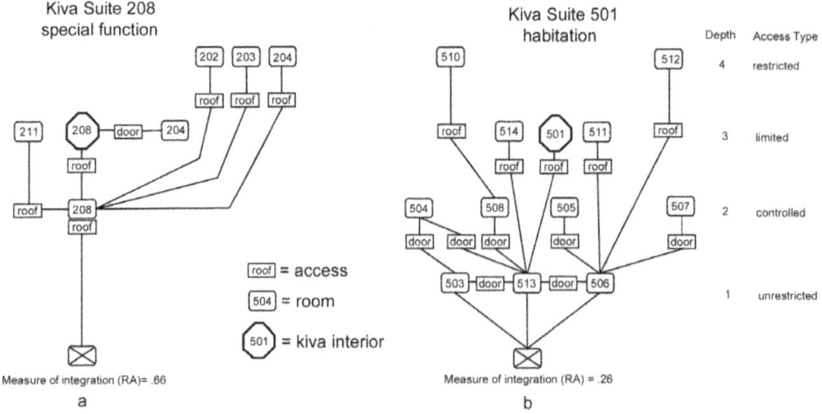

Fig. 4.5 Examples of differences in kiva suite accesses: a) a poorly integrated, special function architectural unit; and b) a well-integrated domestic habitation unit. Illustration by Bruce A. Bradley.

Two of the excavated architectural units in Sand Canyon Pueblo illustrate these differences. Structures excavated in Architectural Block 100 include two circular aboveground kivas (102 and 108), a subrectangular kiva (107), a D-shaped tower (101), and two rooms (104 and 105). These structures are bordered by the site-enclosing wall to the north, internal open space to the south and east, and an unexcavated kiva to the west. With a kiva suite being a kiva and associated nonkiva structures, this excavation area includes three separate kiva suites. The overall room-to-kiva ratio is 2:3. The site-enclosing wall, an important landscape architectural feature, and an unexcavated kiva to the west preceded the construction of Kiva 102 in or soon after A.D. 1274. This was followed by the addition of Kivas 107 and 101, and finally, Rooms 104 and 105 and Kiva 108 were added. Each of these construction episodes represents the addition of a new kiva suite. The time intervals between these construction episodes is unknown.

The function of these kiva suites is inferred to have been specialized and nonhabitational based on the lack of domestic features, such as primary food processing facilities (mealing bins), the scarcity of storage space, the relative intensity of construction effort, special symbolic investment in architectural petroglyphs (rock art incorporated in structure walls or below structure floors), and the poor integration of the structures. Artifact abandonment assemblages and animal bone remains (Muir 1999) support this interpretation.

In contrast, Kiva Suite 501 was constructed in or after A.D. 1252; it began as a large room that was partitioned into two rooms (figure 4.6a), followed by the addition of two rooms and a southern retaining wall (figure 4.6b). Finally, a subterranean room and a kiva were added into the outlined area (figure 4.6c). At this stage, there were five rooms and a kiva. A prepared courtyard was present

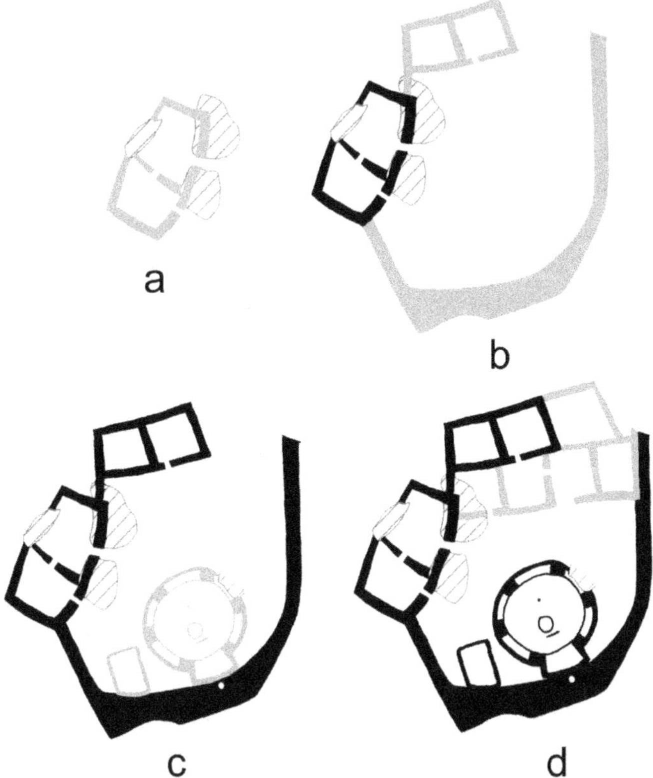

Fig. 4.6 Construction sequence of Kiva Suite 501: a) first building stage; b) second building stage; c) third building stage; and d) additions to core unit. Map by Bruce A. Bradley.

in front of the rooms extending across the top of the kiva roof. I consider this architecture to be the core unit of Kiva Suite 501. Although wall abutments suggest that this core unit was constructed by accretion, there is no direct evidence to indicate that any of the structures were in use while the others were being built. From this I conclude that the core unit was constructed to a plan, which was completed in three stages. I don't know if each of the building stages was done in a different year as seen in Kiva Suite 1206. Secondary refuse accumulated east of the north rooms while they were in use, after which five rooms were added in front and extending to the east (figure 4.6d). These new rooms utilized the courtyard surface and a thin secondary refuse deposit for floors. At abandonment, Kiva Suite 501 included nine ground-level rooms, a subterranean room, a courtyard, and a kiva.

In terms of functional space, this kiva suite includes storage rooms, a living room, a primary food processing room, an adjacent courtyard space, a kiva, and a small subterranean room. Structure access ranged from unrestricted to restricted and the unit as a whole is well integrated. Construction effort was relatively low. Remodeling is present but not extensive. Architecturally, this kiva suite is a classic "unit type" pueblo that functioned as a habitation for a single household. The size and membership of the household probably varied through time. The artifact abandonment assemblage in the kiva suggests that ritual activities may have been taking place at that time.

The presence of this domestic suite in what is otherwise a kiva-dominated architectural block (see figure 4.2) is of interest. If the surrounding architecture (consisting of individual kivas) was also domestic in function, it would indicate that traditional kiva suite form was changing fundamentally. Although possible, it is just as likely that there were different functions for the other kiva suites in this block.

The amount of preplanning that went into the construction of an architectural unit at Sand Canyon Pueblo is difficult to determine, but it is clear that core units of unit type kiva suites took several years to complete, were preplanned, included enclosed open space, and were not the result of haphazard or expedient construction. There is even tree-ring evidence that logs were being stockpiled one to two years in advance of construction.

I have assessed site-wide planning in terms of the distribution of kiva suite types (defined by room-to-kiva ratios), architectural blocks, open spaces, and public architecture. Planning of community-level construction is present at the beginning of site formation as evidenced by the enclosing wall, the great kiva, and the D-shaped building (figure 4.7a). Although it would take total excavation of the site to determine the construction sequence of each of the architectural blocks, I see pioneer units (figure 4.7b) followed by additions through time. Domestic architecture (that is, habitation units) is present in both sides of the site; however, the western component has a greater proportion of kiva-dominated suites (greater than five rooms per kiva), as well as all of the public architecture. This distribution indicates to me that site-level planning was essentially functional zoning and that it was accomplished before any construction began.

The degree to which comparisons can be made between Sand Canyon Pueblo and contemporary sites on Mesa Verde is limited by the comparability of the available data. Generally speaking, there are a large number of similarities but there are also some distinct differences. Architectural units at Sand Canyon Pueblo consist either of single household kiva suites or special-function kiva suites and public architecture. Single household and multihousehold kivas suites are the rule in the Mesa Verde cliff dwellings where room-to-kiva ratios are consistently between 8:1 and 12:1.

Another matter that needs evaluation is the scale at which comparisons are made. Sand Canyon Pueblo may be considered either a site or a community. As a site, comparisons are made between it and other sites, such as Cliff Palace. On

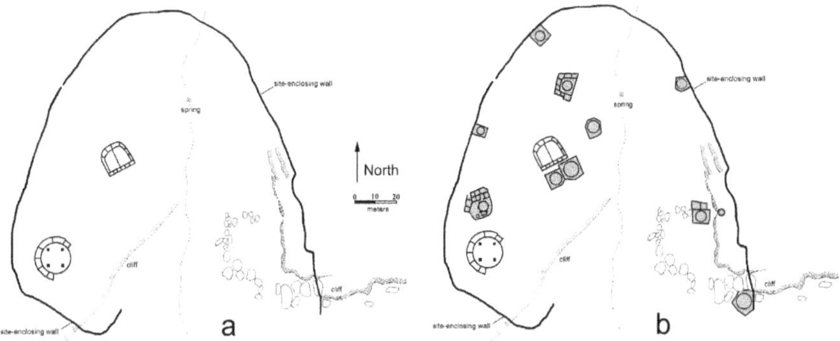

Fig. 4.7 a) Initial construction and b) pioneer kiva suites. Map by Bruce A. Bradley.

the other hand, if Sand Canyon Pueblo is thought of as a community, a more valid comparison is between it and the Cliff Palace Community (figure 4.8). I consider the Cliff Palace Community to include Fire Temple, New Fire House, Oak Tree House, Mummy House, Sun Temple, Cliff Palace, and Sunset House. At this scale there are some striking similarities, not just in general content, but also in overall layout and locations of functional units.

At Sand Canyon Pueblo there are two distinct community structures: the D-shaped building and the great kiva. The D-shaped building is situated near the center of the site, on top of and near the edge of a cliff. It commands a dominant position. The same is true for Sun Temple in the Cliff Palace Community. These two structures share many internal features such as a D-shape (a half-radial structure) with a straight side on the south, surrounding rooms, and two internal circular structures. The great kiva at Sand Canyon Pueblo is near the southwestern area of the site and west of the D-shaped building. An equivalent structure is found in a similar relative position to Sun Temple. This is the site called Fire Temple, which has been interpreted as functionally a great kiva (Ferguson and Rohn 1987:99).

In both communities there are clear habitation units and it is curious that the largest (Block 1200 at Sand Canyon Pueblo and Cliff Palace in the Cliff Palace Community) in both are to the northeast of the D-shaped buildings. All of this may be coincidence, but I think it unlikely. Several years ago I proposed a theory that envisioned a region-wide revitalization movement that incorporated architectural symbolism (Bradley 1996:241–55). I submit that the similarities between Sand Canyon Pueblo and the Cliff Palace Community are expressions of this symbolism.

In conclusion, site planning is evident at Sand Canyon Pueblo in terms of overall boundaries, as indicated by the site-enclosing wall, east and west divisions, siting of public architecture, and the distribution of architectural blocks dominated

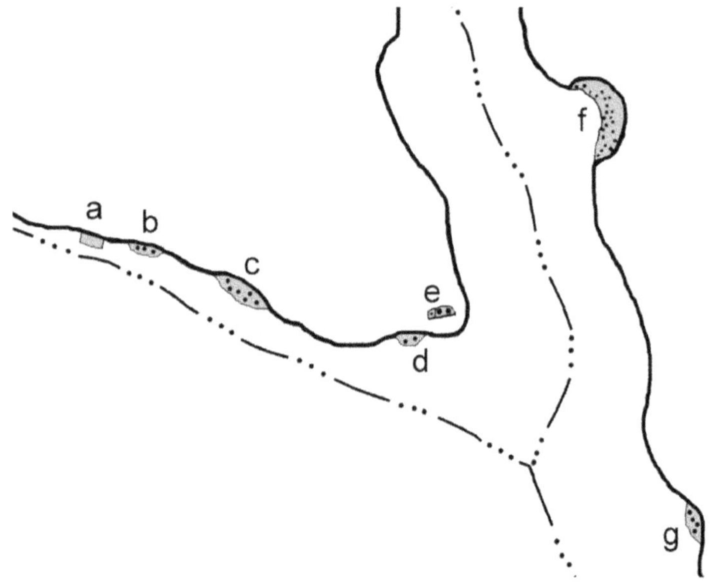

Fig. 4.8 Cliff Palace Community on Mesa Verde: a) Fire Temple; b) New Fire House; c) Oak Tree House; d) Mummy House; e) Sun Temple; f) Cliff Palace; and g) Sunset House. Illustration by Bruce A. Bradley.

by special-function kiva suites. The systematic design and construction of both structures and open space are essential aspects of settlement development and are, of course, primary characteristics of thoughtful landscape planning. The content and layout of the site may have been part of a regional development and may have had symbolic meaning. Standard domestic/habitation architectural suites were built with preplanned core units that grew through time by the addition of rooms and other features. Kiva suites range from the standard form of eight to ten rooms per kiva to individual kivas not associated with any rooms. Multihousehold courtyard units do not seem to be present. Their occurrence in the large cliff dwellings on Mesa Verde may be the result of the need to pack people into a restricted space or may represent a different social organization.

Kiva suites ranged in use from domestic habitations to specialized, probably ritual functions. The ritual kiva suites may have been used intermittently and may have involved activities of non-kin-related groups such as sodalities and/or medicine societies. Sand Canyon Pueblo also served as a locus of habitation for a large proportion, perhaps 75 percent, of the members of a complete community. It also may have served the community as a religious center that functioned to integrate the community, and possibly even a larger area, economically, socially, and politically.

Comparative architectural studies with contemporary Mesa Verde sites are possible because of the relatively large amount of work that has been done in the past century, as well as innovative theoretical approaches (Rohn 1977). What is lacking is comparable excavation data from the large aggregated Pueblo III sites in southwestern Colorado and southeastern Utah. Without this information it will be very difficult to ascertain whether the differences between Sand Canyon Pueblo and the large cliff dwellings on Mesa Verde represent different cultural expressions or if they may be parts of a larger integrated subregional system. Large-scale excavations and analyses will need to be done to even begin to answer many of the questions posed here. Are the specialized architectural forms a product of different organizational or belief systems? Is there a size threshold at which aggregations of people need additional mechanisms of social integration? Could the specialized architectural forms at Sand Canyon Pueblo represent the development of a new social order that is also expressed on Mesa Verde? Additional research is needed to answer these questions and will undoubtedly raise even more of them. Ancestral Puebloan architecture and landscape architecture are indeed a durable legacy, but unless they continue to be studied on an adequate scale and new data are collected, the history of the Ancient Ones will continue to remain a mystery.

Funding and support for this research were provided by the Crow Canyon Archaeological Center, the National Science Foundation, and National Geographic. Excavations were conducted under the authority of antiquities permits issued by the Bureau of Land Management, San Juan Area Office, Colorado.

References Cited

Adler, Michael A.

1990 Communities of Soil and Stone: An Archaeological Investigation of Population Aggregation among the Mesa Verde Region Anasazi A.D. 900–1300. PhD diss., University of Michigan, Ann Arbor.

Bradley, Bruce A.

1992 Excavations at Sand Canyon Pueblo. In *The Sand Canyon Archaeological Project: A Progress Report*, ed. William D. Lipe. Occasional Papers of the Crow Canyon Archaeological Center, no. 2. Cortez, CO: Crow Canyon Archaeological Center.

1993 Planning, Growth, and Functional Differentiation at a Prehistoric Pueblo: A Case Study from Southwestern Colorado. *Journal of Field Archaeology* 20:23–42.

1996 Pitchers to Mugs: Chacoan Revival at Sand Canyon Pueblo. *Kiva* 61 (3): 241–55.

Cattanach, George S., Jr.

1980 Long House, Mesa Verde National Park, Colorado. Publications in Archaeology 7H. Washington, DC: National Park Service, U.S. Department of the Interior.

Ferguson, William and Arthur Rohn

1987 *Anasazi Ruins of the Southwest in Color*. Albuquerque: University of New Mexico Press.

Hillier, Bill, and Julienne Hanson

1984 *The Social Logic of Space*. Cambridge: Cambridge University Press.

Huber, Edgar K.

1993 Thirteenth-Century Pueblo Aggregation and Organizational Change in Southwestern Colorado. PhD diss., Department of Anthropology, Washington State University, Pullman.

Lipe, William D., and Bruce A. Bradley

1988 Prehistoric Pueblo Organization, Sand Canyon Locality, Southwestern Colorado. Research proposal submitted to the National Science Foundation. Cortez, CO: Crow Canyon Archaeological Center.

Muir, Robert James

1999 Zooarchaeology of Sand Canyon Pueblo, Colorado. PhD diss., Department of Archaeology, Simon Fraser University, Burnaby, British Columbia, Canada.

Prudden, T. Mitchell

1903 The Prehistoric Ruins of the San Juan Watershed of Utah, Arizona, Colorado and New Mexico. *American Anthropologist* 5:224–88.

Rohn, Arthur H.

1971 Mug House. Archaeological Research Series, no. 7-D. Washington, DC: National Park Service, U.S. Department of the Interior.

1977 *Cultural Change and Continuity on Chapin Mesa*. Lawrence: Regents Press of Kansas.

Chapter Five

Tewa Fields, Tewa Traditions

by Kurt F. Anschuetz

To understand how Ancestral Puebloan and Pueblo peoples went about "earning a living" in the difficult climate and terrain of the Southwest, it is necessary to temper old concepts like the "abandonment" of sites brought on by drastic and seemingly permanent changes in climatic conditions with a more realistic understanding of flexibility, impermanent migration, and modulated change. Archaeologist Kurt Anschuetz amasses evidence that suggests the agricultural practices and technologies of Tewa speakers in northern New Mexico were cycled through seasons of drought and plenty in which fields were never completely abandoned. In this description, horticulture, wild plant harvesting, and water retention and conservation were year-round activities that embodied the "day to day practice of Pueblo religion."

Why the Agricultural Landscape?

Archaeological research into the Pueblos' past in the northern Southwest historically has focused on the study of large villages and the rich cultural assemblages that investigators have recovered during excavation. Such a focus makes ready sense given that pueblos characteristically represent containers of rich, diverse assemblages of archaeological traces. By working in the Pueblos' old houses, investigators not only assure themselves of the recovery of abundant remnants of people's past activities, they also are able to document much needed contextual information with which to construct interpretive histories.

Armed with excavation data obtained from the study of villages, archaeologists have offered insightful accounts of Pueblo settlement across space and over time. The discipline has witnessed expanded interest in the formal study of small-site phenomena, including limited activity areas, camps, field houses, farmsteads, and agricultural fields, during recent decades to complement their big-village focus. In broadening their pursuits, investigators have tackled increasingly difficult questions about the evolution of Pueblo settlement sensitive to fine-grained spatial and temporal patterns of similarity and difference. Moreover, the increased sophistication in the kinds of questions that archaeologists now ask and in the refined techniques that they have at their disposal have led to much fruitful examination of how Pueblo people *made their living* in the region's unpredictable and ever-changing climate.

Equipped with advances in method and theory, researchers have documented broad patterns of Pueblo history with ever-greater description and quantified measurement. Nevertheless, even as they recognize variation across the dimensions of space and time, archaeologists have struggled in their attempts to explain the complexly intertwined natural, social, and cultural processes underlying the patterned changes among the surviving traces of past Pueblo people's lives.

My choice of the phrase "people made their living" in reference to archaeologists' traditional assessments of the Pueblos' past is deliberate. The characterization of a people devoted to *making their living* focuses attention principally on how the Pueblos brought together all the elements necessary to build their livelihood. Such constructions cast the Pueblos as forcibly imposing themselves upon their physical environments to obtain the resources that they needed to support their everyday lives.

Together, archaeology, history, and ethnography have taught us that the Pueblos historically formed communities of agrarian peoples who relied on technologically simple hand tools for growing a triad of domestic cultigens—corn, beans, and squash—fed by summer rains and the intermittent runoff the storms produced. Moreover, archaeologists' prevailing cultural-historical constructions have conditioned us to view the Pueblos' relationships with their environments literally from the ground up.

Ascending the conceptually compartmentalized rungs of Hawkes's (1954) "Ladder of Reference," archaeologists have informed us that we should place our highest confidence in constructions that address people's economic interactions with their physical environment as they made their living. We expect that our comprehension of past Pueblo societies is dependent on what we first can learn about the people's economic activities. We presume further that our understanding of how the Pueblos looked in their past depends on what we can know about their economies and societies. We perceive that the Pueblos' agricultural landscapes constitute a record of subsistence farmers planting, tending, and harvesting domestic cultigens. The details offered by "talkative tree-rings" (Douglass 1929; see also Dean 1988; Dean et al. 1985; Orcutt 1991, 1993; Plog et al. 1988; Rose, Dean, and Robinson 1981; Rose, Robinson, and Dean 1982; Van West 1994) and other quantitative methods of environmental construction (for example, Dean et al. 1985; Euler et al. 1979; Karlstrom 1988; Orcutt 1991, 1993; Plog et al. 1988) have contributed greatly to our knowledge of the past. Nevertheless, in its application of these data, the discipline generally has treated early Pueblo peoples as automatons who waited passively for the rains to come—or not come—before taking action. Moreover, whenever environmental vagaries such as drought befell them, we expect that people would have reacted in the hierarchical order of Hawkes's (1954) "Ladder of Reference" to dampen threats to their existence. That is, when faced with the challenge of explaining transformations in the settlement histories of sites, localities, and regions, we have been taught that pragmatic concerns structuring the economic strategies and tactics with which people interacted with their physical environment conditioned how they modified the organization of their societies and possibly even ultimately informed the revision of their worldviews.

Because "destroy" is an antonym of "make," it is not surprising that archaeologists typically interpret evidence of residential instability as a likely outcome of deteriorating farmland productivity over time, if not sustained cycles of outright crop failure. Citing widespread patterns of villages falling into destructive ruin, investigators concomitantly equate the withdrawal of Pueblo populations from localities as the *abandonment* of environments from which it was no longer materially possible for people to make their livelihood.

My purpose here is not to question whether Pueblo people historically invested great labor in constructing, using, and maintaining agricultural fields for the production of plants needed to sustain their subsistence economy. We know that Pueblo people, in some places and at some times (for example, in the central San Juan Basin [Vivian 1974, 1990] and the northern Rio Grande valley [Anschuetz 1998a; see also below], among others), significantly made over their physical environments for growing crops. Nor is it my purpose to question the general interpretation that the movements of people out of their large villages and wholesale withdrawals from localities at various points in time were actions linked to downturns in farmland production. The concentration of populations into fewer but larger villages and the intensification of economic production in circumscribed geographic districts may be viewed, in part, as high-order Pueblo strategies for buffering productive risk (see review in Anschuetz 1998a).

It is fair to question, however, the fixity and finality that are embedded in the archaeologists' interpretive schema, particularly when general frameworks are applied uncritically across narrowly defined samples of space and time within the Pueblos' overall landscapes. Does evidence of residential instability at the big villages invariably mean some kind of intractable environmental deterioration, if not outright destruction, of the people's agricultural base? Is the depopulation of pueblos within a locality necessary and sufficient evidence of the Pueblos' abandonment of a place? Might not the ways that people understand the nature of their cosmos and their purpose in the natural world influence how they *earn their living*?

By posing these questions, we position ourselves to ask how worldview and society, the higher steps of Hawkes's (1954) "Ladder of Reference," might effectively condition the organization of peoples' perceptions of their world and the structure of their interactions with their environment, including their agricultural strategies and tactics. Rather than rigidly viewing people as imposing themselves upon their environments, the idea of *earning a living* acknowledges the possibility that ideation and society define idealized behavioral principles, based on traditional cultural knowledge, for sustaining family and community in the present and into the future by working in considered relationship with the environment. In this process, the top and middle rungs of Hawkes's (1954) "Ladder of Reference" interact with both the economy and the physical setting directly to cast people in the creative roles of actors who anticipate and prepare for future environmental states, and respond as well to realized perturbations that they perceive as important.

Recent anthropological consideration of Tewa agricultural landscapes in the northern Rio Grande region of New Mexico suggests that major aspects of Southwesternists' common interpretive archaeological constructions have bumped against a paradigmatic wall. Landscape approaches not only place doubt on the appropriateness of the hierarchical reasoning embedded in the ways that social scientists characteristically frame their questions about the Pueblos' histories and their explanations of linked cycles of construction and destruction, they also reveal that many prevailing archaeological constructs minimize, if not overlook, the web of relationships embedded in the tactics and strategies with which the Pueblos have occupied their landscapes across the generations.

The landscape offers the potential to yield a new understanding of the complex mix of natural, social, and cultural processes through which the Pueblos came to be who they are today (after Peckham 1990), as it acknowledges the contributing role of tradition as a unifying thread when we consider how communities of people interact dynamically with their environments across the dimensions of space and time. The landscape, of which water management and agricultural field works are an integral part, allows us the opportunity to assess the active role that Pueblo people played in changing their own economic, social, and cultural conditions for living to the extent that formally benign or mild environmental perturbations had increasingly significant consequences (for example, see Minnis 1985). It also enables us to begin comprehending the importance of place in Pueblo culture that underlies—and gives meaning to—the Pueblos' insistence on their continued occupation of homeland areas beyond the land grant or reservation boundaries variously defined and redefined by the Spanish colonial, Mexican, and U.S. governments since the end of the sixteenth century.

The Tewa Homeland

The Tewa cultural landscape in north-central New Mexico is the product of a Pueblo people's long history of occupation of a myriad of discrete places, both large and small, among the mountains defining the flanks of the Rio Grande rift valley. The traditional and historical Tewa homeland centers in the Española Basin. This physiographic setting extends roughly between Velarde and Tesuque along the Rio Grande main stem and includes the lower Rio Chama, Santa Cruz, Pojoaque, Nambe, and Tesuque valleys. The physiographic boundaries of this locality coincide with the area still inhabited today by the six autonomous Tewa communities of San Juan, Santa Clara, San Ildefonso, Pojoaque, Nambe, and Tesuque. Nonetheless, all Tewa people view their world as being enclosed by peaks in the Sangre de Cristo, Sandia, and Jemez mountains, as well as prominent summits near the New Mexico–Colorado state line far beyond the sightlines of any of the villages.

Paleoclimatic studies throughout the region reveal that the Tewa perpetuated their communities in the face of ever-changing climatic conditions and rapidly expanding populations over the three centuries leading up to Spanish contact (A.D. 1250–1540). Ongoing studies of architecture and pottery fragments indicate the Tewa maintained their communities in the face of periodic transformations in economy, society, and worldview over this same time span. Spanish contact (1540–98) and colonization (1598–1822), unpredictable moisture and temperature regimes, and catastrophic community population losses to a host of introduced diseases, slavery, and Hispano intermarriage confronted the Tewa with still greater challenges to their existing economic, social, and cultural orders. Throughout these centuries of flux and uncertainty, the Tewa left compelling historical records, both in their oral accounts and on the physical environment in the form of often subtle archaeological traces that reveal how they successfully sustained a sense of continuity in their landscapes despite manifold vectors of change. Moreover, the traceable genesis of Tewa agricultural landscape in the late thirteenth century and its evolution through the early eighteenth century offer valuable insights into how these people laid the foundations for traditions upon which contemporary Tewa culture rests.

Looking at the Landscape from the Ground Up

In recent decades, investigators increasingly have recognized and documented dense remnants of old Tewa agricultural fields and facilities, which apparently date from as early as ca. A.D. 1250 to as late as ca. 1730, in many different physiographic settings throughout the Española Basin (for example, Anschuetz 1998a,

Fig. 5.1 Stone-lined squares, forming garden "grids," are excellent containers for ancient Puebloan vegetables, grains, and other crops. Photo by Kurt F. Anschuetz.

1998b, 2001; Anschuetz and Hena 1991; Anschuetz, Maxwell, and Ware 1985; Anschuetz, Dominguez, and Camilli 2000; Bugé 1984; Fiero 1978; Lang 1981; Maxwell 2000; Maxwell and Anschuetz 1992; Moore 1992; Ware and Mensel 1992, among others). These features include a mix of gravel-mulched plots, rock-bordered grids (figure 5.1), cobble step terraces, short terraces, diversion dams/spreaders constructed across washes to slow runoff, stone-lined ditches, and constructed swales, pits, and broad mesa-top planting areas (as identified through the study of agricultural hoes, axes, and associated tool-sharpening slicks in combination with soil and pollen analyses [figure 5.2]). Archaeological studies of agricultural feature morphology and function demonstrate that the Tewa relied upon integrated systems of technologically diverse farming tactics and strategies to harvest and conserve water for agricultural production (for example, Anschuetz 1998a; Anschuetz, Dominguez, and Camilli 2000; Dominguez 2000; Hudspeth 2000; Maxwell 2000; Maxwell and Anschuetz 1992). The archaeological information also indicates that, just as in the ethnographic present, the Tewa manipulated all four principal moisture resources available in their natural settings: direct precipitation, intermittent runoff, groundwater, and permanently flowing river, spring, and seep water during the late pre-Columbian and early historic periods (after Anschuetz 1998a:139–51).

Through the framework of meaning structured by their worldview (see below), the Tewa understood that they could not sit back passively and assume that there would be adequate moisture for crop production (Anschuetz 1995,

Fig. 5.2 Stone implements such as these were commonly used in stone-lined gardens. Photo by Kurt F. Anschuetz.

1998a). Their observation of the natural history of water in their environment over the generations had taught the Tewa (and their forebears) that they could ill afford to overlook winter precipitation in constructing and occupying their agricultural landscapes. They knew that if they were able to enhance the absorption and retention of snowmelt into the soil, such ample moisture would be available in the spring, and more rapid seedling development could occur than otherwise would be possible (Anschuetz 1998a, 2001; Anschuetz and Hena 1991). The Tewa also knew that they had to capture and to conserve water received during the summer's often high-intensity but brief monsoons to ensure their cultigens would have sufficient moisture to mature fully. They needed to prevent natural runoff processes from robbing valuable water from their fields. The Tewa mastered techniques responsive to their Southwestern ecological setting for enhancing the ground's capacity to absorb both winter and summer precipitation (figure 5.3). The people treated the land as a sponge throughout the year (see Anschuetz 2001).

The evolution of Tewa agricultural landscape engineering depended on more than just the hydrological integration of disparate technologies and planting strategies, however. In the face of marked increases in regional population densities between the thirteenth and fifteenth centuries, Tewa farmers actively managed both quantitatively and qualitatively different sources of moisture for crop production (Anschuetz 1998a; Hudspeth 2000). Archaeological evidence suggests that the Tewa continually added to their earlier field complexes over the fourteenth

Fig. 5.3 Stone terraces channel and contain water in sandy soils, even on steep slopes. Photo by Kurt F. Anschuetz.

and fifteenth centuries (figure 5.4). Moreover, they even began harvesting seepage moisture, runoff flowing down larger watersheds, and water held in deep sand deposits, which function as natural mulches, on mesa tops that they previously had not used (for example, see Anschuetz 1998a; Dominguez 2000; Maxwell 2000).

Looking at the Landscape from the Top Down

While anthropologists traditionally have identified rain making as the principal referent of Pueblo ritual and religious belief (e.g., Beaglehole 1937:45), this perspective is too narrow. Cross-culturally, Pueblo religion rests on a coherent system of belief about how water mediates between the natural and supernatural worlds of the cosmos through a constantly repeating cycle of transformations in form and power (for example, see Anschuetz 1992, 1998a). In this metaphorical ebb and flow of energies, water is not simply a material product and time is not a linear sequence. Rather, they are components in a continual process of *becoming* based on the renewal of supernatural associations (for example, see Ortiz 1969).

Given this essential link between religious belief and economic practice, it is unsurprising that the Tewa occupation of their agricultural landscapes is complicated by the occurrence of numerous shrines consisting of boulders with pecked and ground cupules, incised cobbles, petroglyph panels, and semicircular rock rings (Anschuetz 1995, 1998a). Many of these manifestations occur near old fields and next to the archaeological remnants of farmsteads and field houses. Other shrines enclose villages or top certain hills or mountains that the Tewa still regard

Fig. 5.4 Grid gardens were often laid out in piñon-juniper woodlands, creating ideal small spaces for intensive cultivation. Photo by Kurt F. Anschuetz.

as holy places today. Researchers (for example, Douglass 1917; Hill 1982; Jeançon 1923; Ortiz 1969; Parsons 1939) who worked with the Tewa during the previous century report that such shrines represent places where people solicit supernatural powers for their assistance in providing water to the natural world.

Rooted in the ideas of renewal and process, water in its various material and ethereal forms unifies the contrasting seasons of the annual cycle and reaffirms the interdependency of people and their cultigens, especially maize (Anschuetz 1992, 1998a; Ford 1994). Among Pueblo people generally, large harvests of corn and other cultivars throughout the summer and fall stand as irrefutable evidence that the movement of life energy, as it flows between the natural and supernatural worlds of their cosmos, is unimpeded (after Anschuetz and Dean 1994:124). In this sense, agricultural work stands as the day-to-day practice of Pueblo religion because it embodies both physical and mental energies.

Earning a Living

Although rather general, this review of the ground up and top down views of Tewa agricultural landscapes provides a framework for challenging our own thinking about the organization and structure of Tewa farmland traditions. We can begin this task by considering how agricultural practice refers both to a living, dynamic process and a series of seemingly unrelated products over the span of the annual cycle.

Within Tewa systems of belief, the preparation of fields, the tending of crops, and the harvesting of ripened produce are more than a series of economic activities whose common purpose is the achievement of a particular material gain. Given that the Tewa view harvesttime simultaneously as the end of one agricultural cycle and the beginning of the next, each of these activities becomes a time of transformation and recommitment to a continuing process involving manipulation of water. For example, people build or refurbish, plant, and then leave their fields, and this prepares the earth to absorb moisture for sustaining plants over the span of the annual cycle. As such, agriculture is a year-round activity and the permanent fixture of the Tewa landscape.

If we acknowledge the tactical and strategic diversity in farming technologies but steadfastly hold on to the idea that every planting bed simply represents a place of domestic crop production, we miss a second indispensable principle of Tewa agricultural landscapes: a field is not just a field. The water harvesting and conservation properties built into the Tewa agricultural landscape would have contributed to the historical ecology of the localities they occupy by enhancing groundwater resources for the benefit of native flora and fauna, as well as domestic cultigens (Louie Hena, director, Picuris Pueblo Environmental Program, pers. comm. 1999; see also Mollison 1988). So even as we now begin to comprehend how the Tewas' traditional agricultural technologies harvested and conserved moisture over the span of the annual cycle, we confront the challenge of building an understanding of how fields provided economically, socially, and culturally useful products throughout the year.

Ethnography teaches us that Pueblo farmers traditionally polycropped their fields with a mixture of domesticated and various "wild" plant taxa (or plant species) for edible greens and seeds, tools, twine, dyes, pot herbs, medicines, and ceremonial uses (for example, see Ford 1968; Nabhan 1989). Archaeological study of sediment collected from old fields suggests Pueblo populations cultivated a variety of wild plant taxa, including little barley grass, panic grass, grain amaranth, sunflower, tobacco, and devil's claw (for example, Bohrer 1991; Fish 1984; Ford 1985; Smith 1998).

By acknowledging ethnohistoric evidence (for example, Benavides 1916:36; Domínguez 1956:126; Winship [1904] 1990:146) that the Tewa (and the other Pueblos') fields characteristically were still full of stubble and wild plants after a harvest, we can begin to evaluate the possibility that the people supplied themselves with plant products, such as edible prickly pear pads, whose availability is not determined by the frost-free season. This field use pattern has other significant ecological implications: a rich admixture of plants might serve to maintain the kind of biodiversity that sustains the soil's fertility. Some species might repel insect predators and diseases, while others might attract the kinds of beneficial insects, birds, and animals needed for successful pollination. Fields left full of plants over the fall and winter might attract game birds and animals that the people can harvest for food (Richard Ford, University of Michigan Museum of Anthropology, pers. comm. 1998). If we extend this ecological logic further, we can grasp the idea that fields left in both short- and long-term fallow can also be productive in the sense that their disturbed habitats can produce plants directly useful to people, attractive to game birds or animals, or needed to restore the soil's fertility.

The final undertaking of this essay is to contextualize and evaluate widespread archaeologically observed patterns of residential instability and movement (see Anschuetz 1998a; Anschuetz and Scheick 1996). As outsiders looking back upon the Pueblos' past from a putatively objective scientific perspective, archaeologists reasonably can view these repeated cycles of people's movement in and out of the big villages as productive and organizational strategies for sustaining their populations through perpetual change (see above).

Contemporary Tewa landscape constructions and understandings provide useful perspectives for evaluating historical ecological processes. For example, Tewa oral traditions commonly employ the concepts of rest and renewal when referring to population movement, houses, agricultural land, and foraging and collecting areas. As stated by Tito Naranjo and Rina Swentzell, "Movement is the revered element of life" (Naranjo 1998:261). Tessie Naranjo adds, "Movement, clouds, wind and rain are one. Movement must be emulated by the people" (248). Such concepts of rest and renewal coincide nicely with the idea of fallow cycles for hunting and gathering territories as well as agricultural land.

Traditional community histories, in combination with archaeologically visible patterns across the agricultural landscape, instruct us that the Tewa characteristically did not develop lands for agricultural production only to abandon them easily, or without further regard, after a few years or even a few generations of use. The idea that the Tewa would farm a locality, allowing it to rest and renew its fertility, carries the implication that the people would return to this location at some time in the future.

The likelihood that Tewa (and other Pueblo) populations cycled across their landscapes in a series of settlement shifts over the course of their lives as part of a formal long-term strategy for sustaining agricultural production is intriguing. Importantly, this strategy was not limited to the pre-Columbian past: a body of archaeological and ethnohistorical evidence indicates that the Tewa periodically reoccupied some of their pre-Columbian home and agricultural field sites in the Española Basin's secondary watersheds between the seventeenth and early eighteenth centuries (for example, Anschuetz 1998a, 1998b; Ford and Anschuetz 1995; Hammond and Rey 1966: Enrico Martínez Map of 1602; Harrington 1916; Naranjo 1998; Schroeder 1979; Ramenofsky 1998).

On the one hand, these findings challenge still-prevalent cultural-historical constructions suggesting that the Tewa quit their occupation of major portions of their traditional Española Basin homeland during the century preceding Spanish colonization. While the intensity of these early historic period reoccupation cycles likely was markedly reduced compared to pre-Columbian times, these periodic forays were crucial socially and politically for maintaining the Tewas' ties to their traditional lands. Accompanying the Pueblos' continued use of the land for domestic cultigen and wild plant production is, of course, their system of water management tactics and strategies.

Conclusions

Identifiable Tewa communities have sustained their occupation of New Mexico's Española Basin since the thirteenth century. Ancestral Puebloan communities whose cultural affiliations are unknown (at least to archaeologists) date back to the seventh century. For the better part of a millennium before this, Archaic hunters and gatherers tended domestic cultigens and began building the knowledge—and lifeways—needed to sustain both their plants and their communities as the people became ever more dependent on cultigens for their livelihood.

Judging from recent archaeological and ethnographic findings, it is reasonable to suggest that the Tewas' physical and symbolic associations of themselves with maize occurred long ago in their history of becoming the people we know today. In domesticating themselves to an agricultural lifeway, the people transformed their landscapes through their physical labors and the cultural histories that they passed on from one generation to the next that gave meaning to the places they inhabited. As was the case with the water that their forebears worked so hard to harvest and conserve, the Tewas' history, their culture, and their cosmological understanding of their very being are an inseparable part of the agricultural landscape that their families have occupied since time immemorial.

References Cited

Anschuetz, K. F.

1992 Corn in the Flow of Life: Further Consideration of Hopi Concepts of *Zea mays*. Paper presented at the Fifteenth Annual Conference of the Society of Ethnobiology, National Museum of Natural History, Smithsonian Institution, Washington, DC.

1995 Two Sides of a Coin: Early Pueblo Indian Farming Practices in the Rio Arriba and the Rio Abajo of the Northern Rio Grande Region. Paper presented

at the 60th Annual Meeting, Society for American Archaeology, Minneapolis.
1998a Not Waiting for the Rain: Integrated Systems of Water Management by Pre-Columbian Pueblo Farmers in North-Central New Mexico. PhD diss., Department of Anthropology, University of Michigan, Ann Arbor.
1998b *Pre-Columbian Pueblo Agricultural Plots (AR-03-02-0460 [LA111461]) within the Proposed Las Clinicas del Norte Special-Use Permit Parcel, El Rito Ranger District, Carson National Forest, Rio Arriba County, New Mexico.* Community and Cultural Landscape Contribution 2. Santa Fe, NM: Rio Grande Foundation for Communities and Cultural Landscapes.
2001 Soaking It All In: Northern New Mexican Pueblo Lessons of Water Management and Landscape Ecology. In *Native Peoples of the Southwest: Negotiating Land, Water, and Ethnicities*, ed. Laurie Weinstein. Westport, CT: Greenwood Publishing Group.

———, and G. Dean
1994 North American Desert People. In *Deserts: The Illustrated Library of the Earth*, ed. M. Seeley, 122–27. Sydney: Weldon Owen.

———, S. R. Dominguez, and E. L. Camilli
2000 *An Archaeological Study of Pre-Columbian Agricultural Features at LA125767, Taos Resource Area, Albuquerque District, Bureau of Land Management and New Mexico State Lands in Rio Arriba County, New Mexico.* Prepared for U.S. Department of Justice, Denver, CO, and U.S. Department of Interior, Bureau of Indian Affairs, Albuquerque, NM. Albuquerque, NM: Ebert and Associates.

———, and L. Hena
1991 *A Tradition of Farming: Northern Rio Grande Pueblo Lessons of Land Stewardship and Sustainable Agriculture.* Community and Cultural Landscape Contribution 4. Prepared for the Early Pueblo Agricultural Traditions and Landscape Project through a grant by the New Mexico Endowment for the Humanities (NMEH Grant No. 1905-1056-1424). Santa Fe, NM: Rio Grande Foundation for Communities and Cultural Landscapes.

———, T. D. Maxwell, and J. A. Ware
1985 *Testing Report and Research Design for the Medanales North Project, Rio Arriba County, New Mexico.* Laboratory of Anthropology Note 347. Santa Fe: Museum of New Mexico.

———, and C. L. Scheick
1996 Part 1: The Espanola Basin Geographic Subdivision. In *A Study of Pre-Columbian and Historic Uses of the Santa Fe National Forest: Competition and Alliance in the Northern Middle Rio Grande.* Vol. 1, *The Archaeological and Historical Cultural Resources*, ed. C. L. Scheick, 107–90. Southwest Archaeological Consultants Research Series 253. Santa Fe, NM: Southwest Archaeological Consultants.

Beaglehole, E.
1937 *Notes on Hopi Economic Life.* Publications in Anthropology 15. New Haven, CT: Yale University Press.

Benavides, F. A. de
1916 *The Memorial of Fray Alonso de Benavides, 1630*, trans. E. E. Ayer and annot. F. W. Hodge and C. F. Lummis. Chicago: Privately printed.

Bohrer, V. L.
1991 Recently Recognized Cultivated and Encouraged Plants among the Hohokam. *Kiva* 56:227–35.

Bugé, D. E.
1984 Prehistoric Subsistence Strategies in the Ojo Caliente Valley, New Mexico. In *Prehistoric Agricultural Strategies in the Southwest*, ed. S. K. Fish and P. R. Fish, 27–34. Anthropological Research Papers 33. Tempe: Arizona State University.

Dean, J. S.
1988 Dendrochronology and Paleoenvironmental Reconstruction on the Colorado Plateaus. In *The Anasazi in a Changing Environment*, ed. G. J. Gumerman, 25–44. Cambridge: Cambridge University Press.

———, R. C. Euler, G. J. Gumerman, F. Plog, R. H. Hevly, and T. N. V. Karlstrom
1985 Human Behavior, Demography, and Paleoenvironment on the Colorado Plateaus. *American Antiquity* 50:537–54.

Domínguez, F. F. A.
1956 *The Missions of New Mexico, 1776: A Description by Fray Francisco Atanasio Domínguez, with Other Contemporary Documents*. Trans. and annot. E. B. Adams and F. A. Chavez. Albuquerque: University of New Mexico Press.

Dominguez, S. R.
2000 Assessing the Hydrologic Functions of Prehistoric Grid Gardens in North Central New Mexico. PhD diss., Department of Anthropology, University of New Mexico, Albuquerque.

Douglass, A. E.
1929 The Secret of the Southwest Solved by Talkative Tree Rings. *National Geographic* 56 (6): 737–70.

Douglass, W. B.
1917 Notes on the Shrines of the Tewa and Other Pueblo Indians of New Mexico. In *Proceedings of the Nineteenth International Congress of Americanists*, ed. F. W. Hodge, 344–78. Washington, DC.

Euler, R. C., G. J. Gumerman, T. N. V. Karlstrom, J. S. Dean, and R. H. Hevly
1979 The Colorado Plateau: Cultural Dynamics and Paleoenvironment. *Science* 205:1089–1101.

Fiero, K.
1978 *Draft Final Report: Prehistoric Garden Plots along the Lower Rio Chama Valley: Archaeological Investigations at Sites LA 11830, LA 11831, and LA 11832, Rio Arriba County, New Mexico*. Laboratory of Anthropology Note 111e. Santa Fe: Museum of New Mexico.

Fish, S. K.
1984 Agriculture and Subsistence Implications of the Salt-Gila Aqueduct Project Pollen Analysis. In *Hohokam Archaeology along the Salt-Gila Aqueduct Arizona Project*. Vol. 7, *Environment and Subsistence*, ed. S. K. Fish, P. R. Fish, and J. H. Madsen, 73–87. Tucson: University of Arizona Press.

Ford, R. I.
1968 An Ecological Analysis Involving the Population of San Juan Pueblo, New Mexico. PhD diss., Department of Anthropology, University of Michigan, Ann Arbor.

1985 Patterns of Prehistoric Food Production in North America. In *Prehistoric*

Food Production in North America, ed. R. I. Ford, 341–64. Anthropological Papers 75. Ann Arbor: Museum of Anthropology, University of Michigan.
1994 Corn is Our Mother. In *Corn and Culture in the Prehistoric New World*, ed. S. Johannessen and C. A. Hastorf, 513–25. Boulder, CO: Westview Press.
———, and K. F. Anschuetz
1995 Pesedeuinge Pueblo Pottery Identifications. J. A. Jeançon Collection, Colorado Springs Pioneers Museum. Manuscript on file, Museum of Anthropology, University of Michigan, Ann Arbor.
Hammond, G. P., and A. Rey
1966 *The Rediscovery of New Mexico, 1580–1594*. Albuquerque: University of New Mexico Press.
Harrington, J. P.
1916 *The Ethnogeography of the Tewa Indians*. Twenty-Ninth Annual Report of the Bureau of American Ethnology for the Years 1907–1908, 29–636. Washington, DC.
Hawkes, C. F.
1954 Archeological Theory and Method: Some Suggestions from the Old World. *American Anthropologist* 56:155–68.
Hill, W. W.
1982 *An Ethnography of Santa Clara Pueblo, New Mexico*. Ed. and annot. C. H. Lange. Albuquerque: University of New Mexico Press.
Hudspeth, W. B.
2000 The Evolutionary Ecology of Behavioral Response to Risk among Prehistoric Agriculturalists of the Lower Rio Chama, New Mexico. PhD diss., Department of Anthropology, University of New Mexico, Albuquerque.
Jeançon, J. A.
1923 *Excavations in the Chama Valley, New Mexico*. Bulletin 81. Washington, DC: Bureau of American Ethnology.
Karlstrom, T. N. V.
1988 Alluvial Chronology and Hydrologic Change of Black Mesa and Nearby Regions. In *The Anasazi in a Changing Environment*, ed. G. J. Gumerman, 45–92. Cambridge: Cambridge University Press.
Lang, R. W.
1981 *A Prehistoric Pueblo Garden Plot on the Rio Ojo Caliente, Rio Arriba County, New Mexico: Ojo Caliente Site 7, Features 1–2*. Contract Archeology Division Report O65. Santa Fe, NM: School of American Research.
Maxwell, T. D.
2000 Looking for Adaptations: A Comparative and Engineering Analysis of Prehistoric Agricultural Technologies and Techniques in the Southwest. PhD diss., Department of Anthropology, University of New Mexico, Albuquerque.
———, and K. F. Anschuetz
1992 The Southwestern Ethnographic Record and Prehistoric Agricultural Diversity. In *Gardens in Prehistory: The Archaeology of Settlement Agriculture in Greater Mesoamerica*, ed. T. W. Killion, 35–68. Tuscaloosa: University of Alabama Press.
Minnis, P. E.
1985 *Social Adaptation to Food Stress: A Prehistoric Southwestern Example*. Chicago: University of Chicago Press.

Mollison, B.
1988 *Permaculture: A Designer's Manual.* Tyalgum, Australia: Tagair Publications.
Moore, J. L.
1992 *Archaeological Testing at Three Sites West of Abiquiu, Rio Arriba County, New Mexico.* Archaeology Notes 33. Santa Fe: Office of Archaeological Studies, Museum of New Mexico.
Nabhan, G. P.
1989 *Enduring Seeds, Native American Agriculture, and Wild Plant Conservation.* San Francisco: North Point Press.
Naranjo, T.
1998 Brief Ethnohistory of El Rito, New Mexico. In *Pre-Columbian Pueblo Agricultural Plots (AR-03-02-02-0460 [LA114161]) within the Proposed Las Clinicas del Norte Special-Use Permit Parcel, El Rito Ranger District, Carson National Forest, Rio Arriba County, New Mexico*, ed. K. F. Anschuetz, 106–20. Community and Cultural Landscape Contribution 2. Santa Fe, NM: Rio Grande Foundation for Communities and Cultural Landscapes.
Orcutt, J. D.
1991 Environmental Variability and Settlement Changes on the Pajarito Plateau, New Mexico. *American Antiquity* 56:315–32.
1993 Villages, Field Houses, and Land Use on the Southern Pajarito Plateau. In *Papers on the Early Classic Period Prehistory of the Pajarito Plateau, New Mexico*, ed. T. A. Kohler and A. R. Linse, 87–104. Reports of Investigations 65. Pullman: Department of Anthropology, Washington State University.
Ortiz, A.
1969 *The Tewa World: Space, Time, Being, and Becoming in a Pueblo Society.* Chicago: University of Chicago Press.
Parsons, E. C.
1939 *Pueblo Indian Religion.* 2 vols. Chicago: University of Chicago Press.
Peckham, S.
1990 *From This Earth: The Ancient Art of Pueblo Pottery.* Santa Fe: Museum of New Mexico Press.
Plog, F. T., G. J. Gumerman, R. C. Euler, J. S. Dean, R. H. Hevly, and T. N. V. Karlstrom
1988 Anasazi Adaptive Strategies: The Model, Predictions, and Results. In *The Anasazi in a Changing Environment*, ed. G. J. Gumerman, 230–76. Cambridge: Cambridge University Press.
Ramenofsky, A. F.
1998 Decoupling Archaeology and History: Northern New Mexico. *Papers of the 1998 Chacmool Conference.* Calgary: Archaeological Association of the University of Calgary.
Rose, M. R., J. S. Dean, and W. J. Robinson
1981 *The Past Climate of Arroyo Hondo, New Mexico, Reconstructed from Tree Rings.* Arroyo Hondo Archaeological Series 4. Santa Fe, NM: School of American Research Press.
———, W. J. Robinson, and J. S. Dean
1982 *Dendroclimatic Reconstruction for the Southeastern Colorado Plateau.* Tucson: Laboratory of Tree-Ring Research, University of Arizona.

Schroeder, A. H.
1979 Pueblos Abandoned in Historic Times. In *Southwest*, ed. A. Ortiz, 236–54. Handbook of North American Indians, vol. 9. Washington, DC: Smithsonian Institution.

Smith, S. J.
1998 AR-03-02-02-0460 (LA111461) Pollen Analysis. In *Pre-Columbian Pueblo Agricultural Plots (AR-03-02-02-0460 [LA114161]) within the Proposed Las Clinicas del Norte Special-Use Permit Parcel, El Rito Ranger District, Carson National Forest, Rio Arriba County, New Mexico*, ed. K. F. Anschuetz, 73–84. Community and Cultural Landscape Contribution 2. Santa Fe, NM: Rio Grande Foundation for Communities and Cultural Landscapes.

Van West, C. R.
1994 *Modeling Prehistoric Agricultural Productivity in Southwestern Colorado: A GIS Approach*. Reports of Investigations 67. Pullman: Department of Anthropology, Washington State University; and Cortez, CO: Crow Canyon Archaeological Center.

Vivian, R. G.
1974 Conservation and Diversion: Water Control Systems in the Anasazi Southwest. In *Irrigation's Impact on Society*, ed. T. E. Downing and M. Gibson, 95–112. Anthropological Papers 25. Tucson: University of Arizona Press.
1990 *The Chacoan Prehistory of the San Juan Basin*. San Diego: Academic Press.

Ware, J. A., and M. Mensel
1992 *The Ojo Caliente Project: Archaeological Test Excavations and a Data Recovery Plan for Cultural Resources along U.S. 285, Rio Arriba County, New Mexico*. Office of Archaeological Studies Note 99. Santa Fe: Museum of New Mexico.

Winship, G. P., trans. and ed.
1990 *The Journey of Coronado, 1540–1542*. Reprinted ed. Golden, CO: Fulcrum Publishing. Originally published 1904, *The Journey of Coronado, 1540–1542, from the City of Mexico to the Grande Canyon of the Colorado and the Buffalo Plains of Texas, Kansas, and Nebraska, as Told by Himself and His Followers*. Alberton, NY: Trail Makers Series.

Chapter Six

The Estancia

The New Mexican Hacienda

by James E. Ivey

The ancient Pueblo style of gardening in intense and extended plots was changed almost overnight in the seventeenth century. Spanish mission farming and livestock raising enlisted Pueblo villages and towns as "labor colonies" in a new hacienda-style form of production that was much different than anything the Pueblos or their ancestors had ever imagined.

The fluidity of landscape history in New Mexico is made clear by research that breaks down long-accepted distinctions between Pueblo Indians and their Spanish conquerors. National Park Service historian James Ivey describes in a groundbreaking essay the unexpected development of many pre–Pueblo Revolt hacienda-like farms and ranches by Pueblo Indians. These haciendas, or, more properly in New Mexico, estancias, were the economic powerhouses of the seventeenth century in the Southwest, and they transformed much of the Ancestral Puebloan style of agriculture into something quite different. New Mexican estancias may also properly be called "ecclesiastical haciendas," because their layout, labor allocation, goods processing, and trade or shipping were often established around a mission station founded by the Franciscans at a pueblo.

A prominent feature of the New Mexico colonial landscape was the ranch. In fact, except for one or two hundred people who lived in the Villa de Santa Fe, most Hispanic settlers in the province lived on ranches (Scholes

1935:96n44, 102; Weber 1992:90). New Mexico was settled during the period when the Spanish ranch in Mexico, usually called an estancia, was growing into the more complex and economically powerful hacienda. Although New Mexico continued the practice of calling the large ranch an "estancia" rather than the newer term "hacienda," during the seventeenth century the New Mexico estancia showed a mixture of traits from both establishments. At the same time, according to François Chevalier, the mission establishments of New Mexico became the equivalent of haciendas, a pattern that was followed all across the frontier (Chevalier 1966).[1]

Estancias were first established in Mexico soon after the conquest; the earliest on record were created in the late 1520s. The rancher received a license to use a particular place (*sitio*) for cattle, which amounted to a simple permit to exclude other ranchers. The usual sizes, fixed by Viceroy Luis de Velasco in 1563, were for cattle a one-league square (4,400 acres), and for sheep a square two-thirds of a league on a side (1,936 acres) (Barnes, Naylor, and Polzer 1981:68).[2] No permanent buildings were allowed, and farming grants could be made within these sitios as long as they were protected by a fence (Chevalier 1966:88–92). By the late sixteenth century, estancia use had stabilized into a fairly standard system. Small structures had become acceptable, but might only be jacals of temporary materials, with no permanent fencing.[3] Gisela von Wobeser says that in the period from 1570 to 1620, estancias had virtually no infrastructure (1983:30–31). Von Wobeser considered this lack of permanent buildings the single most distinctive characteristic of the estancia (31–32). Through continued use, eventually the word "estancia" came to mean one *sitio de ganado mayor* or *menor*, as well as indicating a ranching and farming grant.[4] An estancia became a grant of land for stock raising, usually as *estancias de ganado mayor y menor*, of 4,400 acres and 1,936 acres, respectively, the same size as the sitio de ganado mayor and menor defined by Velasco in 1563 (31–32).

The hacienda began to be important in Mexico about the same time the New Mexico colony was established (1598), and in fact, says von Wobeser, many haciendas began as estancias. The term "hacienda" was first used for a ranching operation in 1579 in northern Mexico, and by 1620 such operations had become major elements of the Mexican economy. Although the term has seen some debate, in regard to ranching a hacienda has been defined as an operation that dominated the natural resources of an area, its work force, and the local and regional mercantile system, although the specific meaning varied considerably over time and place (Nickel 1979:9–10). Walter Taylor, for example, said that the "definition of 'hacienda' used in my study of Oaxaca—a rural estate with a mixed economy of ranching and agriculture, permanent buildings, and some resident labor—was based on colonial usage of the term in southern Mexico" (1985:109). Similarly, Leslie Offut considered it to be "a large estate characterized by extensive tracts of land and numerous buildings at some central location including residences

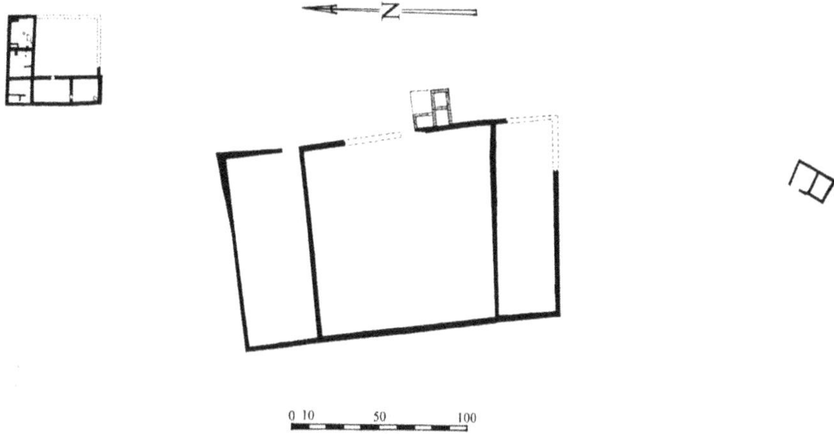

Fig. 6.1 Las Majadas site, LA 591. Illustration by James E. Ivey.

for the owner, his mayordomo, and permanent laborers, storage facilities, barns, stables, and perhaps a chapel" (1991:330–31). These descriptions indicate that as the estancia evolved more farming and permanent buildings it began to be called a "hacienda." Using these definitions, the New Mexico estancias were indeed haciendas. It was a peculiarity of local usage that the New Mexico settlers kept the older name for this new phenomenon.

New Mexican estancias were the primary residences for most families and had from the beginning a full, self-supporting residential establishment. These estancias ranged from a very simple group of structures, such as Estancia Acomilla (LA 286) (Marshall and Walt 1984:199), through ranches with moderate complexity, like the Las Majadas site (LA 591) (Snow and Warren 1973; figure 6.1), to a large and complex set of buildings such as the Sanchez site (LA 20,000) (Smith Williamson and Associates 1993; figure 6.2), but all had the same essential features. These were a dwelling, a barn or shed, and a corral. Although the term "hacienda" never became popular in New Mexico, some of these ranching establishments were large and influential enough that they certainly would have qualified.

By the end of the prerevolt period, the Rio Grande valley had a number of private ranches. For example, don Diego de Vargas specifically mentioned the ruins of eight ranches, which Vargas called haciendas, just in the area along the road between Socorro and Santa Fe (Kessell and Hendricks 1992:375–87).

Supporting Chevalier's contention that in New Mexico the missions were the equivalent of haciendas, one of the most complex farming and ranching compounds in the province is found at the mission of Nuestra Señora de los Ángeles de Pecos (figure 6.3). The residence portion of this estancia was begun during the 1630s as a small plaza, or enclosed house built around a courtyard, and in the

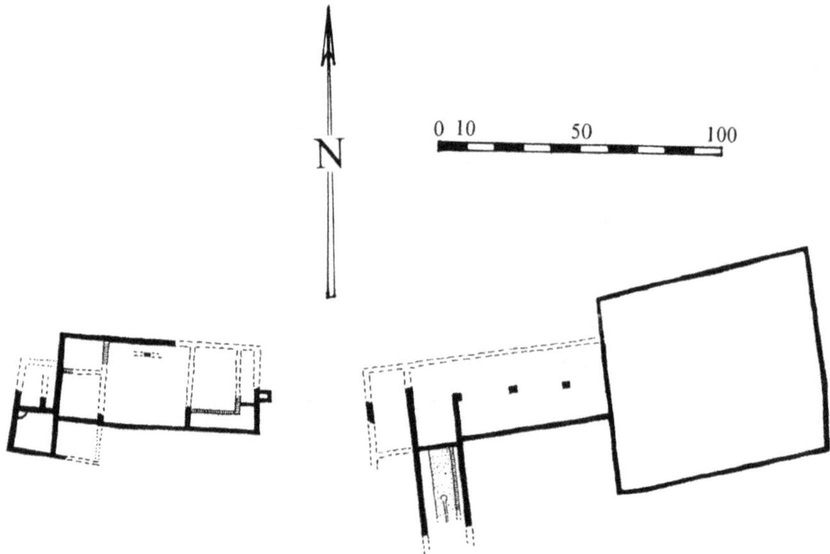

Fig. 6.2 Sanchez site, LA 20,000. Illustration by James E. Ivey.

late 1640s was enlarged by the addition of a second plaza to its north side, with larger rooms built around a bigger patio. The corral complex began as several enclosures of adobe walls on stone foundations, and in its final version, built about the same time as the enlargement of the residence soon after 1645, consisted of a large main corral with several smaller enclosures on its south side and a series of pens, barns, sheds, and possibly bunkhouses along the north side. The strong resemblance between the Pecos estancia complex and the estancia at LA 20,000 (see figure 6.2) leaves little doubt that both these structural groups were used for the same purposes.

In addition to the estancia compound at Pecos, the pueblo shows other developments dating from the same period. West of the estancia is Square Ruin, built about 1625 of the same bricks and mortar used in the huge Pecos church, and changed several times over the next fifty years. North of the estancia is the "Ancient Walled Area," as the Park Service has called it, a large irrigated garden with a water storage tank in the northeastern corner (figure 6.4). This garden is raised above the surrounding landscape about eight feet, built within retaining walls of rubble stone (figure 6.5). The earth to fill this terraced garden was hauled in by hand, rather like the cemetery in front of the church of Acoma. We also have references indicating that the irrigated fields of Pecos ran for two miles to the northwest along Glorieta Creek. These landscape constructions at Pecos indicate the extent to which the Franciscans were willing to develop the resources of a pueblo.

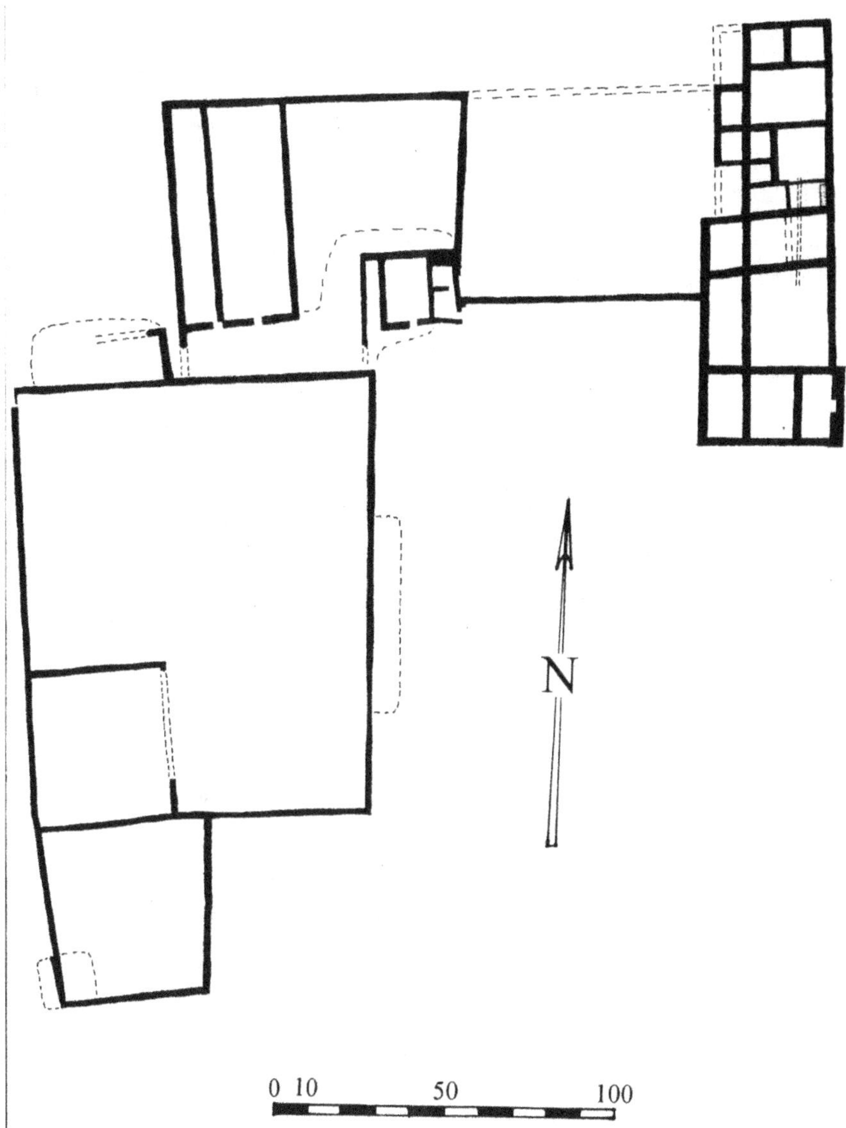

Fig. 6.3 Pecos Mission estancia. Illustration by James E. Ivey.

The estancia compound and other structures at Pecos form a major collection of buildings associated with the economic operations of a frontier mission and pueblo. Many seventeenth-century missions are known to have one or more associated buildings that might have been supporting activity structures. But because archaeologists (basing their expectations on the view of the missions presented by historians) have thought that these were primitive frontier establishments with no sophistication in their physical plant development, in most cases

Fig. 6.4 Upper reach—seventeenth-century priests' garden at Pecos. Photo by Baker H. Morrow.

no clear attribution of date or use of these buildings, or even a reasonable plan, is available. Pecos offers a fairly complete set of such structures, and careful consideration of the group allows reasonable guesses about similar structures, previously unidentified or misunderstood, to be found at other missions. These include such peculiar buildings as the "barrack-stable" at Awatovi (Montgomery, Smith, and Brew 1949:91–92, 229–38), the "low compound" at Las Humanas (now Gran Quivira, a unit of Salinas Pueblo Missions National Monument) (National Park Service 1932), and an unnamed compound north of the church at Hawikuh (Kubler 1972:figure 50; Mindeleff [1891] 1989:plate 46).

It appears that the Pecos estancia complex and others like it are representations of a previously unsuspected category of estancia, those operated by the Native American pueblos. Although it has been thought that all estancias in New Mexico were privately owned by Hispanic landowners, the evidence suggests that the Pueblos operated similar systems under the direction of the missionaries staffing the mission associated with a pueblo, who were acting as the guardians of the pueblo's interests as required by Spanish law (Kubler 1972:figure 50; Mindeleff [1891] 1989:plate 46).

If this interpretation of the evidence is true, then the mission/pueblo system would have been a principal landowner and estancia operator in prerevolt New Mexico. Some of the evidence suggesting this consists of two lists of estancias associated with particular pueblos and missions (Marquez ca. 1641:85–88;

Fig. 6.5 Site of seventeenth-century priests' garden at Pecos. Photo by Baker H. Morrow.

Cardoso 1667). For example, in the list dating from about 1642, the mission at Santa Clara "tiene más ocho estancias y labores y su gente de servicio" (has eight estancias and farms and their people of service). The last phrase appears to be a specific reference to staff working the ranch and farm for the missionary. Another example was Sandia in 1663, where the lists said there were two friars, one of whom was a priest who administered the said pueblo, two *visitas*, and thirty estancias.[5] At Isleta in the same year, there was one priest, who among other responsibilities had care of fourteen estancias. The lists give a total of about twenty-five estancias associated with the missions and pueblos circa 1642, and about sixty in 1663, virtually all in the Rio Grande valley.

The available information is ambiguous—it is possible that these are privately owned estancias in the general area of a mission and that the list indicates that the priest was responsible for the people who lived there, keeping records of their births, deaths, and marriages, hearing their confessions, and having them at Mass at least once a year. If that were the case, there are far too few estancias. Perhaps two thousand people were living on these estancias scattered across New Mexico, suggesting that something like one hundred to as many as four hundred estancias probably existed. In a few areas where we know of private estancias in operation outside the Rio Grande valley, especially in the areas of the Salinas missions near Quarai and Tajique, where we have references to six estancias, no estancias are mentioned in the lists (Ivey 1991:27).

Moreover, the emphasis of the lists is not on the people of these estancias, but rather on their ranching and farming concerns. The only reference to people is in the Santa Clara listing of about 1642, which simply mentions "service people" in passing. It is extremely unlikely that a Franciscan from the Sandia mission, for example, visited thirty privately owned estancias along with two visitas while conducting the main mission at the pueblo itself. If these were individually owned estancias within the responsibility of the Sandia mission, then the individual landowners and their staff would certainly have been expected to come to Sandia for Mass and other church business, rather than to be visited individually by the priest. But it seems unlikely that these estancias would have been specifically mentioned if their families were simply part of the congregation at the mission, arriving on occasion for Mass and an annual confession and communion (Ivey 2000:7–26). The phrasing of the references to these estancias suggests that the better explanation is that they were ranches and farms belonging to the pueblo and operated by the mission. In this case, the reference to the Sandia estancias in the 1663 list, for example, would indicate that the priest administered the pueblo mission, two visitas, and a ranch of thirty estancias belonging to the pueblo. This would have amounted to 132,000 acres of granted or licensed land if the mission and pueblo were running cattle, or 58,080 acres if sheep. Most other mission/pueblo estancias were smaller.

There are comparative examples of precisely this sort of Franciscan ranch management elsewhere on the northern frontier. Although we do not have a clear statement from New Mexico about land law and how it was applied, we can examine a case from the settlement of Texas a century later. In the area of San Antonio, Texas, three new missions, Concepción, San Juan, and Espada, were established in the San Antonio area in 1731. Fray Gabriel de Vergara, father president of the Queretaran missions, reviewed the laws that defined their legal rights to land and water for Captain don Juan Antonio Pérez de Almazán, commander of the Presidio de San Antonio de Bexar and *alcalde mayor*, or "chief judge," of the civilian settlement associated with the presidio (Vergara 1731). Here, the mission ranches began operations adjacent to the mission.

Eventually, these mission ranches were moved away from the San Antonio River valley when population there became too dense. By the late 1760s, the missions had acquired grants for huge cattle and sheep ranches of 22,000 to 230,000 acres or more. Of these, only approximately five have been found recorded outside the province at the viceregal level, for which the owner would have been issued a deed. Had Texas lost all of its local records, as New Mexico did, only these five or so ranches would have been known to have existed out of thirty or more that were actually in operation.

The physical evidence suggests that a similar sequence occurred in New Mexico, with ranches administered from the *convento* area at first, and later ranch headquarters built farther away from the mission in areas where the population density grew. Pecos represents the earliest version of this, with the ranch headquarters next to the mission, and at Pecos the ranch never had to move out away from the mission, because the valley remained unpopulated except for the pueblo throughout the prerevolt period. In the Rio Grande valley, however, additional crowding would soon have forced the missions to move their ranches away from the areas held by Hispanic ranchers. At Quarai, a reverse situation is known to have occurred: in 1633, while serving as the missionary at Quarai, Fray Estévan de Perea wrote that the governor allowed colonists to set up farms and ranches on the fields of the Indians. In some cases he even permitted encroachment on land used by the conventos. Perea specifically mentioned a colonist who had been allowed to establish a ranch near Quarai, where he built corrals and his residence on the cotton fields shared jointly by the "three neighboring pueblos," and ran his cattle and sheep in the area (Vergara 1731). The "three neighboring pueblos" were probably Quarai, Tajique, and Chililí. Perea was likely describing the founding of the ranch of don Luis Martín Serrano or his wife, doña Catharina de Zalazar, perhaps where the town of Manzano is now located (Vergara 1731).

Of course, additional ranchlands and estancias that may have been granted to missions for development would technically belong to the pueblo. A pueblo would have received at least a governor's grant to the ranching land, and the grant would have been the property of the pueblo, not the mission. But the mission, as guardian of the pueblo, would have administered the grant. As in Texas in the next century, most of these grants would have been recorded only in the records within the province, and most evidence of such grants would have been destroyed by the Pueblo Revolt. Nonetheless, some references to mission/pueblo ranches should have been recorded in other archives outside the province.

Therefore, evidence for or against the existence of mission/pueblo estancias undoubtedly waits to be found in the archival collections of Mexico and Spain. A large quantity of this material was collected by France Scholes and Lansing Bloom (now in the Center for Southwest Research at the University of New Mexico) in the form of microfilm and bound photostats, and may contain some of this evidence.

The ranches managed by the missions, with their powerful trade connections, would have dominated the New Mexican mercantile system with their high productivity. Whether such mission/pueblo ranches existed in prerevolt New Mexico is a critical question for understanding the economy and landscape management of the province. Equally important, their existence would provide information about the early development of a mission practice that became more significant on the northern frontier of New Spain as time passed, leading ultimately to the huge cattle and sheep ranches of Texas, New Mexico, Arizona, and California.

Notes

1. "In well-watered valleys in New Mexico and other northern provinces, the remains of mission enclosures, mills, stables, and workshops reveal that the missions were small economic and social units comparable to the haciendas" (Chevalier 1966:236).
2. A league was 5,000 varas, about 2.6 miles. A vara ranged in size from 2.74 feet in the early eighteenth century to 2.77 feet in the early nineteenth century.
3. Jacal (Spanish): upright juniper or other posts, often covered with mud plaster.
4. Sitio de ganado mayor or menor (Spanish): a place for cattle or horses (ganado mayor) or sheep, goats, pigs, and poultry (ganado menor).
5. A visita was a secondary mission without a resident priest, visited on a regular basis from the primary mission.

References Cited

Barnes, Thomas C., Thomas H. Naylor, and Charles W. Polzer
1981 *Northern New Spain: A Research Guide.* Tucson: University of Arizona Press.

Cardoso, Fray Domingo
1667 Archivo General de Nación, Mexico. Museo Nacional, Asuntos, no. 191, "Certificacion," folios 21–22v; in bound photostats. Albuquerque: Center for Southwest Research, Zimmerman Library, University of New Mexico.

Chevalier, François
1966 *Land and Society in Colonial Mexico: The Great Hacienda.* Ed. Lesley Byrd Simpson, trans. Alvin Eustis. Berkeley: University of California Press.

Ivey, James E.
1991 *In the Midst of a Loneliness: The Architectural History of the Salinas Missions.* Santa Fe, NM: Southwest Cultural Resources Center, National Park Service.
2000 *Ahijados*: The Rite of Communion and Mission Status on the Seventeenth-Century Northern Frontier. *Catholic Southwest* 11 (2000): 7–26.

Kessell, John, and Rick Hendricks, eds.
1992 *By Force of Arms: The Journals of Don Diego de Vargas, New Mexico, 1691–93.* Albuquerque: University of New Mexico Press.

Kubler, George
1972 Hawikuh. Plan of the Pueblo by Bandelier, ca. 1881. In *The Religious Architecture of New Mexico; in the Colonial Period and since the American Occupation.* Albuquerque: University of New Mexico Press.

Marquez, Fray Bartolomé
ca. 1641 Archivo General de Indias. Mexico, legajo 306, "Certificacion de las noticias . . . ," 85–88, in bound photostats. Albuquerque: Center for Southwest Research, Zimmerman Library, University of New Mexico.

Marshall, Michael P., and Henry J. Walt
1984 *Rio Abajo: Prehistory and History of a Rio Grande Province.* Santa Fe: New Mexico Historic Preservation Division.

Mindeleff, Victor
[1891] 1989 Hawikuh. In *A Study of Pueblo Architecture in Tusayan and Cibola*. Washington, DC: Smithsonian Institution Press.

Montgomery, Ross Gordon, Watson Smith, and John Otis Brew
1949 *Franciscan Awatovi: The Excavation and Conjectural Reconstruction of a 17th-Century Spanish Mission Established at a Hopi Indian Town in Northeastern Arizona*. Reports of the Awatovi Expedition, no. 3. Papers of the Peabody Museum of American Archaeology and Ethnology, Harvard University, vol. 36. Cambridge, MA: Peabody Museum.

National Park Service
1932 Low Compound, South of Mound 17, on "Topographical Sheet," NM/Q-4937, Gran Quivira National Monument. In the files of the Cultural Resources and National Register Program, Intermountain Regional Office, National Park Service, Santa Fe, New Mexico.

Nickel, Herbert
1979 *Soziale Morfologie der Mexikanischen Hacienda*. Wiesbaden: Franz Steiner Verlag.

Offut, Leslie
1991 Hispanic Society in the Mexican Northeast: Saltillo at the End of the Colonial Period. *Journal of the Southwest* 33 (3): 330–31.

Scholes, France
1935 Civil Government and Society. *New Mexico Historical Review* 10 (April): 96n44, 102.

Smith Williamson and Associates
1993 Archaeological Site Map of "The Sanchez Site": LA 20,000, 1982–1993. Excavations by Cross-Cultural Research Systems and Colorado College.

Snow, David H., and A. H. Warren
1973 *Cochiti Dam Salvage Project: Archeological Excavation and Pottery of the Las Majadas Site LA 591, Cochiti Dam, New Mexico*. Laboratory of Anthropology Note 75, 75a. Santa Fe, NM: Laboratory of Anthropology.

Taylor, Walter
1985 Landed Society in New Spain: A View from the South. In *Readings in Latin American History*. Vol. 1, *The Formative Centuries*. Durham, NC: Duke University Press.

Vergara, Fray Gabriel de
1731 Letter to Captain Don Juan Antonio Perez Almazan, "Escrito . . . para las tierras y aguas, 1731," May 31, 1731, microfilm roll 9, frames 1299–1310, Old Spanish Missions Historical Research Library, San Antonio, Texas.

von Wobeser, Gisela
1983 *La Formación de la Hacienda en la Época Colonial: El Uso de la Tierra y el Agua*. Mexico City: Universidad Nacional Autónoma de México.

Weber, David J.
1992 *The Spanish Frontier in North America*. New Haven, CT: Yale University Press.

PART TWO
The Influence of the Ancestral Puebloan Landscape in Our Own Time

Chapter Seven

Zuni Maize

by Mary Beath

Studying the agricultural and water preservation strategies of Zuni Pueblo farmers in New Mexico (direct descendants of the Ancestral Puebloans) gives scientists important insights into the sustainability of indigenous people and their crops in the harsh desert environment of the American Southwest. In this handsomely crafted and information-packed essay, author Mary Beath describes her firsthand experiences of cooperative interactions between Zuni farmers and scientific agronomists from Iowa State University at the Zuni Sustainable Agriculture Project (ZSAP) and also analyzes the differences among agribusiness approaches and priorities, modern corn varieties, and the microecological mastery of Zuni farmers and their hardy, indomitable maize. Beath's narrative reveals a flourishing and verdant horticultural landscape that has endured for the better part of a millennium.

It is well to be informed about the winds,
About the variations in the sky,
The native traits and habits of the place,
What each locale permits, and what denies.
— *Virgil,* Georgics, *circa 30 B.C.*

Faint southwest wind, clear October light, toasting sun. Locale: Zuni, New Mexico.

In a field filled with whispering corn stalks bleached pale, I found myself happily surrounded by complication. A race of Zuni blue corn stood in tousled ranks next to a variety of modern hybrid corn; my companions were an equally unlikely mix. I had come to the Zuni Reservation with a corn physiologist from Iowa State and we'd been joined in the field by five Zuni men. The corn physiologist was Deb Muenchrath; this experimental field and the nearby canyon were part of a National Science Foundation–funded collaboration between the Zuni Tribe and a group of scientists trained in the same schools that churned out agribusiness researchers. The five Zunis working with us that morning lived with beliefs and practices stretching back millennia, but they had also become experts in speaking with satellites via the latest GPS technology. Expected categories became fluid and intermingled.

While the Ancestral Puebloan inhabitants of this landscape abandoned many settlements, they *didn't* evaporate into the dry desert air, despite the theatrical appeal of such a mysterious disappearance. Modern Pueblo peoples, especially Zunis and Hopis, have no doubts those Ancient Ones simply moved on and became their immediate ancestors (Stuart 2000). Although Zuni traditional farming can't be mapped directly onto prehistoric Ancestral Puebloan agriculture, enough evidence exists to make a confident leap: Zuni strategies for growing crops in their semiarid environment had their genesis in a past more distant than the heyday of Chaco Canyon's great houses (Brandt 1995).[1] That dynamic continuity over such a time span suggests those strategies succeeded without exhausting the land and could well offer unexpected lessons.

Deb's test field sat at the mouth of a small canyon, in a gently tilting expanse of dried grasses, asters, blooming tangerine globemallow, and indeterminate brush full of pesky prickers. Up into the canyon, the slope increased slightly as the fractured sandstone walls slowly closed in, their burnt orange sides streaked with umber, visible behind scattered piñons and junipers. The central runoff channel, which meandered up and back about a mile, had not cut downward and its braided sand patterns smoothly merged into the surrounding ground, unlike the deep erosion I'd seen in most drainages in the Southwest. In the last several years this particular spot had not been farmed, but scattered pot sherds, stone tools, and ruins nearby told archaeologists it had probably been sporadically cultivated for at least eight hundred years.

A dirt track curved away from the field through low sage and spent sunflowers toward the paved road that bisects the reservation. The seven of us had been working about an hour when we all stopped abruptly and turned our faces into the wind. A wavering, high tone seemed to blow past us and up into the canyon. In the bright air, the stalks swished around us like the rush of a fast, rocky stream. Above us, chalky contrails crisscrossed the deep blue distance.

"What *is* that?" asked Deb.

"Someone on the highway, maybe?" said Dixon, tentatively.

The high note glissandoed higher, jumped a major fifth, then stopped abruptly when the wind died.

We all shrugged, shook our heads, and turned back to the harvest. Deb, in a broad-brimmed hat, white T-shirt, jeans, and her multipocket field apron, set a plastic bin filled with blue corn ears on the electronic scale perched on boards suspended between two stepladders. We'd established our harvesting/data-collecting rhythm. Low earthen berms gridded the field into twenty-five plots, and within each plot corn had been planted in nine hills, either Zuni blue or modern hybrid. Deb had treated each plot with one of five water/fertilizer regimes, including the organically rich runoff water from the watershed above the field. Our task was to find each plot's median hill by harvest weight so it could return with Deb to her lab in Iowa: the median hill would provide a statistically significant figure without needing to ship all the corn. In Iowa, Deb would remove all the ears' water to determine each hill's dry weight. One hill at a time, Lowell and Dixon slashed down the stalks with machetes and brought their unwieldy armloads to the green tarp next to the scale. Four of us shucked the ears: me, Deb, Niles, and Monroe. Then each hill's harvest took its turn on the scale. Curtis, whose year-old broken toe had been bothering him, monitored the scale and called out the weights for me to record.

In the quiet fall morning we joked easily as we cut and shucked and weighed the harvest. I felt welcomed and honored to work alongside these five men who were repeating again an activity they knew down to their marrow, but this time repeating it with a twist.

Zuni, a favorite western New Mexico hangout of ethnographers from Frank Cushing in the 1880s to Dennis Tedlock in the 1980s, has lately shifted tribal gears. ("Here come the anthros, better hide the past away," goes a popular song.) In the 1980s, Zuni Pueblo sued the U.S. government for stealing its land and trashing its resources—both intentionally and through high-handed ignorance. During the legal proceedings, the ecological disaster and associated cultural disruption became well documented. In a painful irony, Zuni varieties, grown on Zuni land, with Zuni knowledge and technology, had been producing sustainably for well over two thousand years. At least Zuni agriculture had been sustainable *before* the westward-ho U.S. government had done its damnedest to make Zuni a distant suburb of Kansas City. Even a much condensed list of havoc-wreaking government policies offers some sense of the magnitude of environmental sabotage visited on the Zuni people (Cleveland et al. 1995; Ferguson 1989; Ford 1999; Hart 1995):

> — *Before 1846, the Zunis' aboriginal land covered more than 15.2 million acres.* It extended from Mount Taylor in the east to the San Francisco Peaks in the west, providing territory for grazing, foraging, and farming. Zunis farmed mainly west of the Continental Divide, along the tributary streams feeding the Little Colorado, from near Pie Town in the southeast

and Crownpoint in the northeast, to Winslow, Arizona, in the west.

Without compensation, the government took Zuni land for military uses, National Forests, railroads, and non-Indian homesteading. Today, Zuni trust lands include just under 420,000 acres, less than 3 percent of their original territory; in the mid-nineteenth century Zunis cultivated 10,000–12,000 acres, compared with less than 10 percent of that acreage in 1991.

— *The remaining Zuni land has suffered severe erosion, beginning in earnest around the turn of the twentieth century.* Off-reservation clear-cutting in the Zuni Mountains, combined with a severe region-wide drought, partly caused the extreme land degradation. Overgrazing also played a part, triggered by Zuni flocks squeezed into a smaller and smaller range. In addition, large government-built dams caused extensive down-cutting of rivers and streams.

During the lawsuit, in response to the Zunis' claims that official policies caused erosion, the government at first denied any responsibility. Spokespeople insisted erosion is a natural process in the West and simply "an act of God," despite ample evidence from many locations that human activities influence how, where, and how rapidly erosion occurs.

— *Socially, official policy aimed at assimilating Zunis into mainstream American culture.* Although such cultural sledgehammering is all too familiar throughout Indian Country, at Zuni the policy had a specific effect on farming. Traditionally, Zuni land was held communally, with extended family parcels inherited through women of the family. This communal and female-oriented system of land tenure must have mightily irked the individualistic males who ran the show at the Bureau of Indian Affairs (BIA), and they forcibly changed land control to individual plots (of a mere ten acres) *owned by men.* Those plots then could also be bought and sold, not only precipitating social disruption but also providing another push into a cash economy. Currently, bitter land disputes can be traced directly back to that intrusion into a well-functioning Zuni system, effectively preventing farming on a great deal of otherwise productive land.

— *The most dramatic and ecologically ignorant government encroachment at Zuni has been its attempt at large-scale dam and irrigation projects.* Traditionally, Zuni farmers cultivated relatively modest fields, providing necessary water with small-scale, dynamic water management. Their methods were effective and appropriate to the land, though they often required continual, labor-intensive maintenance. Five farming districts, at some distance from the main Zuni Pueblo, provided most of the land for cultivation: upper and lower Nutria, upper and lower Pescado, Tekapo, Ojo Caliente, and Halono:wa. But small-scale, ecologically effective water management conflicted with the narrow empire-building water attitudes at the Bureau of Reclamation and the BIA. Perhaps the policy makers harbored benevolent visions of providing the Zuni people with lush and fertile fields watered by their new dams. More likely, those bureaucrats were caught up in the twentieth-century rush to dam every flowing watercourse in the West, their technical capacities for impounding water far outstripping their understanding of geology, ecology, soils, sedimentation, or local cultures.

One example will suffice.

Black Rock Dam, just upstream from Zuni Pueblo on the Zuni River, was built between 1906 and 1909 with no consultation with the Zuni people. At the time it was one of the largest public works projects in the country. Its waters were meant to irrigate cornfields downstream, although Zunis knew the intended cornfields were composed of tight clay, badly suited for cultivation. Once filled, the reservoir drowned and destroyed a sacred spring that had been used for traditional ditch irrigation at the settlement of Black Rock.

Though the dam had been built on surface basalt, pure sand lay under the hard rock. As soon as the dam was put into service, it collapsed, causing major erosion downstream. This added to the erosion caused in 1906 when an upstream dam had failed before Black Rock had even been completed. Once repaired, the dam provided enough hope to Zuni farmers to draw them to the new fields, away from the farming districts. Deprived of labor, the carefully maintained water management systems no longer functioned well. The reservoir behind Black Rock Dam silted up quickly and within twenty years held only 27 percent of its original capacity. In 1931 the BIA drained the reservoir to add a sluice gate in an attempt to flush the sediment. Once refilled, the reservoir still could only irrigate 10 percent of the land originally planned for the project. In 1932 the dam failed again.

Dismayingly, blind governmental behavior apparently isn't limited to the early part of the twentieth century. Though twenty feet of fine silt *entirely* filled the reservoir, in the 1980s Black Rock Dam was declared the second most dangerous dam in Indian territory. The $13 million that Congress had appropriated to repair it needed to be spent. When I stopped by with Deb in the fall of 1998 to take a look at the construction, the heavy equipment and hard-hatted men had rebuilt an impressive structure. However, not one of the contractors was from Zuni. When I asked the construction foreman what the plans were for the sediment stretching upstream in a flat, scrub-covered plain *level with the top of the dam*, he shrugged and said, "The Zunis are in charge of that."

With the help of expert witnesses testifying to the unending litany of environmental and social destruction, the tribe finally won their lawsuit in an out-of-court settlement. In 1990, Congress appropriated money for two multimillion-dollar funds to support conservation and restoration efforts, *controlled by the Zuni Tribe*, and in the long term to "promote sustained yield development." As part of the settlement, the Zunis established the Zuni Conservation Project (ZCP) and its component, the Zuni Sustainable Agriculture Project (ZSAP), to work toward transforming the optimistic, generalized language of restoration, sustainability, and community control into living, breathing, growing reality. A difficult task (Enote, Albert, and Webb 1993; Hart 1995; Cleveland et al. 1995).

While Zuni had been struggling through the labyrinthine legal system to claim some small justice, on the margins of Big Agriculture a handful of scientists had been rediscovering the value of "land races," heirloom crop populations whose genetic variability gives them resilience in the face of pests, disease, and erratic environmental conditions. Since the domestication of plants, especially in the biotically diverse Third World, growers have practiced intense artificial selection, season by season, and mingled geographically distant populations. As a result, crops have evolved into many varieties adapted to local conditions. Within any one crop species thousands of genetically diverse land races exist: rich, heterogeneous variations on a theme, much like the members of an extended family. The Zuni blue corn growing in Deb's test field was a land race, not a "pure" single genetic strain like modern hybrid corn, but adapted through centuries to the particular conditions at Zuni (figure 7.1). Usually land races flourish in the fields of small farmers who depend more on their grandparents' knowledge than on official science. Land races also rely on cultivation methods that contrast sharply with the highly mechanized, synthetically fertilized, and pesticide-treated fields of Big Agriculture.

Some early data from this project suggested the nitrogen content *inside* some traditional Zuni fields surpassed the nitrogen in the surrounding ground. Most fields showed more soil microbes (Norton, Pawluck, and Sandor 1998). Both results were exactly opposite those of U.S. Corn Belt fields where persistent nutrient loss

Fig. 7.1 Zuni cornfield. Photo by Mary Beath.

required annual additions of nitrogen and other supplements. And Zuni fields used no synthetic fertilizer, had no pesticide residues, depleted no groundwater, lost no topsoil.

This collaboration challenged a commodified mainstream that had little real understanding of any vision outside a narrow band of acceptability. That challenge to mainstream intolerance most deeply explained why I'd joined Deb at Zuni. Although I relished the particularities of Zuni corn growing and the details of the puzzles Deb and her colleagues worked to decipher, I found solace in their refusal—on the part of both the Zunis and the researchers—to buckle under pressure from the juggernaut of twentieth-century American culture. That juggernaut usually barreled along blindly, dehumanizing, standardizing, simplifying, and destroying any insubordination in its path. Like many other small, quiet ventures, this project questioned business as usual, not with romanticized notions, but with careful, open-minded explorations of a working system.

What the Zunis could teach wasn't an easy lesson for a culture like ours, convinced of the truth of linear reasoning, of singular answers, of quick fixes and absolutes. Loosen that limited set of logical apparatuses, I imagined I heard the Zunis saying, throw out those badly fitting templates, and open your eyes to what will, given time, work: flexibility in the face of inevitable uncertainty, innovation as a response to living on the edge.

Paradoxically, this long-standing, fluid accommodation contrasted with the immutability given to traditional practices absorbed into religion. Where to unbend? Where to hold firm?

Corn is sacred. The Zunis will not sell their corn.

The eerie whistle renewed its silvery song. We all stopped again, looking for some explanation.

"I know what it is," said Niles finally. "It's the wind in these lines." He tossed his head toward the glittering gossamer threads stretched east to west, every three feet, across the seven-foot-tall enclosure. Deb needed the fence to keep out the hungry elk, the fishing line to spook the marauding crows and ravens. In the center of the field, hanging from one taut line, a large inflated plastic pumpkin grinned at us. The monofilament succeeded in keeping the birds out, but in its delicacy and unexpected regularity, it looked unmistakably like high tech art. And in the wind it sounded like a playful gremlin making mischief from some other realm. No wonder the ravens left it alone.

Deb Muenchrath and her colleagues from Iowa, New Mexico, Montana, and Wyoming approached this canyon and the experimental cornfield as an integrated *system*: "crops, biophysical elements, and human management." Oddly, such systems approaches that encompass multiple factors crossing disciplines are almost anomalies in science today. They're hard to get funded and equally hard to publish in a journal market that seeks short, highly focused articles. Soil journals concentrate on soils not plant physiology, for example, despite the relationship between the two. And not until recently would such a project have embraced indigenous knowledge as the skilled orchestrator of the whole shebang. The pressurized atmosphere of scientific publishing, partly geared toward getting authors jobs or tenure, seemed to add unnecessary roadblocks to legitimate attempts to truly understand the interrelated complications of the real world.

This project had three goals. First, the researchers intended simply to *describe* Zuni runoff farming analytically (the basic hookup to science) and in the process glean a better understanding of semiarid ecosystems. Second, they meant to add to research on sustainable land use. Third, they would offer what they learned to the Zuni Tribe for its agricultural revitalization. A kind of loop-de-loop: from Zuni through the digitized university house of mirrors and back to Zuni.[2]

For nearly three years they'd been measuring rainfall and water flow, analyzing soils, surveying plants, and mapping the topography of the diminutive drainage. Runoff from the rare rains normally would wash nutrient-rich sediments into the field near its mouth, an ancient farming method that used neither conventional irrigation nor artificial fertilizer. But now a temporary, boxcar-sized reservoir caught the runoff so Deb could treat the twenty-five plots in this test field with different water/nutrient regimes.

Despite the Zuni Sustainable Agriculture Project's welcome, some Zunis remained skeptical: after all, before their world had been disrupted, they'd successfully farmed corn, beans, squash, and peppers for a hundred generations. After the Spanish had arrived, they'd added wheat, melons, and peaches to their fields. In waffle gardens closer to houses, women grew coriander, garlic, onions, some cotton, and encouraged wild plants such as amaranth and edible greens. In the mid-nineteenth century, ten thousand acres were planted in corn. Although currently Zunis farmed only about one thousand acres, planting cycles and ceremonial cycles still depended on each other's elaborate rhythms. But ZSAP had spotted issues that needed science's stamp: whether tractors bought with Ford Foundation money worked the soil more effectively than hand tilling; verification for the New Mexico Organic Commodities Commission that their runoff farming produced crops organically without depleting the land; maps of eastern Zuni indicating suitable future farming spots so the inevitable pueblo housing expansion might be wisely located. These were practical Zuni goals, interwoven with the project's more general ones.

Deb's attention to Zunis' traditional farming attracted me, but I'd also caught her contagious fascination with corn.

The plot whose ears we were shucking at the moment had been planted with Zuni blue corn and treated with runoff water, but no sediment, from the drainage—one of Deb's five treatment regimes. The ears had grown long and thin, with mature, filled-out kernels. While we laughed at Niles intoning again "tamale, tamale, tamale, tamale, tamale"—those Southwestern steamed delights of spicy meat and cornmeal wrapped in corn husks—I peeled away one ear's pale, translucent, paper-thin sheaths. Exposed, the dark corn glowed in the October sun, the overall deep blue-violet kernels interrupted in places with red ones the color and richness of burgundy. Five or six yellow ones from cross-pollination with the non-Zuni hybrid in other plots had also shown up. Next to the dark kernels, the hybrid ones looked sallow and opaque. This ear had a rare variation: on certain kernels a delicate starburst of dotted white lines radiated from the center top, down around the kernel's curved sides and bottom. An ear full of jewels (figure 7.2).

"That's from a mutation in one gene," said Deb when we all stopped shucking to admire the ear. Since we needed to harvest and weigh twenty-five plots, nine hills per plot, we tried to work fast, but not so fast we couldn't slow down to exclaim at an oddity—a tassel ear or an extra-large corn worm—or a beauty.

Fig. 7.2 Zuni corn showing multiple "imperfect" ears. Photo by Mary Beath.

Corn. *Zea mays*. Maize. Without maize, what would the Inca, the Aztec, the Maya, the Ancestral Puebloans have been? What would the Rio Grande Pueblos, the Hopi, the Zuni be? How many times have we heard that story? Yet maize still grips us like the sight of a much-loved person, ever renewing its magnetic pull, grounded in need but ultimately mysterious. What, after all, would *we* be without maize (Fussell 1992)?[3]

Corn is so uniquely mysterious that no other crop provides so much to the industrial world. In 1987 the National Corn Growers Association crowed, "Anything made from a barrel of petroleum can be made from a bushel of corn," from biodegradable plastic to ethanol to lightweight building materials. It's been claimed that in a supermarket everything but fresh fish has had contact with some product or by-product of corn. And then there's its use in rubber tires, dynamite, and embalming fluid.

"Corn is our mother," say all the Southwest cultures whose roots extend deep into the land's past (Ford 1994). "King Corn is Supreme," proclaimed Midwestern cities in the booster years after 1880 when corn palaces with domes, flying buttresses, and allegorical mosaics seemed to sprout everywhere. In 1891, Sioux City's corn palace included a balcony scene from *Romeo and Juliet* constructed entirely from white corn. An annually refurbished corn palace still graces Mitchell, South Dakota (figure 7.3).

In the Southwest, tracking corn cultivation has provided work for legions of archaeobotanists, who currently place its arrival from the south at around 1800 B.C. Dating the appearance of corn's companion crops, squash and especially beans,

Fig. 7.3 South Dakota corn palace.

has been even more difficult. But one thing can't be argued: they supplied what corn lacked as a protein source, the amino acids tryptophan and lysine. We can explain molecularly why that made sense, but those ancient chefs had their own ways of knowing. They also discovered that corn must be cooked with an alkali, like wood ash. The lime improves the flavor, but it also promotes the release of the important B-vitamin niacin. Early Europeans who first imported corn neglected to import the alkali processing, and an epidemic of the niacin deficiency pellagra followed, with its skin sores, aching joints, and dizziness. But in a study of fifty-one Native American societies depending on corn, fifty-one used alkali processing (Fussell 1992:176).

During the nineteenth and twentieth centuries, plant breeders have chased after "corn improvement" with high passion, rarely recognizing that the plant they aimed to improve was already highly bred. No one knows what became of the missing link between corn's presumed wild ancestor—teosinte—and its cultivated descendants, but countless myths explain that maize was a gift whose usefulness arrived full blown. The corn geneticist Walton Galinet says, "The American Indians were not simply the first corn breeders. They created corn in the first place" (quoted in Fussell 1992:67).

Unlike other cultivated grains, maize *needs* humans. A human must *plant* corn kernels before a new crop will grow. Wheat or barley or rye will sprout into producing plants if wind broadcasts their seeds, but corn will not. The corn stalks we cut and weighed at Zuni took their place as the most recent installment of an *unbroken* chain of corn-human-corn-human-corn-human that extended back perhaps seven millennia to somewhere in central Mexico.

That staggering continuity hovered in my mind while I wondered about the unspoken, closely guarded, and for me all but unknowable ceremonial and sacred lives of the five Zunis joking with me and Deb as we all weighed and shucked her scientific harvest. I say "her harvest," but after she'd dried and analyzed a portion of the corn, Deb would return it all to Zuni.

"And which one wins a free trip back to Iowa?" Niles asked in his game show voice as I tallied the weights and determined the median hill.

"Number nine, number nine, number nine," I chanted, Beatles-style, though my reference to that sixties album might have been lost on everyone. While Deb and Monroe, in his Nike hat, stuffed the ears and stalks of pile nine into the string cabbage bags the Iowa Agronomy Department bought for just such purposes, Curtis, Dixon, Lowell, and I added the other stalks from this plot to one big heap outside the field. The shucked ears we laid in their new, ears-only group. Five plots down, twenty to go.

I was, of course, an outsider admitting a curiosity shared by generations of curious outsiders, through the long line of ethnographers to the thousands of visitors who until 1995 had been welcomed to watch the intricately costumed and masked kachinas of Sha'lak'o.[4] The best-known Zuni celebration, Sha'lak'o takes place near the winter solstice, the return of light. The dancers dance to ensure harmony and to bless newly built houses, the earth, and all humankind.

But the word "curiosity" is too lightweight and simplistic to describe what I felt. I also admired the tenacity and inventiveness it took to live where summer heat rivaled winter cold, and where meager soils, scarce water, violent spring winds, and dramatically unpredictable weather made farming a chancy venture. That same tenacity had helped maintain the Zuni culture in the face of the devouring, disease-laden European onslaught beginning in 1540 and the even more destructive U.S. government policies after 1846. I envied their attachment to this land of sandstone and light, still largely free from the most unsightly marks of the twentieth century, despite the eroded arroyos, depleted game and forests, and stolen water. I was both attracted and discomfited by the contrast between the inappropriate HUD housing and the Zunis' richly complicated beliefs, which whirled everywhere like the invisible wind through sage and junipers.

The ancient heritage these corn plants embodied mirrored the threads of the past in the Zunis themselves. Culture/agriculture: not exactly the same, but here as closely mated as the husks hugging the ears.

Deb, on the other hand, had grown up in the culture of the Corn Belt, the still-beating heart of the green revolution, where hybrid varieties have been bred for optimum conditions, where air-conditioned John Deere tractors work enormous feed-corn fields nourished with synthetic fertilizer and drenched in pesticides and fungicides. A familiar scene: soil as black as night, corn as high as a crop plane's eye and stretching into infinity. A picture of abundance, with a not so subtle whiff of crushing mass production. The Industrial Revolution turned to chlorophyll.

Sometime in Deb's graduate career, after she'd had a part in developing a new patentable genetic strain, she decided she didn't relish trafficking in the guts of life. She turned then to corn's physiology. Her dissertation research had been on land races of corn from the Tohono O'odham, who live in the Sonoran Desert near Tucson (Muenchrath 1995). During that work, it had dawned on her that Native culture and local growing techniques were inseparable from corn's biology. They had evolved together.

A short foray into the staggering behemoth of industrial agriculture is in order here, to put in proper context local growing techniques, corn's land races, and Native cultures.

Some have suggested that Big Science didn't start with the Manhattan Project but with the successful hybridization of corn in the mid-1930s (Kloppenburg 1988; Kloppenburg, ed. 1988). Modern hybrid corn—the carefully controlled crossing of inbred parent lines—had two immediate physical effects: to dramatically reduce genetic variability and to decouple "grain" from "seed." Farmers could no longer save seed from their own corn crops but needed to buy it anew every year or suffer declining yields. That has meant enormous profits for seed companies who have always promoted hybrids rather than other approaches, such as population improvement, which would have left them without such a saleable and proprietary product. In fiscal 1997, for example, Pioneer Hi-Bred, the planet's largest seed company, sold seed corn worth $1,374,000,000 worldwide (*Feedstuffs* 1997). In 1982 biologist Richard Lewontin flatly stated, "If the same time and effort had been put into [improving open pollinated varieties], they would be as good as or better than hybrids by now" (quoted in Fussell 1992:93).

But hybrid corn has also been linked with two other legs of the so-called high-profit trio: plant more thickly, fertilize more heavily (Kloppenburg 1988). In the United States, between 1950 and 1994, the number of acres in corn *de*creased by 4 percent, the harvest *tripled*, while the tonnage of nitrogen fertilizer applied to corn increased by *1,700 percent* (U.S. Department of Agriculture 1950, 1997; Kloppenburg 1988). More luxuriant corn growth in larger fields encouraged insects, disease, and weeds, which meant more insecticides, fungicides, and herbicides. Over the years pests have adapted to those chemical controls, and applications have increased. More row planting and less fallow time encouraged topsoil loss. In 1992 corn accounted for 58 percent of U.S. agricultural herbicide use (223 million pounds!) and 37 percent of insecticides. Yet since 1940 the price of a bushel of corn in constant dollars has steadily *fallen* (U.S. Department of Agriculture 1995; Lin 1995; Kloppenburg 1988). The term "high-profit" *implied* farmers would be better off. In reality, seed companies and the agrochemical industry made out like bandits. Green, orderly abundance came with a dark underbelly of pollution, erosion, loss of topsoil, and capital concentration. In October 1998, with a near record crop, a depressed Asian market, and a shrunken federal safety net, an Iowa State University survey predicted perhaps as many as 30 percent of Iowa farms would go under (Strauss 1998).

While technology has continued to refine its tools—first hybridization and now gene splicing—commercial seed companies have succeeded in gaining patent protection for plant varieties and genetic strings. With utter solemnity they have engaged in acrobatic doublespeak: their germplasm *sources* (varieties from the gene-rich Third World or from Native America) are the "common heritage of mankind" and therefore should be free to all comers, while their saleable seeds should be protected by property rights laws. Once again, the already powerful are attempting to increase their power and profits by manipulating the law.

When I asked Deb how she connected her research in the outback of the arid Southwest to more mainstream agriculture, she said, "There's lots to learn from traditional systems," and paused. "But it's not easy to convince people in Iowa of that."

In the Southwest, nothing is more important to agriculture than water. Traditionally, Zunis would have used storm runoff from the small watershed above Deb's test field to provide it with sufficient moisture. Runoff fields concentrated the rain from an area significantly larger than the field: in some examples of similar "akchin" fields at Hopi, the planted area at the mouth of a canyon measured less than 2 percent of the watershed's total area (Hack 1942; figure 7.4).

At Zuni, until the end of March and during the monsoons beginning in July, short and intense rainstorms quickly saturated the thin soil over rock. Then the rainwater washed across fallen pine needles, juniper berries, gritty sand, and cryptobiotic soil clinging to bare earth; past sage, saltbush, and mullein; finally tumbling down the watershed to the field at its mouth. These floods, rare but usually frequent enough, not only brought necessary water to the corn, but also supplied what Zunis call "tree sand"—the decaying organic matter that slowly made its way down the drainage. A moving compost pile delivered without pitchforks.

These storm runoff fields struck me as ingenious and quirky. The land, often with a few added low rock barriers, focused the flash floods where they could be used, the way a lens can focus light. Ingenious, maybe, but Deb told me such runoff irrigation wasn't limited to a few out-of-the-way spots in the American Southwest. In Israel's Negev Desert, a group of biologists and archaeologists had renovated ancient runoff irrigation systems into several large, thriving farms with vegetables, wine grapes, and orchards of peach, fig, olive, apricot, and almond trees. Pastures of alfalfa, barley, oats, and wheat stretched out next to barren

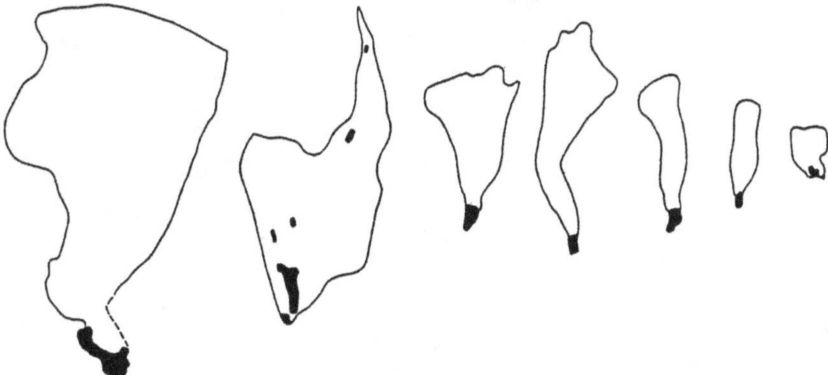

Fig. 7.4 Relationship between areas of cultivated akchin fields and the areas of the watersheds that supply them with water. Illustration by Mary Beath after Hack 1942.

ground. Hardly what anyone would expect in a desert without pumping groundwater or rechanneling a river (Evenari, Shanan, and Tadmor 1982).

Deb and her colleagues weren't oriented to truck farming but to deciphering *this* system, and that depended on understanding the biology of maize, a plant so adaptable it seemed to be a botanical chameleon. Corn's wild promiscuity, extreme even for a flowering plant, partly explains its dramatic adaptability. It's the most widely distributed crop in the world, from 12,000 feet in the Andes to sea level, from the humid tropics to Southwest deserts, and in all climates between (Muenchrath and Salvador 1995).

Fourteen million pollen grains, give or take a few, blow from each of the male tassels that fountain up from the tops of corn's leafy stalks. Carried mostly by the wind, the pollen finds its way to the silks of protoears on the stalk below or on nearby plants: one pale, delicate silk per kernel. On each plant, the tassels usually shed their pollen several days before its ears are ready, which makes cross-pollination between plants more likely. In a land race field, theoretically, each kernel on an ear could have a different set of genes. But corn has an additional trick that keeps its variability high: specialized DNA sequences that shift around a little like jackrabbits. They're called "jumping genes." Not surprisingly, though it is a single species, corn claims more varieties than any other crop—thousands worldwide.

Corn's genetic blueprint, *by itself*, dictates only some corn attributes: the colors of the kernels and whether the "meat" of the kernel will be sugary, flinty, floury, or "dent"—a type mostly used to feed livestock and named for the dimple in each dried kernel's crown.

But everything else, including cob and kernel size, yield of grain, growth and development, height, number of leaves and ears, side stalks, and so on, depends on the genes' interaction with the corn's local environment. No matter what instructions are encoded in a kernel's germplasm, its growing conditions can mean the difference between large, full ears and small, poorly filled ears. Sometimes a few degrees colder during germination can doom a future plant, or not quite enough water when an ear silks out in July can mean fertilization never happens. No fertilization, no kernels, no harvest.

I imagined corn's messy heterogeneity first prompted the *idea* of orderly hybrids, with their matching sets of DNA, long before technology could make it happen. Why not track down the "best" traits and construct ideal, predictable plants, instead of settling for the hodgepodge from promiscuous, open pollination? And that's exactly what has happened: the handful of Corn Belt hybrid varieties will grow uniform plants with one ear per exceptionally stiff stalk, perfectly suited for mechanical harvest, and will produce large yields when all conditions are *optimum*. And that insistence on optimum conditions has led down the path of industrial agriculture. Keep the plants standard, like dolls off the assembly line, and go after the *maximum* yields. But, keeping conditions optimum can require enormous inputs, especially in difficult, variable conditions, and drastically diminishes flexibility.

Deb had planted hybrid dent corn that New Mexico State University had recommended for Zuni's conditions, to compare with the local Zuni blue.

"I once planted some corn from the Extension Service," Niles told us. "Tall, beautiful. Giant stalks, though—two inches across," he circled his thumb and forefinger, "but I didn't get ONE ear." He shook his head half in amazement, half in disgust.

Among most traditional farmers, certainly in the less-than-optimal arid Southwest, the goal has been different from industrial agriculture: to *minimize risk*. When literal survival depends on your harvest, as it did for several thousand years, the less risk the better.

Instead of attempts to *control* the environment, the Zunis, like other traditional farmers, have worked to *buffer* its lack of cooperation. At the same time, they have selected seeds that tolerate their harsh and uncertain world. Maize and Zuni have evolved together.

This distinction bears repeating. Industrial agriculture aims for high yields in the short term, under the best of conditions, no matter what the eventual collateral damage to the environment might be. Traditional farmers have always sought consistency of production through genetic variability and multiple, flexible growing strategies. Minimize risk.

At Zuni, harshness and uncertainty meant scarce and sporadic water, cold temperatures at germination and toward the end of the season, high mid-season heat, low soil nitrogen, spring wind so violent it could rip seedlings right out of the ground, and pests. This year the worst pests had been field-inhaling grasshoppers, elk forced down from the mountains by new houses, and "two-legged deer" in pickup trucks. But Zuni's varied topography—its mesas and canyons, elevations that range from 6,030 feet to 7,000 feet, springs and seasonal streams—partly counterbalanced those difficulties by offering many microclimates.

The Zuni potpourri of planting techniques reminded me of a well-stocked larder, full not of food, but of effective strategies.

Sometimes the Zunis nestled their fields by a mesa for wind protection or next to heat-holding canyon walls that trumped frost; they might locate one field a little higher, one a little lower, hedging their bets.

They planted up to twelve inches deep—where the growing plant would be more likely to reach water and to be protected longer from those late frosts, deep roots providing solid anchor. Zuni varieties had evolved to grow much longer sprouts than varieties planted closer to the surface.

They planted four to ten plants together in widely spaced hills. The stalks supported each other against the violent spring winds and debris-laden swift runoff. The hills' distance apart increased effective moisture and required less labor to plant and tend.

Traditionally—though not since ready tractors—they planted kernels using a digging stick. Undisturbed by plowing, the soil evaporated less of its precious moisture and didn't compact under heavy equipment. They tended to their soils with crop rotation and by allowing fields to lie fallow. Not only do beans, with their microbial collaborators, fix nitrogen from the air, but so do wild plants like larkspur and cliffrose. Lightning also transforms atmospheric nitrogen into a usable form. Cryptobiotic soil, which covertly takes over on ground untrampled for some years, supplies a surprisingly large proportion of the nitrogen available to plants all over the Southwest.

At Zuni, an unexpected regular genetic shake-up takes place, beyond cross-pollination, beyond jumping genes. Night dances include a large communal seed bowl: everyone contributes, everyone leaves with a handful of *different* seeds that have been blessed. Extra care goes into planting and tending those sacred seeds (Carol Brandt, pers. comm.).

My head spun with the details. But I thought of these Zuni farmers beside me who I knew often laughed good-naturedly at this project's effort to translate their "system" into the framework of science. What to me seemed novel and complicated had been codified in their culture, each detail easily related to the others—details of land and weather, of ceremony and the sacred, of corn stalks growing green and kernels ripe with the future.

Yet Zunis are no more monolithic than any other group. Some ZSAP fields closer to the roads, including one of Deb's test fields, had been vandalized this year

(1998)—squash smashed, ears of corn half shucked and thrown on the ground. Reverence abandoned. No one knew who. No one really knew why.

But this year's assistant director of ZSAP could only work until December, when his year-long religious duties kicked in again. Reverence maintained.

And jurisdictional ironies abounded:

> The renovated Black Rock Dam in front of its silted-up reservoir seemed unlikely ever to function, though the Zunis themselves welcomed it, retaining some hope for new irrigation water.
>
> The crop-damaging elk roamed the reservation with impunity, illegal game unless a hunter had a permit, pushed down from the Zuni Mountains in the past five or six years by extensive new house building off the reservation. Even though the New Mexico Department of Game and Fish provided free permits to farmers in the Eight Northern Pueblos in north-central New Mexico, I'd been told, they hadn't extended the same privilege to the Zunis.

I could easily portray this Zuni system as jazz improv counterbalancing the Sousa marches of mainstream agriculture, but that didn't honor the complications and the internal paradoxes. To me, the most positive impulse at Zuni seemed the attempts not to resolve their paradoxes, but to corral them into an encompassed synergy. The success of the Zuni corn system came from its flexibility, responsiveness, redundancy, human resourcefulness and idiosyncrasy, and specificity to local, often wildly unpredictable, conditions. Powerful outside forces *had* interrupted it, but its heart remained intact.

As far as the Zuni effort can be generalized, it seemed meant to buffer their culture against internal nuttiness (such as field vandalism) and external nuttiness (such as capricious policies of the BIA, Game and Fish, HUD, TV, and mainstream culture) just as their corn has been buffered for millennia against the potentially destructive forces of a difficult climate. Much as they cultivated *with* the topography, the soils, the wind, the rain, the heat and cold, they were trying to work *with* the twentieth and twenty-first centuries, *with* science, and not be swallowed. But the going was tough, partly because science can never claim the ultimate certainty of religion, despite its apparent handle on "truth."

A few days before the corn harvest, I'd joined Deb and several others following Niles and his ZSAP boss down a rocky dirt track on a mesa southwest of Zuni Pueblo. The bumper piñon crop hung heavy on the branches, ready to be shaken loose. The smooth, oblong pine nut meats were as rich in protein by weight as

Fig. 7.5 Old peach orchard. Photo by Mary Beath.

beefsteak, with a full complement of amino acids. Chamisa bloomed egg yolk yellow. Prickly pear, dried grasses, and snakeweed mingled with flame-shaped junipers, covered with their own yields: dull purple berries traditionally used as food or flavoring or to make a tea for stomachaches.

The track angled downhill to an outcrop of pale sandstone boulders. To our left the edge of the mesa fell away abruptly to a series of gently sloping benches of maroon, purple, and cream gravels dotted with dark piñons and junipers. Directly ahead and several hundred feet below, a broad, flat expanse of golden desert separated us from two short red mesas, then more distantly, a taller light mesa, its top frosted dark green. The trail rounded the boulders to a steep, winding slot through the rocks. Stepping carefully across stones and dust, we picked our way down to a small basin that faced the warm sun to the southwest. About one hundred yards long and thirty yards wide, the nearly flat shelf nestled below the mesa's faceted persimmon face, but still above the desert floor: a natural porch. Clumps of big sage and more delicate sand sage shared the ground with the pale, delicate grasses. And, remarkably, within the porch's sandstone boundaries grew a reviving peach orchard.

When the Spanish had muscled their way into this territory they'd brought not only a mission to convert the "heathens," but also plants from home. They'd carried with them from Spain several peach varieties that would grow from pits, already adapted to an arid climate, with small fruits perfectly suited for drying. The Zunis had established orchards on many terraces just below mesa tops where

Fig. 7.6 Reviving peach tree. Photo by Mary Beath.

runoff would water deep sandy soils (figure 7.5). They dried their new harvests on their roofs alongside corn and chile and gourds and beans. But in the 1950s a catastrophic freeze had wiped out most of the thousands of trees.

For years the bare branches in this lovely, protected cove had stood neglected, left for dead, with cactuses growing at their feet, and the two stone field houses slowly disintegrating. ZSAP had mined their community's knowledge, consulting with an older Zuni farmer who kept his own flourishing orchard, and had gone to work. They cleared out the cactus and dug around among the roots. If the roots weren't brittle, they still lived. The crew cut away the dead fibers, split the stumps aboveground, and pruned some of the old branches. Around the gray cleft bases they piled up sand. Just downslope from each tree they built a curved earthen berm to catch again the winter snows and summer runoff from the mesa top.

And in a year, or two, or three, these small moribund fruit trees had sprouted back to life, into ragged, five-foot-tall, healthy, leafy peach bushes: truth as convincing as any I could imagine (figure 7.6).

I couldn't miss the obvious analogy. In 1879 the Smithsonian's Bureau of Ethnology had been created to document Native Americans just before they *disappeared completely*. And yet—

The wind whipped up over the raised sandstone lip of the shallow basin, stirring flaxen grasses, lifting the curved, dark green peach leaves, and brushing the higher mesa's steep walls, where rows of ancient petroglyphs scored the soft stone. We all grabbed for our hats.

For a certain sizable segment of the agricultural world, the results of the collaboration between these scientists and the Zuni Tribe would matter little. Most seed companies demeaned traditional systems and land races as insignificant, marginal oddities. Deb had paraphrased their attitude, "If land races had any merit, they'd already have been used." I doubted seed companies could grasp any reason for the Zunis not to sell their corn, either.

But for a small and perhaps growing minority, all the data crunching and correlating, the computer modeling and simulating, would perhaps add evidence that, in part, for practical science as well as for poetic vision, *the way forward is the way back* (Lao-Tzu, *Tao Te Ching*).

"Look at this," said Niles as we shucked yet another pile of corn from Deb's test field. He rubbed off the last silks from a dark ear the color of oxidized silver. The kernels grew entirely to the tip, a perfectly filled potential. All the other ears had either not grown to the end or had been nibbled away by corn worms. "Save this one out," he said as he handed it to me. I took it and turned it and watched the sun reflect off each of its burnished kernels. I bent my head and inhaled its delicate, buttery smell, then laid it carefully in the small cardboard box on top of several dozen new wooden row stakes.

"Hmmm. All done," said Dixon later, with clear pleasure, as he gently turned the perfect ear in his own callused hands.

Asking for his life-giving breath
His breath of old age,
His breath of waters,
His breath of seeds,
His breath of fecundity,
His breath of good fortune,
Asking for his breath.
And into my warm body
Drawing his breath,
I shall add to your breath . . .
May . . . you be blessed with light . . .
May your roads all be fulfilled.

— From a Zuni prayer, translated by Ruth Bunzel, 1932
(in *Zuni Ceremonialism*)

I wish to thank the Zuni Sustainable Agriculture Project and the Zuni men who helped with the harvest for welcoming me as a fellow worker. For this essay, I've changed their names. I also want to express my great gratitude to Deb Muenchrath and to Carol Brandt. Thanks, too, to Jeff Homburg for reviewing an early version of this manuscript.

Notes

1. Although Brandt notes that "ethnographic examples must be used with caution when modeling prehistoric agriculture," she continues, "it is likely that [the Zunis'] technological and biological innovations have their origin in antiquity." Strategies that are common both at Zuni and in the archaeological record include waffle gardens, field locations, features within fields for controlling soil and water erosion, irrigation systems, and crop repertoires.
2. Since this essay was written in 1998, some of the project's results are reaching publication: Muenchrath et al. 2002; Norton, Pawluck, and Sandor 1998, 2000; Stahl et al. 1998. The National Science Foundation grant was in Ecosystem Studies, Award Number 9528458.
3. Exhaustive elaborations of the information in the following five paragraphs can be found in this lively and extensively illustrated book.
4. Sha'lak'o was reopened to non-Natives in 2000.

References Cited

Bowannie, Fred, Jr., and Andrew Laahty

1993 The Nutria Irrigation Unit, the Zuni Sustainable Agriculture Project, and the Nutria Pilot Project. *Zuni Farming for Today and Tomorrow: An Occasional Newsletter of the Zuni Sustainable Agriculture Project* 2:1, 3–5.

Brandt, Carol B.

1995 Traditional Agriculture on the Zuni Indian Reservation in the Recent Historic Period. In *Soil, Water, Biology, and Belief in Prehistoric and Traditional Southwestern Agriculture*, ed. H. Wolcott Toll, 291–301. New Mexico Archaeological Council Special Publication 2. Albuquerque: New Mexico Archaeological Council.

Bunzel, Ruth L.

1992 *Zuni Ceremonialism*. Albuquerque: University of New Mexico Press.

Cleveland, David A., Fred Bowannie Jr., Donald F. Eriacho, Andrew Laahty, and Eric Perramond

1995 Zuni Farming and United States Government Policy: The Politics of Biological and Cultural Diversity in Agriculture. *Agriculture and Human Values* 12 (3): 2–18.

———, Donald Eriacho, Daniela Soleri, Lygatie Laate, and Roy Keys

1994 Zuni Peach Orchards, Part III. *Zuni Farming for Today and Tomorrow: An Occasional Newsletter of the Zuni Sustainable Agriculture Project* 3:25–28.

Cushing, Frank Hamilton

1920 *Zuni Breadstuff.* Reprinted 1974. Indian Notes and Monographs 8. New York: Museum of the American Indian, Heye Foundation.

Eggan, Fred, and T. N. Pandey

1979 Zuni History, 1850–1970. In *Southwest.* Vol. 9 of *Handbook of North American Indians,* ed. Alfonso Ortiz, 474–78. Washington, DC: Smithsonian Institution.

Enote, James, Steven Albert, and Kevin Webb, eds.

1993 *The Zuni Resource Development Plan: A Program of Action for Sustainable Resource Development.* 1st ed. Zuni, NM: Zuni Conservation Project, Pueblo of Zuni.

Evenari, Michael, Leslie Shanan, and Naphtali Tadmor

1982 *The Negev: The Challenge of a Desert.* 2nd ed. Cambridge, MA: Harvard University Press.

Feedstuffs

1997 Pioneer Reports Decrease in Corn Market Share: Net Earnings for the Year Are Up at $243 Million Despite 2% Drop in Market Share. 69 (45) 971103:6.

Ferguson, T. J.

1989 The Impact of Federal Policy on Zuni Land Use. In *Seasons of the Kachina,* ed. J. L. Bean, 85–131. Hayward: Ballena Press/California State University.

Ford, Richard I.

1994 Corn Is Our Mother. In *Corn and Culture in the Prehistoric New World,* ed. S. Johannessen and C. A. Hastorf, 513–25. Boulder, CO: Westview Press.

1999 Ethnoecology Serving the Community, A Case Study from Zuni Pueblo, New Mexico. In *Ethnoecology: Situated Knowledge/Located Lives,* ed. Virginia D. Nazarea, 71–87. Tucson: University of Arizona Press.

Fussell, Betty

1992 *The Story of Corn: The Myth and History, the Culture and Agriculture, the Art and Science of America's Quintessential Crop.* New York: Alfred A. Knopf.

Hack, John R.

1942 *The Changing Physical Environment of the Hopi Indians of Arizona.* Papers of the Peabody Museum of American Archaeology and Ethnology, vol. 35(1). Cambridge, MA: Harvard University.

Hart, E. Richard

1995 *Zuni and the Courts: A Struggle for Sovereign Land Rights.* Lawrence: University Press of Kansas.

Johannessen, Sissel, and Christine A. Hastorf, eds.

1994 *Corn and Culture in the Prehistoric New World.* Boulder, CO: Westview Press.

Kloppenburg, Jack Ralph, Jr.

1988 *First the Seed: The Political Economy of Plant Biotechnology, 1492–2000.* Cambridge: Cambridge University Press.

———, ed.

1988 *Seeds and Sovereignty: The Use and Control of Plant Genetic Resources.* Durham, NC: Duke University Press.

Lin, Biing-Hwan

1995 U.S. Department of Agriculture, Economic Research Service. *Pesticide and Fertilizer Use and Trends in U.S. Agriculture*. Washington, DC: U.S. Department of Agriculture, Economic Research Service.

Matson, R. G.

1991 *The Origins of Southwestern Agriculture*. Tucson: University of Arizona Press.

Maxwell, Timothy D.

1995 A Comparative Study of Prehistoric Farming Strategies. In *Soil, Water, Biology, and Belief in Prehistoric and Traditional Southwestern Agriculture*, ed. H. Wolcott Toll, 3–12. New Mexico Archaeological Council Special Publication 2. Albuquerque: New Mexico Archaeological Council.

Muenchrath, Deborah Ann

1995 Productivity, Morphology, Phenology, and Physiology of a Desert-Adapted Native American Maize (*Zea mays* L.) Cultivar. PhD diss., Iowa State University, Ames.

———, M. Kuratomi, J. A. Sandor, and J. A. Homburg

2002 Observational Study of Maize Production Systems of Zuni Farmers in Semiarid New Mexico. *Journal of Ethnobiology* 22 (1): 1–33.

———, and Ricardo J. Salvador

1995 Maize Productivity and Agroecology: Effects of Environment and Agricultural Practices on the Biology of Maize. In *Soil, Water, Biology, and Belief in Prehistoric and Traditional Southwestern Agriculture*, ed. H. Wolcott Toll, 303–33. New Mexico Archaeological Council Special Publication 2. Albuquerque: New Mexico Archaeological Council.

Nabhan, Gary Paul

1979 The Ecology of Floodwater Farming in Arid Southwestern North America. *Agro-Ecosystems* 5:245–55.

1989 *Enduring Seeds: Native American Agriculture and Wild Plant Conservation*. New York: North Point Press.

Netting, Robert McC.

1993 *Smallholders, Householders: Farm Families and the Ecology of Intensive, Sustainable Agriculture*. Stanford, CA: Stanford University Press.

Norton, Jay B., Roman R. Pawluck, and Jonathan A. Sandor

1998 Observation and Experience Linking Science and Indigenous Knowledge at Zuni, New Mexico. *Journal of Arid Environments* 39:331–40.

2000 Farmer-Scientist Collaboration for Research and Agricultural Development. In *Soil Science Society of America Special Publication*, ed. W. A. Payne and D. Keener. Madison, WI: Soil Science Society of America.

Sandor, Jonathan A.

1995 Searching Soil for Clues about Southwest Prehistoric Agriculture. In *Soil, Water, Biology, and Belief in Prehistoric and Traditional Southwestern Agriculture*, ed. H. Wolcott Toll, 119–37. New Mexico Archaeological Council Special Publication 2. Albuquerque: New Mexico Archaeological Council.

Stahl, P. D., C. I. Havener, S. E. Williams, J. B. Norton, J. A. Sandor, and D. A. Muenchrath

1998 Influence of Zuni Agricultural Practices on Some Soil Biotic Properties. Unpublished manuscript.

Strauss, Gary
1998 Green Acres Turn into Lean Acres; Strong Global Financial Climate Slashes Crop Prices; Many Farms Could Be in Final Season. *USA Today*, October 13.
Stuart, David E.
2000 *Anasazi America*. Albuquerque: University of New Mexico Press.
U.S. Department of Agriculture
1950 *Agricultural Statistics, Yearbook 1950*. U.S. Department of Agriculture, Washington, D.C.
1995 *Agricultural Resources and Environmental Indicators*. Washington, DC: U.S. Department of Agriculture, Economic Research Service.
1997 *Agricultural Statistics, Yearbook 1997*. U.S. Department of Agriculture, Washington, D.C.

Web Pages

Annotated Bibliography of Publications Relating to Indigenous Peoples and Traditional Resource Rights
http://users.ox.ac.uk/~wgtrr/bib1.htm
Food and Agriculture Organization of the United Nations
http://www.fao.org
Indigenous Agricultural and Environmental Knowledge Systems
http://www.ciesin.org/TG/AG/iksys.html
International Development Research Centre
http://www.idrc.ca
The Maize Page, Iowa State University
http://maize.agron.iastate.edu
Native Americans and the Environment
http://www.cnie.org/nae/
Native Seeds/SEARCH
http://www.nativeseeds.org

Chapter Eight

The Narrative Construction of Landscape

Hopi, 1879–94

by Louis A. Hieb

In the desert-and-mesa country of northern Arizona, the ancient and enduring Hopi learned how to coax a good living from an amazing series of corn gardens planted in the sand. They knew that "the sand is the only fertile land" in their part of the world. Anglo-American interference in the 1890s threatened the highly successful Hopi way of gardening. In this study of a number of elegant Hopi insights into the nature of the desert, Louis Hieb looks at language and its relationship to a landscape to explain hidden aspects of the culture of a remarkable people.

Landscape per se does not exist; it is amorphous—
an indeterminate area of the earth's surface and a chaos
of details incomprehensible to the perceptual system.
A landscape requires selective viewing and a frame.
— *Hildegard Binder Johnson*

Landscape is never passive. People engage with it, rework it, appropriate and contest it. It is part of the way in which identities are created and disputed, whether as individual, group or nation-state. Operating at the juncture of history

and politics, social relations and cultural perceptions,
landscape is a concept of high tension.
— *Barbara Bender*

Between 1879 when A. M. Stephen first visited the Hopi and the Bureau of American Ethnology's first expedition reached the Southwest and 1894 when the second Hemenway Southwestern Archaeological Expedition ended and Stephen died, a number of narratives "describing" (representing and constructing) the "landscape" near the Hopi villages were written or recorded. I have chosen three that differ markedly in their form and content: the aesthetic landscape of the artist Frederick S. Dellenbaugh, the moral landscape of the Hopi religious leader Wiki, and the political landscape of ethnologist Stephen in his role as advocate for the Hopi. My interest is in the language and structural design of these narratives rather than the exterior real-world place to which reference is made.

In the epigraph above, art historian Hildegard Binder Johnson underscores the point that landscape—to be comprehensible—requires "selective viewing and a frame." Dellenbaugh, Wiki, and Stephen made (or found) comprehensible the incomprehensible. Through their narratives, what is "amorphous . . . indeterminate . . . a chaos of details" is represented or presented as meaningful and valuable. At the same time, as anthropologist Barbara Bender notes above, landscape is created and contested and is a "concept of high tension." Dellenbaugh's landscape—as painting or as narrative—differs markedly from that of Dan Namingha, a modern Hopi artist, whose selection of color and form is at once more abstract and metaphysical (for example, Namingha's *View of First Mesa*; Hoving 2000:55). The image of Masau's footprints, part of that chain of memories narrated by Wiki, has taken on new significance in land claims and litigations in the twentieth century.[1] And the contested nature of landscape is explicit in Stephen's advocacy for the Hopi in the face of federal efforts to "civilize" Hopi land-use practices, practices Stephen knew were informed and shaped by a different but equally valid social organization and more effective agricultural economics.

I have chosen to focus on written *narrative* as a vehicle for the representation of "landscape." Like paintings and photographic images, narratives construct realities. This is to say two things: that a "narrative is a representation of a reality" as well as that a "narrative is itself a reality" (Shuman 1996:236). It is my intent to explore the form as well as the culturally and historically situated nature of these narrative constructions of landscape. Like the historian Alun Munslow, I regard these written landscapes as "socially constituted narrative representations" (1997:15). As such, narratives constitute aspects of the landscape as objects of meaning, understanding, and comprehension. This is a perspective equally valid, I would suggest, for other forms of representation or presentation of the Hopi landscape, including various, more recent scientific narratives (for example, Forde 1931; Hack 1942; McIntire 1968) as well as visual media.

The Aesthetic Landscape of Frederick S. Dellenbaugh

"It is such an extraordinary place," Dellenbaugh wrote in a letter to his mother at his arrival on the Hopi First Mesa, October 28, 1884.

> Perched high above all the world on this narrow, barren ledge of rocks, with perpendicular precipices all around, one seems actually out of the world as we know it—and he is. The vast expanse of treeless desolation, stretching into infinity everywhere, is each day, morning noon and night, the same. The apparent movement of the sun through the heavens is the only changing thing except to a limited extent the shadows about the houses. (1884)

At age seventeen, Dellenbaugh had joined John Wesley Powell's second Colorado River expedition as an oarsman and artist. That was 1871. Thirteen years later he returned to the Southwest, this time to the Hopi villages, with brushes, canvas, and tubes of paint. Although sensitive to the silence ("no songs of the wind through branches") and the sounds (the "crying of babies, the yelping of dogs... the long agony-like howls of the donkeys" and "the strange language of the strange people"), his focus was the visual landscape and the creative role of the sun in light and shadow (figure 8.1). Recalling this trip in "An Artist's Glimpse of Northern Arizona," primacy is given to sight and to view ("we began to see," and "at last they were quite plain to our eyes"):

> As far as the eye could reach, a land of desolation, apparently boundless, lay stretched out under the burning sun. Leagues away, the waves of civilization are advancing toward the valley, but we heard no sound of them there. The life of another race and of another time pervades the air—we are out of the world. Another language startles the ear, and curious customs, familiar to this people for untold ages, surprise the eye. (1889:854)

It was not long before Dellenbaugh discovered no one would pose for him in the villages; consequently, "I was obliged to content myself with making studies of houses and inanimate objects" (1889:855). Soon ill and ill at ease, he moved to more comfortable surroundings at Keam's Canyon, ten miles east, bringing with him a Hopi who agreed to pose with a throwing stick (figure 8.2):

Fig. 8.1 Eagle Cage (from Dellenbaugh 1889).

> [O]nce there, I stretched a large canvas and drew him on it, life size.... In the illustration he is seen in the act of throwing the putch-kohu [throwing stick]; behind him are the remains of ruined houses, of which there are many in the country. The Moki [Hopi] Buttes are seen at the left, and the first mesa can be distinguished in the distance. (1889:855)

Dellenbaugh constructed images of the landscape—both natural and cultural—with paint and words that reflect the perspectives of late nineteenth-century studio cultures of Paris and New York of which he was a part. Implicit in his work is a concept of "landscape" as "the artistic representation of nature in terms of the physical 'view'" (Fitter 1998:86). For Dellenbaugh, "landscape" is a genre of art, not a term referring to landform, landmarks, land use, or topography. Rather, as Christopher Fitter suggests, "landscape is the definition of nature that organizes material features of the land [including the people] into a composite whole set into defined spatial relations." Dellenbaugh's "glimpse," the perspective he brought as an artist, was "an eager dwelling upon appearances, an engrossment in surfaces, an absorption in things, as we say, 'in themselves'" (Geertz 1973:111) and a "contemplation of sensory qualities without *their usual meanings*"

Fig. 8.2 Moki Indian (from Dellenbaugh 1889).

(Langer 1953:49, quoted in Geertz 1973, emphasis added). It is to the question of "their usual meanings" that I turn next.

The Moral Landscape of Wiki

The anthropologist Walter Hough later recalled Wiki (or Samiwiki, ca. 1850–1910) as "a man whose brain contained a vast stock of ancient lore, of legend, myth and song" (1915:223). For most of his life, Wiki was the chief priest of the Antelope Society. To him was entrusted its most sacred knowledge (*wiimi*), the beliefs and practices of the Snake/Antelope ceremony.

Hopis distinguish two major categories of traditional narrative: *novati*—teachings, traditions, bodies of knowledge, cultural beliefs—and *tuutuwutsi*—stories, legends (Hopi Dictionary Project 1998; Curtis 1922:184, n.2). Within novati there are two recognized subcategories. While there is no established way of referring to these, the following are possible Hopi glosses and translations (Emory Sekaquaptewa, pers. comm. 1997): the emergence narrative (*qatsiyamakiwqat novati*, or "traditional knowledge relating to the emergence of life") and clan migration narratives (*qatsihepnumyaqat novati*, or "traditional knowledge relating to their search for a settlement/place to make life"). Emergence narratives record events prior to and including the emergence of the Hopi and other peoples on the earth's surface. Clan migration narratives describe the movements of the various clans at the emergence from *sipaapuni* to the village of Walpi (or some other place considered as the "center").[2] These accounts become more specific as to the directions taken and the locations of places where clans stayed as they approached the "center" ("a settlement/place to make life"). The narratives provide a moral topography, and in the Snake Clan migration narrative particular importance is placed on the "land pact" or "covenant" (inadequate glosses) made between the Hopi and the sacred being Masau whose footprints define Hopitutsqua, the sacred lands of the Hopi. As Wiki told Jeremiah Sullivan, a young doctor living on First Mesa in 1885:

> For four days our uncles searched for the maker of the footprints, when our oldest uncle saw, coming over the west mesa, a who-was-it. Our uncle went to meet the stranger.... *They kept walking toward each other, when they came together our uncle took hold of him, and it was Masau....Masau spoke first and said, You are strong of heart and know no fear—Good—let us sit down....Masau then said: You and your people are strong of heart. Look in the valleys, the rocks and the woods, and you will find my footprints there. All this is mine, but by your courage you have won it. All this I give you, all this is yours forever, because you met me and were not afraid.* (Sullivan 1886, original emphasis)

For the Hopi, their social memory and sacred knowledge was, and continues to be, embodied and represented in significant places in the natural landscape, in the architectural forms of their villages, in the bodily memory of ritual performance, and in a variety of unwritten but memorized songs and narratives that were (and are) the property of the clans and ceremonial societies. The landscape, especially, serves as an archive, a repository of "mementos" (Sullivan's word) both cultural (for example, shrines, petroglyphs, ancestral dwellings) and natural (for example, springs, significant places) that give meaning and, more importantly, create and maintain "a place to make life."

The Political Landscape of A. M. Stephen

A. M. Stephen had lived at Keam's Canyon continuously since 1880, managing Keam's trading post. In 1891 he began ethnological research among the Hopi under the direction of Jesse Walter Fewkes, as part of the Hemenway Southwestern Archaeological Expedition.

Even before the 1880s, the "landscape" surrounding the Hopi villages was the subject of a number of narrative proposals that sought to define it, to specify ownership of it, to serve purposes of federal control. On December 16, 1882, President Chester A. Arthur signed an executive order, a narrative construction of the landscape invisible to those living there:

> It is hereby ordered that a tract of country, in the Territory of Arizona, lying and being within the following described boundaries, Viz: beginning on the one hundred and tenth degree of longitude west from Greenwich, at the point 36°30" north, thence due west to the one hundred and eleventh degree of longitude west, thence due south to a point of longitude 35°30" north, thence due east to the one hundred and tenth degree of longitude west, thence due north to the place of beginning, be and the same is hereby withdrawn from settlement and sale, and set apart for the use and occupancy of the Moqui [Hopi], and such other Indians, as the Secretary of the Interior may see fit to settle thereon.

In the months and years following, interpretation and implementation of the executive order has been the subject of continuous conflict and litigation. In 1887 the Dawes Act was passed and in 1892 an allotment agent was sent to the reservation to enumerate the Hopi people and to survey and allot the lands in severalty. The Dawes Act provided for the division of the land into 160-acre plots for male heads of families, 80-acre plots for single males over eighteen years of age, and 40-acre plots for boys.

It was in this context that A. M. Stephen wrote a petition "to the Washington Chiefs" on behalf of the Hopi. Although aware of the Hopis' pact with Masau, Stephen chose what he regarded as a more politically effective logic of protest, one based on his knowledge of Hopi social organization and agricultural practices. It is as follows:

> During the last two years strangers have looked over our land with spy-glasses, and made marks upon it, and we know but little of what this means.
>
> As we believe that you have no wish to disturb our possessions, we want to tell you something about this Hopi land. None of us ever asked that it should be measured into separate lots and given to individuals, for this would cause confusion.
>
> The family, the dwelling-house, and the field, are inseparable, because the woman is the heir of these, and they rest with her. Among us the family traces its kin from the mother, hence all its possessions are hers. The man builds the house

but the woman is the owner, because she repairs and preserves it; the man cultivates the field, but he renders the harvest into the keeping of the woman, because upon her it rests to prepare the food, and the surplus of stores for barter depends upon her thrift.

A man plants the fields of his wife, and the fields assigned to the children she bears, and informally he calls them his, although in fact they are not. Even of the field which he inherits from his mother, its harvests he may dispose of at will, but the field itself he may not. He may permit his son to occupy it and gather its produce, but at the father's death, the son may not own it, for then it passes to the father's sister's son, or nearest mother's kin, and thus our fields and houses always remain with our mothers.

According to the number of children a woman has, fields for them are assigned to her, from some of the lands of her family group, and her husband takes care of them. Hence our fields are numerous but small, and several belonging to the same family may be close together, or they may be miles apart, because arable localities are not continuous. There are other reasons for the irregularity in size and situation of our family lands, as interrupted sequence of inheritance caused by extinction of families, but chiefly, owing to the following condition, and to which we especially invite your attention.

In the spring and early summer there usually comes from the Southwest a succession of gales, oftentimes strong enough to blow away the sandy soil from the face of some of our fields, and to expose the underlying clay, which is hard, and sour, and barren; as the sand is the only fertile land, when it moves the planters must follow it, and other fields must be provided in place of those which have been devastated. Sometimes generations pass away and these barren spots remain, while in other instances, after a few years, the winds will again restore the desirable sand upon them.

In such event its fertility is disclosed by the nature of the grass and shrubs that grow upon it. If these are promising, a number of us unite to clear off the land and make it again fit for planting; when it may be given back to its former owner, or if a long time has elapsed to other heirs, or it may be given to some person of the same family group more in need of a planting place.

> These limited changes in land holdings are explored by mutual discussion and concession among the elders, and among all the thinking men and women of the family groups interested.
>
> In effect, the same system of holding, and the same method of planting, obtain among the Tewa, and all the Hopi villages, and under them we provide ourselves with food in abundance.
>
> The American is our Elder brother, and in everything he can teach us, except in the method of growing corn in these waterless, sandy valleys, and in that we are sure we can teach him.
>
> We believe that you have no desire to change our system of small holdings, nor do we think that you wish to remove any of our ancient land-marks, and it seems to us that the conditions we have mentioned afford sufficient grounds for thus requesting to be left undisturbed.
>
> Further it has been told to us, as coming from Washington, that neither measuring nor individual papers are necessary for us to keep possession of our villages, our peach orchards, and our springs. If this be so, we should like to ask what need there is to bring confusion into our accustomed system of holding our corn fields.
>
> We are aware that some ten years ago, a certain area around our lands was proclaimed to be for our use, but the extent of this area is unknown to us, nor has any Agent ever been able to point it out, for its boundaries have never been measured.
>
> We earnestly desire to have one continuous boundary ring enclosing all the Tewa and all the Hopi lands [apparent reference to a proposed modification of the 1882 Executive Order Reservation], and that it shall be large enough to afford sustenance for our increasing flocks and herds. If such a scope can be confirmed to us by a paper from your hands, securing us forever against intrusion, all our people will be satisfied. (Stephen n.d.)

The narrative is practical and pragmatic and, ultimately, self-serving: Stephen wanted to complete his research before Hopi culture changed. The petition was apparently never sent. In his last letter to Fewkes, written just weeks before his death in April 1894, Stephen noted that Hopis continued to come to his room to sign. Ironically, although the allotting agent felt he had completed his work as best he could, he had been ordered to return to Washington in February. Others had voiced their support of the Hopi. In his Annual Report for 1894, the commissioner of Indian affairs acknowledged that the attempt to allot the Hopi lands had failed and he had therefore discontinued the plan, owing to opposition of a small number of the Indians and "the formal objections to the approval of any of the allotments presented to this office by friends of the Indians" (Commissioner of Indian Affairs 1894:20).

As Barbara Bender concludes in the epigraph at the beginning of this essay, "landscape is a concept of high tension." I have arranged the *written* narratives in chronological order but priority is to be given to the ancestral memories of Masau's footprints given expression by Wiki, a keeper of Hopi tradition, for it is this construct and covenant that constitutes what is most important in the Hopi landscape (cf. Hervieu-Leger 2000:86–89 on the power of tradition in society).

The external real world in which the Hopi live *does* exist. What I have contended here is the notion that it is the language and structural design of these (and other) narratives that constitute aspects of this landscape as objects of meaning, understanding, and comprehension, and that it is primarily by attending to the *narrative* construction of landscape that cross-cultural understanding and appreciation is possible.

Notes

1. Masau: A Pueblo deity.
2. The "emergence points," or holes, from which Pueblo people come out into the world.

References Cited

Bender, Barbara

1996 Landscape. In *Encyclopedia of Social and Cultural Anthropology*, ed. Alan Barnard and Jonathan Spencer, 323–24. London: Routledge.

Commissioner of Indian Affairs

1894 *Annual Report of the Commissioner of Indian Affairs*. Washington, DC: Government Printing Office.

Curtis, Edward S.

1922 *The North American Indian*. Vol. 12, *The Hopi*. Cambridge: Privately published.

Dellenbaugh, Frederick S.

1884 Letter to his mother, October 29. Dellenbaugh Papers, Special Collections,

University of Arizona Library, Tucson.
1889 An Artist's Glimpse of Northern Arizona. *St. Nicholas Magazine*, 854–56.

Fitter, Christopher
1998 Landscape: Landscape from the Ancients to the Seventeenth Century. In *Encyclopedia of Aesthetics*, Vol. 3, ed. Michael Kelly, 86–93. New York: Oxford University Press.

Forde, C. Daryll
1931 Hopi Agriculture and Land Ownership. *Journal of the Royal Anthropological Institute* 41:357–405.

Geertz, Clifford
1973 *The Interpretation of Cultures*. New York: Basic Books.

Hack, John T.
1942 *The Changing Physical Environment of the Hopi Indians of Arizona*. Papers of the Peabody Museum of Archaeology and Ethnology, Harvard University, vol. 35, no. 1. Cambridge, MA: The Museum.

Hervieu-Leger, Daniele
2000 *Religion as a Chain of Memory*. New Brunswick, NJ: Rutgers University Press.

Hopi Dictionary Project
1998 *Hopi Dictionary/Hopiikwa Lavaytutuveni: A Hopi-English Dictionary of the Third Mesa Dialect*. Tucson: University of Arizona Press.

Hough, Walter
1915 *The Hopi Indians*. Cedar Rapids, IA: Torch Press.

Hoving, Thomas
2000 *The Art of Dan Namingha*. New York: Harry N. Abrams.

Johnson, Hildegard Binder
1979 The Framed Landscape. *Landscape* 23 (3): 26–32.

Langer, Suzanne
1953 *Feeling and Form*. New York: Scribners.

McIntire, Elliot G.
1968 The Impact of Cultural Change on the Land Use Patterns of the Hopi Indians. PhD diss., University of Oregon, Eugene.

Munslow, Alun
1997 *Deconstructing History*. London: Routledge.

Shuman, Amy
1996 Narrative. In *Encyclopedia of Cultural Anthropology*, Vol. 3, ed. David Levinson and Melvin Ember, 836–40. New York: Henry Holt.

Stephen, Alexander M.
n.d. Copy of Petition, J. W. Fewkes–A. M. Stephen Correspondence. National Anthropological Archives, Washington, DC.

Sullivan, Jeremiah
1886 The Hopi Indians of Arizona. MS.5.291. Southwest Museum, Los Angeles.

Chapter Nine

Conflicting Landscape Values

The Santa Clara Pueblo and Day School

by Rina Swentzell

Landscape and architecture, the built environment as a whole, embodies and conveys the values of the cultures out of which it is produced. Santa Clara Pueblo architectural historian Rina Swentzell contrasts the sterile and authoritarian physical landscape of the Bureau of Indian Affairs–designed and –operated Santa Clara Day School with the open, welcoming, humane environment of the pueblo itself. In this classic essay, Swentzell examines the psychological legacy of these conflicting landscape values. With the day school colonizing the emotional lives of Santa Clara children, the pueblo landscape they returned to each night cleansed, revived, and buttressed the security and self-respect of the Santa Clara matriarchy and its communitarian value structure.

Two very different relationships to the land are represented by the Santa Clara Pueblo, in New Mexico, and the Bureau of Indian Affairs (BIA) day school established next to it. These relationships reflect the divergent worldviews of two cultures as well as their differing educational methods and content.

Pueblo people believe that the primary and most important relationship for humans is with the land, the natural environment, and the cosmos, which in the Pueblo world are synonymous. Humans exist within the cosmos and are an integral part of the functioning of the earth community.

The mystical nature of the land, the earth, is recognized and honored. Direct contact and interaction with the land, the natural environment, is sought. In the pueblo, there are no manipulated outdoor areas that serve to distinguish humans from nature. There are no outdoor areas that attest to human control over nature, no areas where nature is domesticated.

Santa Clara, where I was born, is a typical Tewa pueblo, with myths that connect it to the nearby prehistoric sites and that also inextricably weave the human place into a union with the land whence the people emerged. The people dwell at the center, around the *nansipu*, the "emergence place" or "breathing place." The breath flows through the center as it does through other breathing places in the low hills and far mountains. These symbolic places remind the people of the vital, breathing earth, and their specific locations are where the people can feel the strongest connection to the flow of energy or the creation of the universe. The plants, rocks, land, and people are part of an entity that is sacred because it breathes the creative energy of the universe.

The physical location of Santa Clara Pueblo is of great importance—the Rio Grande snakes along to the east of the pueblo; the mysterious Black Mesa, where the mask whippers emerge, is to the south; the surrounding low hills contain shrines and special ceremonial areas; and the far mountains define the valley where humans live.

This world, for me as a child, was very comfortable and secure, because it gave a sense of containment. We roamed in the fields and nearby hills. At an early age we learned an intimacy with the natural environment and other living creatures. We learned of their connectedness to rocks, plants, and other animals through physical interaction and verbal communication. We gained tremendous confidence and an unquestioning sense of belonging within the natural ordering of the cosmos. Learning happened easily. It was about living. In fact, the word for learning in Tewa is *haa-pu-weh*, which translates as "to have breath." To breathe or to be alive is to learn.

Within the pueblo, outdoor and indoor spaces flowed freely and were hardly distinguishable. One moved on bare feet from interior dirt floors enclosed by mud walls to the well-packed dirt of the pueblo plaza. In this movement, all senses were utilized. Each of the various dirt surfaces (interior walls, outdoor walls, plaza floor) was touched, smelled, and tasted. Special rocks were carried in the mouth so that their energy would flow into us. Everything was touchable, knowable, and accessible.

There was consistency in that world because the colors, textures, and movements of the natural landscape were reflected everywhere in the human-made landscape. Reflection on the cosmos was encouraged. Separation of natural and human-made spaces was minimal, so conscious beautification of either outdoor or indoor spaces was not necessary. Landscaping—replanting, bringing in trees, shrubs, and grass for aesthetic reasons—was thought to be totally unnecessary. The mobility of humans and animals was accepted, but the mobility of plants rooted in their earth places was inconceivable.

The pueblo plaza was almost always full. People cooked outdoors, husked corn, dried food, and sat in the sun. The scale of the pueblo plaza was such that I never felt lost in it even when I was the only person there.

The form and organization of the pueblo house reinforced the sense of security and importance of place. One sat on and played on the center of the world (the nansipu) and thereby derived a sense of significance. Houses were climbed on, jumped on, slept on, and cooked on. They were not material symbols of wealth but were rather, in Thoreau's terminology, a most direct and elegantly simple expression of meeting the human need for shelter.

Construction methods and materials were uncomplicated. The most direct methods were combined with the most accessible materials. Everyone participated, without exception—children, men, women, and elders. Anybody could build a house or any necessary structure. Designers and architects were unnecessary, since there was no conscious aesthetic striving or stylistic interest.

Crucial elements of the house interiors were the low ceilings; rounded and hand-plastered walls; small, dark areas; tiny, sparse windows and doors; and multiple-use rooms. All interior spaces were shared by everybody, as were the exterior spaces. The need for individual privacy was not important enough to affect the plan of pueblo houses. Privacy was viewed in a different way; it was carried around within the individual, and walls and physical space were not needed to defend it. Sharing was crucial.

Within the house, as without, spirits moved freely. Members of families were sometimes buried in the dirt floor, and their spirits became a part of the house environment. Besides those spirits there were others who had special connections with the house structure because they assisted in its construction or because they were born or died in it. Since houses survived many generations, the spirits were many. Houses were blessed with a special ceremony similar to the ritual performed for a baby at birth. There was also an easy acceptance of the deterioration of a house. Houses, like people's bodies, came from and went back into the earth.

Ideas that characterize the Pueblo human-made and natural environments, then, are that humans and nature are inseparable, that human environments emulate and reflect the cosmos, that creative energy flows through the natural environment (of which every aspect, including rocks, trees, clouds, and people, is alive), and that aesthetics and the cosmos are synonymous.

How Western Education Shaped the BIA Day School Landscape

The goal, from the beginning of attempts at formal education of the American Indian, has been not so much to educate him as to change him.
— *Committee on Labor and Public Welfare*

Santa Clara Day School was introduced to such a world in the early 1890s, during the BIA's golden age of constructing schools for Native Americans. In the very early years of European settlement in America various religious groups attempted to "civilize" and Christianize Native Americans. In 1832 that responsibility was assumed by the commissioner of Indian affairs and the focus narrowed to civilizing Native Americans.

From 1890 to 1928, the goal was to assimilate Native Americans; the tactics were dissolving their social structure through Western education and destroying their land base. After 1928, when an influential government study asked for "a change in point of view" in how Native Americans should be educated, programs in bilingual education, adult basic education, training of Native American teachers, Native American culture, and in-service teacher training were initiated across the country. But these programs were halted almost as quickly, and certainly before the ideas reached Santa Clara Day School.

The years after 1944 saw a new determination to terminate Native American reservations and abolish the special relationships between Native Americans and the federal government, relationships that had been guaranteed by centuries of law and treaties (Committee on Labor and Public Welfare 1969:13). It was during this time, from 1945 to 1951, that I attended Santa Clara Pueblo Day School (figure 9.1).

The government school grounds and buildings, built during the 1920s, not only reflected that attitude of changing and civilizing Native Americans but also characterized the general Western European attitude of human control that seems to stem from the Renaissance glorification of human capabilities. Everything had to be changed to make it accord with the Western way of thinking and being. The BIA school compounds reflected a foreign worldview that opposed the Pueblo world and its physical organization.

At Santa Clara, the BIA school complex was located a quarter of a mile from the center of the pueblo and had a barbed-wire fence around its periphery. That fence defined the complex and effectively kept the two worlds separate. The cattle guards and the double-stiled ladders built over the fence provided the only openings into the compound. They kept out both animals and old people. All large rocks and natural trees had been removed a long time

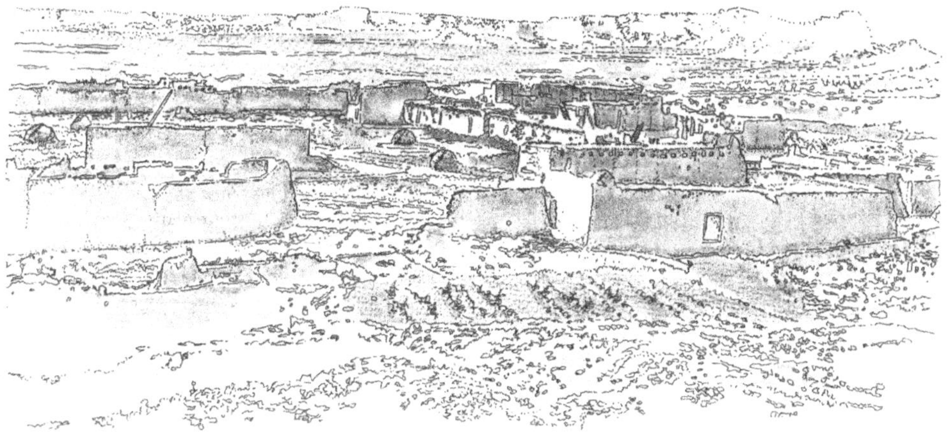

Fig. 9.1 Santa Clara Pueblo. Sketch by Baker H. Morrow, based on a nineteenth-century photograph.

before I was a student, and there were but a few foreign elm trees in the barren, isolated landscape.

The loss of trust that occurred when people moved from the pueblo to the school setting was most striking. Within the pueblo, preschool-aged children were allowed enormous freedom of activity and choice; to a great extent they were trusted as capable of being in charge of themselves. This liberal assumption created its own self-fulfilling prophecy. Since pueblo children were expected to care for themselves in an adequate, responsible way, they generally did.

But within the BIA school, there was a different attitude: the overall atmosphere was one of skepticism. The fence was an expression of the lack of respect and trust in others. Although the formal reason given for the fence was that it kept out animals, everyone in the pueblo knew its purpose was also to keep people out. It was unsettling to know that other people had to protect themselves physically from the community.

As the school grounds were separate from the life and environment around them, so were the various structures located within the compound separate from each other. There were separate laundry and shower buildings—as part of the civilizing effort, everybody, including adults, was supposed to take showers. Also included in the compound were a health clinic, a maintenance shop, the main school building, and small separate houses for the teachers. All of them were scattered seemingly randomly in the approximately five-acre compound.

Within the school building, children were grouped into rooms according to grade level. Inside the various classrooms, the divisions continued. Those who could read well were separated from those who could not. Individual desks and mats were assigned. Individual achievement was praised. Concentration on the individual, or the parts, which has become the hallmark of modern American society, was strongly emphasized. This was in contrast to the holistic concepts of the pueblo, which emphasized togetherness and cooperation and which were expressed in connected and multiple-function structures.

The floor plan of the school was efficient and designed to create an aspiration of moving up—the good old American attitude of upward mobility—from one room and grade level to the next. The move, however, was always disappointing, because there were expectations that something special would happen in the next room, but it never did. The whole system had a way of making people unhappy with the present situation. Again, this was totally foreign to pueblo thinking, which worked toward a settling into the earth and, consequently, into being more satisfied with the moment and the present.

Inside the schoolhouse the ceilings were very high. The proportions of the rooms were discomforting—the walls were very tall relative to the small floor space. The Catholic church in the pueblo also had high ceilings, for Spanish priests sought to maximize both interior and exterior height in the missions they built. But in the church there was no sense of overhead, top-heavy space. It had heavy, soft walls at eye level to balance its height, as well as dark interiors that made the height less obvious.

Although there were plenty of buildings on the school grounds, it seemed that there were never enough people to make the spaces within the grounds feel comfortable. Everything seemed at a distance. The message was, "don't touch, don't interact." The exterior formality of the structures, as well as the materials used, discouraged climbing on them, scratching them, tasting them, or otherwise affecting them. There was no way to be a part of the place, the buildings, or the lives of teachers who lived there.

The creation of artificial play areas on the school grounds within the pueblo context and community was ironic. The total environment (natural as well as human-created) was included in the pueblo world of play. Play and work were barely distinguishable. Every activity was something to be done and done as well as possible; the relaxation or joy that play gives was to be found in submerging oneself in the activity at hand.

Play and work were distinguished from one another in the BIA school, and specific time was assigned for both. There were recesses from work, yet play was constantly supervised, so that the children could not discover the world for themselves. Every possible danger was guarded against. Lack of trust was evident in the playground as opposed to the pueblo setting, where we roamed the fields and hills.

It was apparent that the Anglo teachers preferred indoor and human-made spaces over the outdoors, and they tried to instill this preference in us. In the pueblo, the outdoors was unquestionably preferred.

The saddest aspect of the entire school complex was the ground. There was no centering, no thought, no respect given to the ground. The native plants and rocks had been disturbed a long time ago, and the land had lost all the variety one finds in small places created by bushes, rocks, or rises and falls of the ground. The ground had been scraped and leveled, and metal play equipment was set upon it. It was also a gray color, which was puzzling because the ground in the pueblo plaza, only a quarter of a mile away, was a warm brown.

The sensation of being in the pueblo was very different from that of being on the school grounds. The pueblo plaza had soulfulness. It was endowed with spirit. The emergence place of the people from the underground was located within the plaza, and the breath of the cosmos flowed in and out of it. The land, the ground, breathed there; it was alive. The school grounds were imbued with sadness, because the spirit of the place, the land, was not recognized. Nothing flowed naturally. The vitality of the school came from faraway worlds, from the lands described in books. Appreciation of the immediate landscape was impossible.

The Legacy of Conflicting Landscape Values

The pueblo and the school grounds were imbued with different cultural values, attitudes, and perceptions, and the students who moved from one setting to the other were deeply affected by those differences.

The school was part of a world that was whole unto itself, and its orientation toward the future, time assignments, specialized buildings, artificial playgrounds, and overall concern with segmentation were elements of a conscious worldview that was not concerned with harmony and acceptance of spirituality in the landscape.

The government did not come to Santa Clara Pueblo out of inner kindness or benevolence. Rather, the government was dealing with Native Americans in what it considered to be the most efficient manner. This efficiency, which was so apparent in the structures, took away human interaction and dignity. We had to give ourselves totally to this order.

BIA authoritarianism assured the absence of any human-to-human or human-to-nature interaction. The monumental structures and sterile outdoor spaces in no manner stimulated the community to enter and exchange communications at any time or at any level of equality. In that people-proof environment, the natural curiosity that children have about their world was dulled, and respect for teachers far exceeded respect for the larger forces in the world.

Santa Clara Day School was a typical American school of its era—isolated and authoritatively emphatic. Its visual landscape read accordingly with the surrounding fence, the barren land, and the tall pitched-roof structures scattered within the compound.

But the longest-lasting impact may not be visual. The two physical settings taught different types of behavior to pueblo children. Consequently, lack of confidence and feelings of inadequacy have become characteristic traits of children who lived in the pueblo and went to the BIA school.

This chapter was originally published in 1990 in *Vision, Culture, and Landscape: Working Papers from the Berkeley Symposium on Cultural Landscape Interpretation*, ed. Paul Groth. Berkeley: Department of Landscape Architecture, University of California–Berkeley. It was one of the papers given at the symposium on March 2–3, 1990, at UC–Berkeley.

References Cited

Committee on Labor and Public Welfare
1969 Indian Education: A National Tragedy—A National Challenge. Washington, DC: U.S. Government Printing Office.

Chapter Ten

Mary Jane Colter and the Ancestral Puebloan Tradition

by Kenneth A. Romig

National Park Service architect and interior designer Mary Colter understood nearly one hundred years ago that Ancestral Puebloan and Pueblo design strategies were not merely decorative. She thought they should not be consigned to some museum of national nostalgia and commercialism. An inveterate investigator and explorer of indigenous sites in the Southwest, Colter brought to her National Park buildings and Fred Harvey hotels around the Grand Canyon and elsewhere a deep knowledge of, and respect for, what ancient builders achieved. Author Ken Romig reviews Colter's pioneering recognition of the intelligence and sophistication of indigenous designers and builders. In contrast to many modern designers, if Colter were alive today she would likely not reduce Ancestral Puebloan buildings and landscape forms to the level of quaint sources for an aging regional style.

Even the most nonchalant observer of today's National Park environment can recognize the pastoral, even bucolic, atmosphere created by a park's older, rustic architecture. The setting aside of wilderness areas for purely scenic purposes in the late 1800s led park advocates to urge an "American" style of architecture suitable to these spectacular landscapes. Mary Jane Colter's work as architect and interior designer with the Fred Harvey Company, the concessionaire for Grand Canyon National Park, indicates that no architect has more claim to the title "Architect of the National Parks" than Colter. Colter infused the structures and landscapes of the newly developing National Park system with a distinct vision of indigenous and pioneer history. In essence, Colter's architectural designs contributed to the development of an invented American landscape, an American rustic "theme park" within the National Park system.

Mary Jane Colter was born in 1869 in St. Paul, Minnesota, to a modest Irish household, the daughter of a sewer inspector. She grew to be part of the explosive growth of a nation bent on taming the North American wilderness via the "Iron Horse." The railroad would reach across the continent from St. Paul to Oregon by 1883, the year Mary graduated from high school.

Colter was trained in the American Arts and Crafts tradition, a tradition that sought an alternative to the numbing effects of mechanized labor through hand craftsmanship. The Arts and Crafts tradition came to America from England, where its primary advocate was the social theorist and art critic John Ruskin. Ruskin promoted the rehumanization of industrial arts by casting the craftsman as an ideal individual who unified art and labor, fashioning utilitarian objects with inherent beauty. The English Arts and Crafts movement looked back to the medieval master craftsman as the person who best synthesized spiritual and material reality.

In short, these romantic currents of thought promoted the idea that happiness and well-being decrease as civilization becomes more complex. The extension of such logic would tend to glamorize a return to the wilderness as a panacea to civilization's ill effects. This notion, sometimes called "primitivism," took hold in America through the writings of Henry David Thoreau and others.

Nineteenth-century America was in an identity crisis because, in American eyes, its relatively short history and weak traditions tended to compare poorly with those of Europe. Intellectuals brooded over the articulation of a distinct culture for the United States. In 1850, Thoreau expressed the general sentiment that contact with wilderness kept a culture virile and virtuous. America's salvation might lie in its wilderness and in the slow recognition of such distinct, indigenous cultures as those of the Southwest. American Arts and Crafts advocates like Mary Jane Colter looked to the "primitive" as the figure unifying humankind and nature.

Those American architects and landscape architects who were influenced by the Arts and Crafts movement of the early 1900s rejected the emerging International Style of architecture, which promoted severe geometric shapes and modern materials. Arts and Crafts architecture sought to be true to local context in form and material, to contextualize a building within its landscape by incorporating cultural and historical elements into the design. For example, California architects drawn to Spanish Mission architecture began designing modern homes in the Mission Style (Grattan 1992; Wilson 1997). Replicas of Southwestern cliff dwellings and pueblo village exhibits were constructed at the World's Columbian

Exposition in Chicago in 1893, and again at the Louisiana Purchase Centennial Exposition in St. Louis in 1904. These exhibits fueled the curiosity of wealthy middle class city dwellers about Native American architecture and lifestyles. Before long, curious tourists were traveling by railroad to experience the western American landscape and its indigenous culture. In landscape architecture, Frederick Law Olmsted forged a sturdy, rustic style of park building structures for Central Park, in New York City, in the 1860s.

In the midst of these developments, Mary Jane Colter (1869–1958) gave architectural form to the intellectual excitement of the American Arts and Crafts movement and capitalized on American popular fascination with Southwest landscapes and indigenous cultures. Colter's unique empathy for Native American imagery was likely a result of early exposure to Sioux drawings when she was a child. Her interests in Native arts and crafts never waned as she pursued studies in art and design in San Francisco at the California School of Design and then apprenticed herself to an architect. Early Spanish Mission architecture was an acceptable style in California by the time Colter graduated from college, and she went on to teach technical drawing in Menominee, Wisconsin, and later in St. Paul, Minnesota (Grattan 1992). She took classes in archaeology in St. Paul while teaching. Colter's opportunity to express her version of America's innate architecture and the Arts and Crafts ideal came when the Fred Harvey Company hired her in 1902 to decorate the interior of the Indian Building at the Alvarado Hotel in Albuquerque, New Mexico.

By the early 1900s, the Harvey Company was working hand-in-hand with the railroad to make travel across America more pleasant. The company built restaurants that emphasized good food and good service along the length of the new railroad passenger routes. The construction of the Alvarado Hotel (a prime example of the California Mission Style) initiated the Harvey Company's commercial interest in Native American crafts. Future Harvey Houses would continue to be graced with rugs, pottery, jewelry, and furniture made by Native Americans. Through its establishment of the Indian Building at the Alvarado, the Fred Harvey Company set up the first of its retail shops to display objects that were not for sale. It was the beginning of the museum-shop sales floor. Mary Jane Colter recognized the Indian artisan as the American version of the master craftsman articulated by the Englishman John Ruskin, an artist whose creation of utilitarian objects was unified with a sense of beauty. Indians maintained contact with nature's educational and moral influence, thus giving America indigenous inspiration. A unique commercial promotion was born.

It should not be surprising, then, that when Mary Jane Colter got her first opportunity to be lead architect of a new Fred Harvey building she chose to recreate Native architecture. With its 1905 construction of El Tovar Hotel, built in the Swiss chalet manner at the Grand Canyon, the Harvey Company became a

National Park concessionaire. Mary Colter's task was to construct a neighboring building to house and showcase Native handicrafts. Colter imagined a building that would introduce the lifestyle of the Indian to the tourist through the experience of Native architecture.

Colter designed Hopi House, at the edge of the Grand Canyon, as a literal re-creation of a building at the Hopi village of Oraibi. Hopi House was an authentic reproduction down to the details; it was even constructed by a Hopi construction crew. Architectural features such as stair-step buttresses, projecting roof beams, undulating rock coursings, and chimneys fashioned of old pottery made the building an authentic replica of its predecessor. The interior followed Hopi structures with its low doorframes, thatched ceilings, and hand-plastered walls. Programmed exterior space attempted to emulate the Hopi use of the landscape with its weaving and jewelry-making demonstrations on rooftop terraces (figure 10.1), baking exhibits in *hornos* (outdoor ovens), and dance exhibitions on a raised terrace. As a living museum, Hopi House provided a stage for Native American artisans to demonstrate their craftsmanship, thus joining romantic notions of Native American culture to commercial architecture. It can be argued that some Indian crafts, such as the making of pottery and the weaving of rugs, might have been lost or considerably diminished if it were not for the commercial aspect of such tourist spots.

Hopi House went on to do something more than just house Native American crafts. The structure was in stark contrast to its neighbor, El Tovar Hotel, which resembled European resort architecture. Hopi House with its Ancestral Puebloan precedents posed an American design form against an inherited European standard. Hopi House was architecturally derivative, but it boldly stated an indigenous building tradition to a receptive and identity-hungry American public. Colter would take even stronger steps in this direction as her work at the canyon continued.

Her next opportunity to design at the rim of the Grand Canyon involved creating two buildings to act as destinations for sightseeing tours at points along the South Rim Trail. Colter lobbied her bosses and received permission to further elaborate on the theme of indigenous-feeling structures (Grattan 1992). She began with an invented history, the story of a miner's encampment, to develop the theme of Hermit's Rest. Hermit's Rest was constructed to look as though it were haphazardly built by untrained hands into the canyon's edge, with columns of jutting rock and hand-hewn beams holding up the porch. The structure disguises itself in the landscape and fittingly gives the impression of a local builder making rough-and-ready lodging in the wild.

Lookout Studio, a third structure designed by Colter, followed the same theme—an emulation of pioneer building through the use of naturally occurring, mostly uncut stone to shape an indigenous, "primitive" structure that melted

Fig. 10.1 Hopi artisans on the rooftop terrace of Hopi House. Fred Harvey handicraft demonstrators. Grand Canyon National Park Museum Collection #9847. Photo by Detriot Photographic, ca. 1905.

back into the canyon walls. Grasses and cactus were encouraged to grow on the roof for this purposeful rusticity (figure 10.2).

In 1900 there was actually very little in the way of real pioneering structures that could stand as examples of frontier history on the rim of the Grand Canyon. Invented histories imposed upon the landscape were Colter's specialty, and they made a person think that the architectural past could have looked and felt like these pioneer structures. The grand openings of these buildings drew crowds, generated considerable press attention, and initiated a thematic historicism, an imagined Native architecture that seemed to fit many National Park landscapes.

While Mary Colter continued to work as an interior designer and architect for the Fred Harvey Company, she traveled extensively with archaeologist Herman Schweizer to many Pueblo ruins to study prehistoric architecture. Although these travels were undertaken for commercial reasons, Colter's participation was motivated by genuine curiosity and her interest in Ancestral Puebloan history. Colter was an avid explorer, at times chartering an airplane to locate Ancestral Puebloan ruins. She often marked their locations on maps and later returned to find them on horseback or in cars via rough road trips (Grattan 1992). These extraordinary outings are not recorded by her in private notes or drawings but in Harvey Company albums, which clearly lay out Pueblo construction methods

Fig. 10.2 Lookout Studio view north. Front entrance and stairway down to observation areas. Grand Canyon National Park Museum Collection #9722b. Santa Fe Railroad Photo, ca. 1915.

and the extraordinary siting of Ancestral Puebloan structures. The albums note in detail the placement of towers and structures at the edges of cliffs and mesas. Hovenweep, nicknamed the "playground of towers," is considered the best example of Four Corners–area tower forms. Colter's trips to Ancestral Puebloan ruins at Hovenweep, Chaco Canyon, Mesa Verde, and Aztec inspired her next work at the Grand Canyon in 1932 (figure 10.3).

Desert View Watchtower

In Desert View Watchtower, Mary Colter intended to re-create a prehistoric structure that belonged to the region of the Grand Canyon. She even went so far as to state that the chosen rocky point and the rim of the canyon might have been the site of a similar prehistoric structure (Colter 1933). The form of the building followed the lines and shape of the round tower of Cliff Palace at Mesa Verde (figure 10.4). The masonry incorporated within its stone coursing examples from the ruins of Mesa Verde, Aztec, Hovenweep, and Chaco Canyon. The kiva took its form and ceiling construction from the log cribbing of the Great Kiva at Aztec (Colter 1933). This was a collection of everything that Colter thought best in Ancestral Puebloan design. She wanted to use it in a watchtower/curio shop situated on the south rim of the Grand Canyon.

However, changes to certain elements of the prehistoric towers were necessary to convey the right amount of drama. For instance, variations on the tower's

Fig. 10.3 Mary Jane Colter looking out a door of Twin Towers Ruin, Hovenweep National Monument. Grand Canyon National Park Museum Collection #13315. Santa Fe Railroad Photo, ca. 1931.

surface were broken up to add shadows and vigor to the walls (Colter 1933). The height of the tower deviated from normal as well. At seventy feet, the size of Desert View Watchtower was unparalleled in Southwestern ruins; but the proportion, according to Mary Colter, was not alien to Ancestral Puebloan design (Colter 1933). The height, Colter explained, accommodated a view to the southern San Francisco Peaks, the residence of Hopi kachinas for part of the year. The 360-degree views from the watchtower seem to support the depth of Mary Jane Colter's perception of the sacred landscape of the Hopi. Although Colter never wrote about her understanding of such matters, she admired Frank Waters's novel *The Man Who Killed the Deer*, which portrayed the Pueblo landscape as filled with ancestral spirits and mythic powers (Waters 1942).

Masonry styles and decorative rockwork from ruins in the Four Corners area as well as rocks resembling Zuni animal fetishes were displayed on the exterior of the Desert View Watchtower (figure 10.5). Hopi and Navajo painting, petroglyph imagery, and examples of Native crafts graced the interior. Colter attempted, within the constraints of Harvey Company marketing, to design a human container for the symbolic landscape of the Hopi (Thompson et al. 1997) that would also incorporate the European tradition of the folly. (Follies were part of the landscape of European estates—peculiar, ruinous structures that accented views and made gardens look "picturesque.")

Fig. 10.4 The Round Tower in Cliff Palace, Mesa Verde National Park. Pictured is Mr. Herman Schweitzer, director of the Fred Harvey Indian Department. He accompanied Mary Jane Colter on her exploratory trips to Southwestern sites. Grand Canyon National Park Museum Collection #16968. Santa Fe Railroad Photo, ca. 1931.

The successful integration of the watchtower into the landscape is partially based on Colter's control of views and vistas. Focused, framed, and open views and vistas are given different contexts by virtue of surrounding materials and particular methods of approach. The deeply recessed windows found in the tower are employed to narrow and focus views through rough rock casements. The kiva itself is a viewing room looking into the canyon, a sheltered refuge with open, expansive views. On the roof of the kiva Colter placed reflectoscopes, devices created by the French pastoral landscape painter Claude Lorraine in which a darkened mirror focuses and narrows a portion of the landscape, increasing contrast and heightening colors.

Framed and controlled views of the landscape were employed to contrast the overpowering panorama of the canyon with the concentrated glimpse of just a segment of it. The intent was to inspire wonder. Colter sought, and in some measure achieved, a feeling of empathy with the landscape. The structure does not "create a discordant note against the time eroded walls of the promontory" (Colter 1933). The watchtower opened its doors to the public in 1933 with a Hopi ceremony that included dancing and cornmeal blessings.

Just west of the watchtower lies a constructed ruin that serves to create the sort of atmosphere one would encounter in a real Ancestral Puebloan building

Fig. 10.5 Desert View Watchtower, 2001. Photo by Ken Romig.

(Grattan 1992). The conspicuously located "ruin" (or folly) is common in landscapes designed in the English Landscape Garden tradition of the eighteenth century, an allusion to the sort of antiquity found in the rustic hills and valleys of Italy. Colter's folly at the Grand Canyon alludes to the demise of an old indigenous culture—the Ancestral Puebloans. Her sensitive and respectful historicism here becomes the key to her successful design and, remarkably, to an evolving design ethic for the National Parks.

The Harvey Company's concessionaire architecture was so successful that the company saw itself as the progenitor of an "American" style of building. Fred Harvey laid out some cardinal rules for great architecture in albums recording employees' visits to Ancestral Puebloan ruins. They were:

- Architecture is to adapt to existing conditions.

- Use native materials.
- The building should be suited to the purposes it is intended to serve. (Harvey Album, date unknown)

Of course, Mary Jane Colter was an ardent advocate and practitioner of these principles. But she would add another tenet of good architectural design:

- Use historic structural forms and site design.

Colter looked for contextually sound building forms consistent with the image of the landscape and building precedents set by her treasured Ancestral Puebloan ruins.

Although Mary Colter is almost wholly known for rustic architecture, she also designed an extraordinary hotel—El Navajo—in Gallup, New Mexico. The year was 1916. Colter was well aware of modernist regional impulses in the Southwest, but her work for Fred Harvey allowed few instances to explore modern forms. El Navajo, finally built in 1921, exhibited Colter's talent for abstracting Spanish Pueblo forms. El Navajo had strong horizontal and vertical groupings of windows and geometric massings of architectural elements. Sadly, it was destroyed in 1923. El Navajo is credited with influencing such noted architectural works as the Franciscan Hotel and the KiMo Theatre in Albuquerque (Berke 2002).

Early National Park architects and landscape engineers, later called landscape architects, perpetuated the principles followed by Fred Harvey's concessionaire architects, often consulting Mary Colter to further explore design issues. For example, Ed Maier, architect and acting region three director of the National Park Service, followed the example of Colter's architecture at the rim of the Grand Canyon in his design for Yavapai Point. He laid out the Yosemite Museum in the same rustic vein (McClelland 1998). Daniel Hull, landscape engineer for the National Park Service after 1920, spent two years collaborating with Mary Colter at the Grand Canyon. Hull experimented with Native building materials and construction methods to adapt to local natural conditions (McClelland 1998). Colter maintained a running correspondence about Ancestral Puebloan architecture with pioneer archaeologist Jesse Nusbaum, the first director of Mesa Verde National Park. Nusbaum later designed Mesa Verde Village in the park, drawing from Ancestral Puebloan architectural and cultural allusions (McClelland 1998).

Ed Maier focused National Park design into a framework practiced by archaeologists such as Cecil Doty and Albert Good and by the landscape architects Thomas Vint and Harvey Cornell. National Park Service architect and writer Albert Good wrote Ed Maier's thoughts down in a three-volume work, *Park and Recreation Structures*, which influenced park design until World War II. Park Service publications stated that "the habits and primitive ingenuity of the

American Indian persist and find varied expression in park construction" (McClelland 1998). The architecture and site design of National Park Service structures continued to romanticize the landscape in the middle years of the twentieth century, reforming Native American and pioneer history into a type of idyllic pastoralism.

Concessionaire architects fell short in two arenas of site design that only the public servant could rectify: the establishment of a consistent architectural style for each park and the construction of community space. Horace Albright, Park Service director in the 1930s, formalized the process by directing landscape engineer Thomas Vint to establish the Park Service's master planning process and the attendant design criteria that still characterize National Park site design today (McClelland 1998).

It took the New Deal construction efforts of the 1930s to push this National Park design theme to its next level—the level of national nostalgia. New Deal construction projects not only fed a weak economy but also were politically promoted as healing agents for a national spirit disheartened by the Depression. Furthermore, scenic places for public recreation were expected to do much the same thing. The National Parks provided broad experiences with raw landscapes. In rustic recreational structures, subordinate to natural and cultural influences, the Park Service thought that the tourist would encounter an awe-inspiring landscape and be refreshed; the national spirit would thus be rekindled. Opening ceremonies for recreation areas were often announced in such terms as, "Along the slopes of La Cueva Canyon, which originates among the precipitous cliffs high in the Sandias, have been arranged and constructed every facility and convenience for picnicking in the shade of oak and cedar with plenty of cool running water. From these lofty battlements of nature an excellent panorama greets the eyes of those fortunate to view the scene" (Lilleland and Chatterson 1936–37).

Today, visitation to National Parks continues to climb and new efforts are continually employed to improve facilities for visitors, while protecting the landscape. The environmental movements of the 1960s, which continue in vigorous form, have expanded the mission of the Park Service from protection and preservation of individual landscapes to the protection of ecosystems. The National Park Service recognized decades ago that historic preservation must include historic settings—landscape—to convey historic context adequately to visitors. It is in this sense that architecture that suits its place has never left the Park Service's "manual" for good architecture.

These official Park Service concerns and the regional experimentation of Mary Jane Colter have led to unexpected results.

Rural National Park landscapes only lightly touched by Indian designers and pioneering hermits in the distant past make up a theme to be found in Colter's architecture at the Grand Canyon and in contemporary National Park Service architecture. The images represent the successful promotion of a compelling idea that creates tourism. Mary Jane Colter articulated this notion better than anyone in the last century as a designer of Southwestern structures with explicit allusions to prehistoric architecture. Such unapologetic, thematic architecture is a hallmark of the modern resort complexes to be found in such places as Las Vegas, Nevada, or the city of Santa Fe, New Mexico. Colter and then the National Park Service quite consciously created the primary elements of the American theme park with their strong romantic historicism, complete with appealing and defining architectural images and their associated emotive power.

References Cited

Berke, Arnold
2002 *Mary Colter, Architect of the Southwest*. New York: Princeton Architectural Press.

Carr, Ethan
2000 Landscape Architecture in the National Parks. *Landscape Architecture* (October): 56–63.

Colter, Mary Jane Elizabeth
1933 *Manual for Drivers and Guides of the Indian Watchtower at Desert View and Its Relation, Architecturally, to the Prehistoric Ruins of the Southwest*. Grand Canyon National Park, AZ: Fred Harvey.

Grattan, Virginia L.
1992 *Mary Colter, Builder on the Red Earth*. Flagstaff, AZ: Northland Press.

Lilleland and Chatterson
1936–37 Recreation Site Promotion, Cibola National Forest Historic Recreation Files.

McClelland, Linda Flint
1998 *Building the National Parks*. Baltimore, MD: Johns Hopkins University Press.

Nash, Roderick
1967 *Wilderness and the American Mind*. New Haven, CT: Yale University Press.

Thompson, Ian, Mark Varien, Susan Kenzle, and Rina Swentzell
1997 Prehistoric Architecture with Unknown Function. In *Anasazi Architecture and American Design*, ed. Baker H. Morrow and V. B. Price, 149–58. Albuquerque: University of New Mexico Press.

Waters, Frank
1942 *The Man Who Killed the Deer*. Chicago: Swallow Press.

Wilson, Chris
1997 *The Myth of Santa Fe*. Albuquerque: University of New Mexico Press.

Chapter Eleven

AMREP and the Pueblos

River's Edge and La Luz

by Anthony Anella

Architect Anthony Anella, AIA, compares two development patterns on Albuquerque, New Mexico's booming West Mesa. One embodies the short-term, high profit, "anyplace" standard subdivision model of development that is as oblivious to local culture as it is to the existing natural patterns of the land. The other is a rare example of a contemporary designer—architect Antoine Predock, FAIA—blending both Modernist and indigenous landscape strategies to create a cluster development that exhibits a classic sensitivity to place that Ancestral Puebloan builders would have appreciated. Anella grounds his narrative in a site-mapping strategy called "conservation land planning," in which a piece of rural land to be developed is examined minutely to determine the ecologically ideal location for construction. In his own practice, Anella observes that sites determined to be ideal for modern development tend to have already Mimbres or Ancestral Puebloan ruins associated with them.

Examine each question in terms of what is ethically and
esthetically right, as well as what is economically expedient.
A thing is right when it tends to preserve the integrity,
stability, and beauty of the biotic community.
It is wrong when it tends otherwise.
— *Aldo Leopold*

Two different models for contemporary land development in the Ancestral Puebloan landscape lie along the Rio Grande in the greater Albuquerque Metropolitan Area. One is the conventional single-family detached housing development of "River's Edge I," developed by AMREP Southwest Inc., a subsidiary of the New York–based AMREP Corporation, between 1987 and 1993. The other is the clustered housing development of "La Luz," developed by Ray Graham and designed by Antoine Predock between 1969 and 1974. The context for each is the same. Both developments share an identical relationship to the river and the adjacent cottonwood bosque that grows along it. Both are situated on the west side of the Rio Grande above the river's floodplain in a semiarid grassland characterized by alkali sacaton, sand dropseed, and Indian ricegrass with scattered four-wing saltbush. And both have spectacular views of the Sandia Mountains to the east. Each development is distinguished by a different business plan, reflecting fundamentally different attitudes regarding human relationships to the land and the creation of long-term versus short-term economic value.

River's Edge I is an expression of a conceptual framework that views land as a commodity and ownership as an individual privilege to be exploited (figure 11.1). This relationship is rooted in the historical circumstances that made the 1862 Homestead Act possible when land was abundant, non-Native settlers were scarce, and land ownership was the incentive for settling a continent. Even though these circumstances have changed, the criteria for land development that grew from this relationship still prevail. River's Edge I is an artifact of the contemporary culture that occupies the ancient Pueblo landscape; it is premised on a relationship of perceived abundance between people and the land that is strictly market oriented.

La Luz, on the other hand, expresses a different conceptual framework (figure 11.2). It follows in the Ancestral Puebloan tradition that clusters housing in order to preserve the remaining land for open space. It is a conservation-based development that maintains local character and conserves resources. It shifts the conventional paradigm of extracting immediate value from the land as an individual privilege to a new paradigm of creating long-term value by protecting the land for future generations through ecologically based design and planning.

A comparison of the property value appreciation at La Luz (built in 1969) with the property value appreciation at River's Edge I suggests that La Luz is a more financially rewarding long-term investment. The average price of a 1,740-square-foot La Luz townhouse appreciated by 17.71 percent per year from $77.90 per square foot in 1993 to $96.74 per square foot in 2000.[1] The average price of a 1,425-square-foot River's Edge I detached house appreciated by 16.88 percent per year from $55.89 per square foot in 1993 to $75.53 per square foot in 2001.[2] It is important to note that the average age of the River's Edge I house sold in 2001 was only twelve years

Fig. **11.1** River's Edge. Illustration courtesy Morrow Reardon Wilkinson Miller Landscape Architects.

whereas the average age of a La Luz townhouse sold in 2000 was twenty-four years.[3] The fact that, since they were first constructed in 1969, the average annual appreciation for La Luz townhouses has been 13.89 percent makes a powerful statement about the long-term value of La Luz as an investment.[4] It remains to be seen whether or not the River's Edge I development will continue to appreciate at the same rate as the houses grow older and the construction deteriorates. Nevertheless, the land development pattern represented by River's Edge I is by far the dominant one. This paper will explore why the River's Edge I model works, and why the land development pattern exemplified by La Luz has not been emulated in the marketplace. It will question the conventional wisdom regarding the inevitability of the River's Edge I pattern of development. And it will conclude with a discussion of an alternative pattern for land development based on a design process known as "sieve mapping," which identifies the conservation value of the land and demonstrates how to capitalize on this value.

The River's Edge I development responds to the need for affordable housing in Albuquerque. This is why River's Edge I is so successful. For a young family just getting a start it provides the opportunity to build equity as an attractive alternative to paying rent. In part, AMREP achieves affordability through the economies of scale and mass production. A limited number of house models are offered for sale to the prospective buyer. Further, the land is bulldozed to create identical house pads for each of these models, thereby avoiding the added expense of customizing the house to fit a specific site. There is no question that this pattern of development has enabled thousands of New Mexicans to realize

Fig. 11.2 Aerial photo of La Luz. Courtesy Ovenwest Corporation.

the enduring dream of home ownership. However, what makes River's Edge I affordable is a false economy. Cheap land at the fringe of the metropolitan area and development and construction practices designed to last no longer than a thirty-year mortgage may be the real reasons River's Edge I is affordable.

American homebuilders have operated on the assumption that abundant supplies of inexpensive energy make it easier to pump vast amounts of cold air into houses in the summer and hot air into houses in the winter than to pay for site-sensitive buildings designed by architects in direct response to the climatic conditions found in a particular location. The advantage of site-specific and environmentally sensitive house design has been rarely considered in the modern history of homebuilding in this country. The exigencies of mass production result in "anywhere" design and construction. This is why the house designs of River's Edge I are similar to those in any other part of the country. They show no more awareness of the climatic, geographic, or cultural conditions particular to their site than do new houses in Phoenix or Amarillo. Albuquerque ends up looking like Los Angeles. To put it another way, the American marketplace favors the short-term advantage of a low down payment on a smaller mortgage over the long-term advantage of energy efficiency resulting from environmentally responsible design and construction. The prevailing attitude in the marketplace is to postpone until the future what you don't have to pay for today. As modern Americans we have grown fat from our indulgences at the expense of creating the legacy of a healthy environment for our children.

AMREP's purchase in the early 1960s of about ninety thousand acres of West Side land at or near rock-bottom prices is one of the reasons for the low prices. Another is that AMREP has not provided basic improvements such as sidewalks, residential street lighting, or underground storm drainage—not to mention amenities, such as parks, recreation facilities, or libraries, which contribute to making a community. Over the years the AMREP Corporation and its subsidiaries have been accused of negligence on everything from improper sewage disposal and inadequate house foundations to using inferior indoor plumbing pipe (Michael Hartranft, *Albuquerque Journal*, 22 February 1991). In 1978, AMREP settled a class-action lawsuit brought by area landowners that accused AMREP of deceptive land sale practices by donating 161 acres of land and $350,000 in cash to the City of Rio Rancho as part of the settlement (Staff Report, *Albuquerque Journal*, 22 April 1993). In 1991 a lawsuit brought by the New Mexico Attorney General's Office alleged that AMREP built many homes with lumber that was not pressure-treated for use belowground; this lawsuit was also settled against AMREP (Gayle Geis, *Albuquerque Journal*, 27 June 1992).

Deficient flood control is another one of the false economies that makes AMREP's development of Rio Rancho affordable. Rio Rancho relies almost entirely on using streets to carry storm water (Christopher Miller, *Albuquerque Journal*, 25 June 1989). This has a drastic effect on the dry landscape because the street-level drainage often causes erosion when a street ends abruptly and turns into a dusty mesa or an unlined arroyo (Miller, *Albuquerque Journal*, 25 June 1989). For example, it normally takes between one-half and one inch of rain to create runoff in the desert but after the development of streets, houses, and parking lots, runoff occurs with only one-tenth of an inch of rain. As a result of development, instances of runoff in arroyos jump from an average of once every three years to twenty-three or more times in a year (Miller, *Albuquerque Journal*, 25 June 1989).

Rio Rancho did not establish comprehensive drainage and flood control laws until 1988. Enforcing the laws has been difficult. Part of the problem is that from 1963, when Rio Rancho's first homes were built, until the incorporation of Rio Rancho as a city in 1981, Rio Rancho's destiny was controlled by AMREP. AMREP built the community's homes and roads, and owned and operated the water and sewer system, which, in effect, controlled how and where the city grew (Hartranft, *Albuquerque Journal*, 22 February 1991). In short, AMREP functioned autonomously as a quasi-government. Even after incorporation, the relationship between Rio Rancho and AMREP has been like that between David and Goliath. This is because Rio Rancho is dependent on the large amount of revenues it receives in sales taxes on new AMREP homes. In 1988–89, according to Hal Donovan, the city finance director at the time, just more than $1 million or 16.5 percent of the city's total $6.3 million in revenue came from new home sales with AMREP building 88 percent of the city's new single family homes during that time (Miller, *Albuquerque Journal*, 25 June 1989). "That makes the City of Rio Rancho very vulnerable and tied to AMREP's operations," according to Chuck Easterling, a West Side engineer and mastermind of Albuquerque's drainage laws who has served as a private engineer under contract with Rio Rancho. "It's not a healthy situation" (Miller, *Albuquerque Journal*, 25 June 1989).

Easterling said he refused AMREP's request to approve the first phase of the Vista Hills subdivision after finding that AMREP hadn't built a storm drain at a key intersection as directed. But, he said, then-mayor Richard Wiles approved the subdivision anyway. AMREP said it was simply a difference of opinion between Easterling and the AMREP engineer. Richard Wiles said he couldn't remember the incident (Miller, *Albuquerque Journal*, 25 June 1989). In 1988 the Vista Hills subdivision was scourged by a flood that filled the streets with thousands of tons of sediment and caused an estimated $500,000 in property damage (Greta Guest, *Albuquerque Journal*, 1 August 1988).

When Rio Rancho incorporated in 1981, some residents suspected that the power behind incorporation was AMREP (Hartranft, *Albuquerque Journal*, 22 February 1991). It seemed dubious for AMREP to willingly give up the power it had as an autonomous quasi-government. But in 1990 a second flood swept through the Vista Hills subdivision. Many residents blamed AMREP. Richard Williams, the public affairs director for AMREP at the time, maintained that AMREP was not to blame for any possible drainage problems in the Vista Hills subdivision since its drainage plans were approved by the proper officials. "A lot of this is the City's responsibility, too," Williams said, "because this is an incorporated town now" (Miller, *Albuquerque Journal*, 17 July 1990).

An inadequate water supply is another example of the false economies that make AMREP's development of Rio Rancho affordable. On July 13, 1989, the Rio Rancho City Council, by a five to one vote, approved a sixty-day moratorium on issuing new building permits (Miller, *Albuquerque Journal*, 13 July 1989). They did so because of periodic water outages and low water pressure in some areas of Rio Rancho. The Albuquerque Utilities Corporation was blamed for not pumping enough water to keep up with the residents' needs. The utility was owned by AMREP at the time. (It has since been sold by AMREP to the General Waterworks Corporation.) The next night, on July 14, 1989, the Rio Rancho City Council reversed itself and lifted the ban on building saying the measure penalized the city and its residents without helping to resolve Rio Rancho's water supply problems (Miller, *Albuquerque Journal*, 14 July 1989). According to Martin Block, a member of the State Public Service Commission at the time who attended the council meeting, the residents of Rio Rancho were paying $1.16 per one thousand gallons of water, compared with a state average of about $2.50 per one thousand gallons of water. He told the council that the Albuquerque Utilities Corporation could install more storage tanks, wells, and pumps to meet the demands for water, but that residents must be willing to pay for the extra equipment (Miller, *Albuquerque Journal*, 13 July 1989).

It seems obvious that AMREP ignores the long-term costs of building a community without adequate infrastructure. It also ignores the long-term costs due to commuting and energy consumption that can burden a family's annual budget. And it ignores the consequences to a family that finally pays off the thirty-year mortgage only to find that their equity in home ownership may have evaporated due to poor construction and the depreciation of their property's value in a declining—because poorly planned—neighborhood. AMREP responds to short-term social and economic needs at the expense of creating real long-term value that would benefit not only the family's equity in home ownership but also the community of Rio Rancho as a desirable place to live. This "false" economy has to do with living in an age of instant gratification where success is defined by the realization of short-term goals. Unfortunately, the short-term interests of a large publicly held corporation like AMREP with the responsibility of making quarterly financial reports to its shareholders may not coincide with the long-term interests of a community. In our culture the self-interest of the individual has often supplanted the interests of the community as a whole. And yet sustained and sustainable prosperity is in everyone's interest.

Before the era of abundant and inexpensive energy supplies, there were practices of architecture and planning—evolved out of necessity—that reflected an acute awareness of the climatic and topographic conditions particular to a site or region. Just such an awareness resulted in the building traditions of Ancestral Puebloans in the desert Southwest. The settlement of Mesa Verde, for example, is based on a remarkable human collaboration with topography and climate. The cliff dwellings are built in canyons that dissect a relatively flat tableland or mesa that tilts to the south. Over a fifteen-mile stretch the elevation varies from 8,500 feet at the northern escarpment to about 6,500 feet at the southern end. This gentle tilt of the land toward the sun results in greater solar radiation and accounts for a slightly longer frost-free season for growing corn than that of the surrounding Montezuma Valley (Erdman, Douglas, and Marr 1969:47–58). The longer growing season, in addition to the increased precipitation due to the higher elevation, may explain why Mesa Verde was occupied in the first place. It would take an acute awareness of the environment to recognize this advantage. But in the unforgiving environment of the desert, such an awareness would have been critical for survival. There is an equally elegant relationship between the human settlement of Mesa Verde and its geology. Cliff Palace, for example, is located in an alcove created at an interface between a stratum of sandstone and a stratum of shale that outcrops on the steep canyon slopes (15–16) (figure 11.3). As water seeps down through the sandstone it meets the impervious shale, which forces it to migrate laterally to the canyon walls. There, a process of freezing and thawing undercuts

Fig. 11.3 Cliff Palace at Mesa Verde. Photo by Anthony Anella.

the sandstone cliff where it is in contact with the impervious shale. This weathering process produces not only the alcove that shelters Cliff Palace but also the very stones Ancestral Puebloans used to build it! At Mesa Verde, the architecture is given meaning by an order established by geology and by a synergy that occurs when human design interacts intelligently with nature.

At Chaco Canyon the architecture is given meaning by an order established by astronomy and by a sophisticated awareness of the solar and lunar cycles. The major buildings at Chaco Canyon are part of a complex and intricate building project based on this awareness of astronomy (Sofaer 1997:88). Pueblo Bonito, for example, commemorates the solar cycle in the cardinal orientation of its walls (figure 11.4). According to Anna Sofaer in her essay "The Primary Architecture of the Chacoan Culture," "Each day at meridian passage of the sun, the mid-wall [of Pueblo Bonito] which approximately divides the massive structure casts no shadow. Similarly the middle of the sun's yearly passage is marked at Pueblo Bonito as the equinox sun is seen rising and setting closely in line with the western half

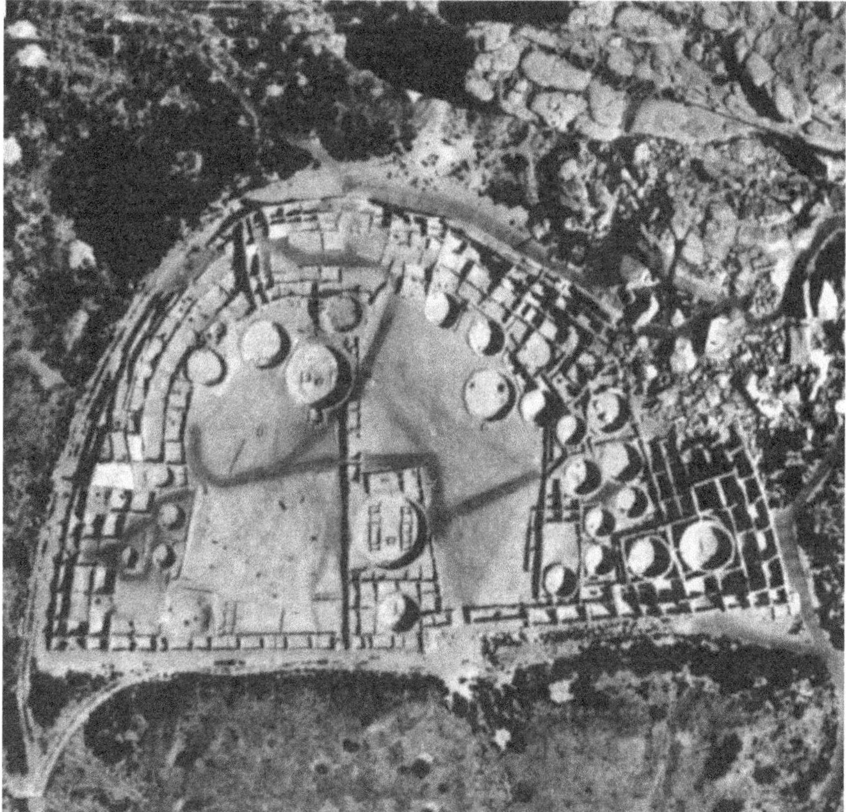

Fig. 11.4 Pueblo Bonito at Chaco Canyon. Photo courtesy National Park Service.

of its south wall. Thus the middle of the sun's daily and yearly journeys are visibly in alignment with the major features of this building which is at the middle of the Chacoan world" (116). Sofaer and others make a compelling case for how the synchronization and integration of the solar and lunar cycles determine the design of the major buildings at Chaco Canyon in terms of their orientation, their internal geometries, and their alignment with each other. It would take an acute awareness of the movement of the sun and moon to recognize these cycles and a profound sensibility to integrate these cycles into the design of Chacoan architecture. Such an awareness and sensitivity was no doubt critical in an environment where survival was a delicate human dance with the elements of sun, wind, and water.

What the Mesa Verde and Chaco Canyon examples teach us is enlightened self-interest predicated on a simple assumption: that man is a part of nature, not separate from it. Out of the necessity of surviving in an arid and unforgiving land, they offer an example of tough-minded pragmatism and grace: the kind of pragmatism that recognizes the ethical and practical expedience of preserving the integrity and stability of the land for future generations; the kind of grace that occurs when human design collaborates with the wonder and the beauty of nature. Places such as Mesa Verde and Chaco Canyon serve as pedagogical models. We may never return to those now forgotten traditional ways of building, but neither can we afford the luxury that has allowed us to be as wasteful of our resources or as oblivious to our environment as we have been in the recent past.

La Luz, designed by architect Antoine Predock with the creative and visionary sponsorship of developer Ray Graham, offers an example of a contemporary housing development looking back at older traditions and reinterpreting them in innovative ways. La Luz asserts not just modern but far-sighted principles of open space and community planning in direct response to the climate and the site. La Luz clusters its housing in order to preserve open space while achieving the housing densities necessary to make it economically feasible. And it did so back in the days when land was still relatively inexpensive in the Albuquerque Metropolitan Area and before "sprawl" had become a buzzword of the "New Urbanists." La Luz was built with a pre-central-air-conditioning sensibility regarding the climate. As an artifact of our culture it is an anomaly: it embodies values that are related to the Ancestral Puebloan building tradition in its reverence for the landscape and nature.

Perhaps one reason La Luz has never been emulated in the marketplace is precisely because it is a cultural anomaly. In spite of the fact that it has been fully occupied since its construction and in spite of the fact that it has appreciated in value over a long period of time at an average annual rate of nearly 14 percent, realtors report that prospective buyers still hesitate at buying a townhouse that shares common walls with its neighbors. Never mind that it is almost impossible to find a single unit that has its privacy or its views compromised by any of the neighboring houses. And never mind that by gracefully stepping the houses up the natural topography so that each house has an unobstructed view of the Sandia Mountains to the east, La Luz conveys a sense of open space lacking in most suburban developments, and at River's Edge I in particular. We Americans like our ranchettes. According to Gary L. Wells, the qualifying broker at the Rio Rancho office of Coldwell Banker Legacy, "Price sensitivity has kept really well-built developments like La Luz from happening. Also, in general, more people prefer detached housing to attached housing."[5]

Another reason La Luz has not been emulated may have to do with the conventions of development. Developers understandably favor quick returns on their investments in order to shorten their exposure to interest payments required by debt financing of the construction loan. La Luz was developed by someone with deep pockets who had the staying power to be patient long enough for the market to first recognize and then accept the innovation. Further, developers are not rewarded by the appreciation of long-term value. They are only rewarded by the profit margin at the time of the initial sale. The appreciation of long-term value rewards the buyer: the homeowner who will invest the lion's share of his or her net worth in paying off the mortgage. It also rewards the community.

In 1891 the landscape architect Frederick Law Olmsted Jr. observed that "a local park adds more to the value of the remaining land in the residential area which it serves than the value of the land withdrawn to create it" (as cited in Fausold and Lilieholm 1996:8). This enhancement value of open space influenced the thinking of developer Ray Graham and architect Antoine Predock who preserved two hundred acres of land to the east of La Luz as perpetual open space. Mr. Olmsted's observation is substantiated by several empirical studies measuring the enhancement value of open space that are cited in a Lincoln Institute of Land Policy Research Paper by Charles J. Fausold and Robert J. Lilieholm. For example, a 1967 study of a ten-acre neighborhood park in Lubbock, Texas, found that "within a two-and-one-half block area around the park, land values declined with distance from the park" (8). This relationship was true for the sales price of land only—not houses and land—a fact with revealing implications for land developers. In Boulder, Colorado, a 1978 study found that "the existence of greenbelts had a significant impact on adjacent residential property values." The relationship proved to be linear: a $4.20 decrease in the price of residential property for each foot away from the greenbelt. The aggregate property value in one of the neighborhoods studied was approximately $5.4 million greater than it would have been without the greenbelt. This resulted in an additional annual neighborhood property tax revenue of $500,000 (9).

These empirical studies quantify the fiscal and economic implications of open space preservation. They demonstrate that, as Mr. Olmsted observed, open space does affect the surrounding land market in positive ways—both for the individual property owners as well as for the local governments that depend on property tax for operating revenue. Unfortunately, the reverse is also true. Poor planning can cancel the enhancement value of open space. Witness River's Edge where the design of open space was an afterthought. Not until the fall of 1992 did the city of Rio Rancho enlist Dekker/Perich and Associates P.A. and their subconsultants Campbell Okuma Perkins Associates Inc. to prepare a development plan for the River's Edge Open Space. At that time River's Edge I and III contained no parkland, and River's Edge II had a small neighborhood park under construction. The result of this poor planning is that the River's Edge Open Space was forced to occupy the leftover space between the river and the preexisting residential development—a missed opportunity. In contrast, when thoughtfully designed to be integrated into a neighborhood, open space preservation contributes not only to the intangible value of making more enjoyable places to live, but also to the economic bottom line. The economic implications of open space preservation and other quality of life issues prompt a reassessment of the conventional wisdom about the consequences of development and conservation.

Two facts lead us to a critical question. First, developers are not rewarded by the appreciation of long-term value; they are only rewarded by the profit margin at the time of the initial sale. Second, the enhancement value of open space contributes positively both to the individual property owner's equity and to the local government, which depends on property tax for operating revenue. The critical question is this: how can the short-term profit that motivates the individual developer be harnessed to the long-term creation of real property value?

Conservation land planning suggests an answer. As an alternative to the conventional pattern of land development typified by River's Edge, conservation land planning is premised on preserving the long-term integrity of the natural landscape as a value-adding principle of development. It is similar to the settlement pattern of Ancestral Puebloans and La Luz in this regard. It is based on a design process known as "sieve mapping," which identifies the conservation value of the land and demonstrates how to capitalize on this value by allowing for carefully designed development to be located in appropriate places on the land. Sieve mapping was refined in the 1960s by Ian McHarg in his widely acclaimed book *Design with Nature*, and more recently by Randall G. Arendt in *Conservation Design for Subdivisions*. It is a process that promotes a *qualitative* analysis of the land to determine where and where not to build rather than the *quantitative* analysis of conventional development. The qualitative analysis of conservation development focuses on what intrinsic qualities of the land enhance the long-term value of the development and on protecting those qualities. In contrast, the quantitative analysis of conventional development focuses on the number of lots and on the other factors of development that influence the short-term conversion of land value into cash.

Conservation land planning is based on the following six-step design process.[6]

Step One: Identify the Conservation Areas

In the design of a conservation development the first and most important step is to identify the land that is to be preserved. A logical criterion for this analysis is to protect the land that most enhances the long-term value of the remaining land to be developed. However, this depends on subjective judgment. What intrinsic qualities of the land are most valuable? To a developer? To a homeowner? To an ecologist? These different value systems may result in conflict and compromise. But what is most important and what cannot be stressed enough is that the conservation design process begins by looking at the land and letting the existing features of the land determine where and where not to build.

This first step helps ensure that the design process is rooted in the landscape and that the final product is not arbitrary. It is best accomplished by

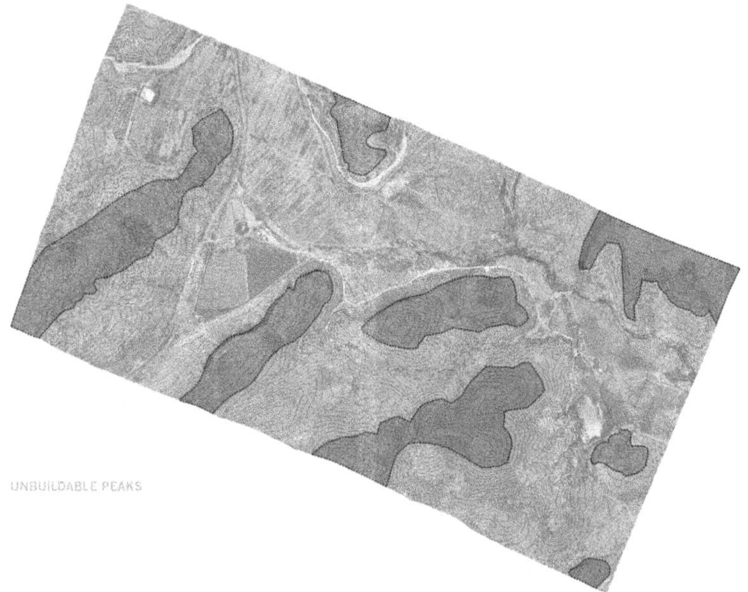

Fig. 11.5 Non-buildable Peaks: To protect the natural horizon from man-made structures, this overlay maps the hills and ridges down to forty contour feet below the top of the hill or ridge as being off-limits to development. Illustration by Anthony Anella.

walking the land in order to gain a thorough personal familiarity with it, and discovering its meaning in the process. This firsthand experience can be supplemented by listening to the insights of the people who have lived on the land during all four seasons. Where does that arroyo go? Where do the seasonal winds come from? What are the most significant features in the landscape in terms of topography, climate, drainage patterns, wildlife habitat, agricultural lands, cultural sites, views into the site from existing public roads, and views from the site toward external landscape features such as distant mountain ranges? All important features are mapped in the field. In this way the maps and the contours stop being mere abstractions.

Step Two: Map the Information

The second step is to create overlay maps. Each overlay corresponds to a separate feature of the landscape to be preserved. Each overlay represents a priority for conservation based on a firsthand understanding of what is special about the landscape. For example, in order to keep the natural horizon free from man-made structures the hills and ridges down to forty feet below the tops are mapped as being off limits to development (figure 11.5). In order to protect historic and archaeological sites these areas are mapped as being off-limits to development (figure 11.6). Prime agricultural land is mapped for protection (figure 11.7) as are

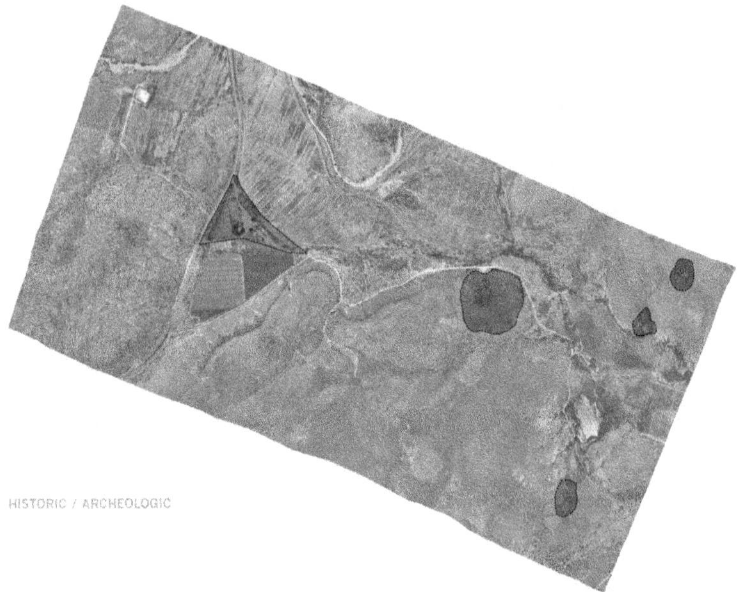

Fig. 11.6 Historic and Archaeological Sites: This overlay corresponds to historic and archaeological sites. This land is being protected from development in order to preserve the cultural heritage left by previous inhabitants. Illustration by Anthony Anella.

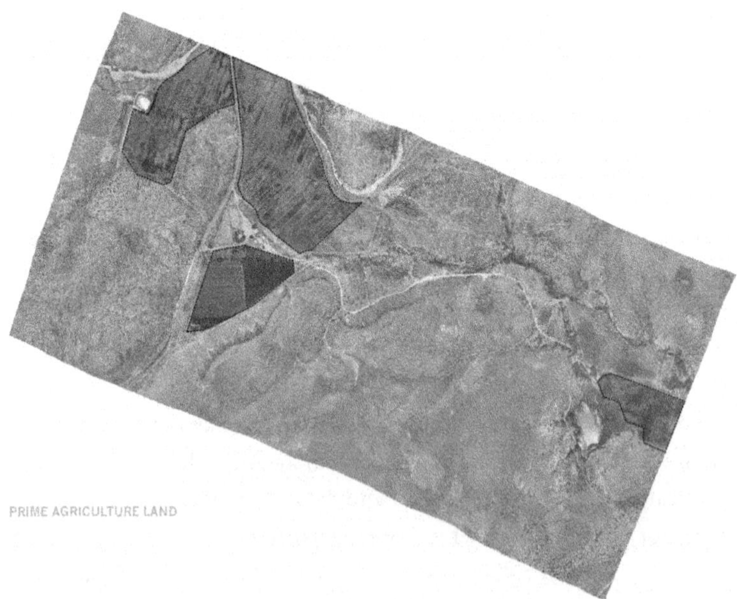

Fig. 11.7 Prime Agricultural Land: This overlay corresponds to prime agricultural land that is being protected from development in order to preserve agricultural productivity. Illustration by Anthony Anella.

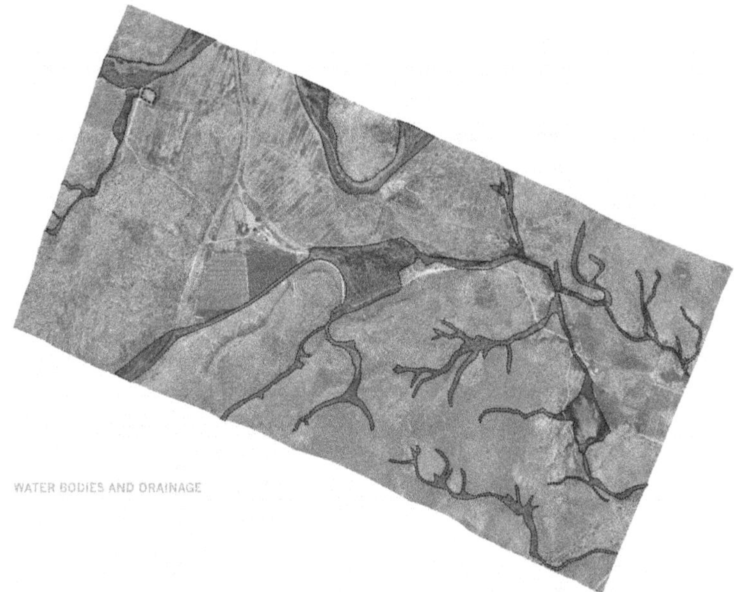

Fig. 11.8 Water Bodies and Drainage: This overlay corresponds to land located within 150 feet on either side of a water body or natural drainage system. This land is being protected from development in order to preserve the natural drainage pattern of the land. Illustration by Anthony Anella.

water bodies and drainage (figure 11.8), wildlife habitat (figure 11.9), and steep slopes (figure 11.10). The public "viewshed" (figure 11.11) is identified as that part of the land that is visible from the highway. By protecting this viewshed, the experience of driving through the rural landscape leading up to the homesites is preserved for both the homeowners and the public.

Step Three: Synthesize the Information

The third step is to create a composite of all the overlays. What is revealed is an overall pattern of conservation priorities. It is an organic pattern based on what is perceived to be important for protection. The land that falls through the "sieve" of conservation priorities is the land that is appropriate for development. *It is also the land whose value is most enhanced by the protection of what is not developed.* The gray area on the composite map of the conservation areas (figure 11.12) becomes the red area on the map of house sites relative to buildable land (figure 11.13).

Step Four: Designate the House Sites

Designating the house sites within the areas identified as being appropriate for development is best accomplished by walking the land and field-verifying the optimal sites based on views to the surrounding landscape, views to the other house

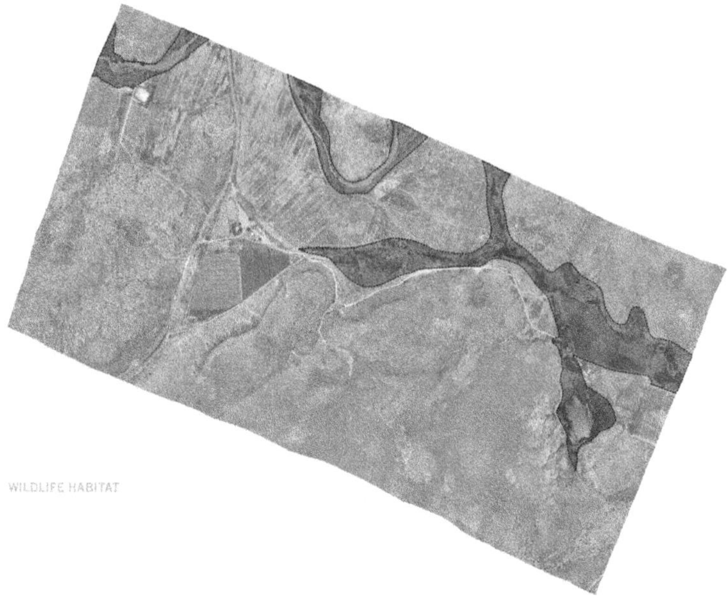

WILDLIFE HABITAT

Fig. 11.9 Wildlife Habitat: This overlay corresponds to wildlife habitat (roughly corresponding to water bodies and drainage). This land is being protected from development in order to preserve the natural habitats of wildlife. Illustration by Anthony Anella.

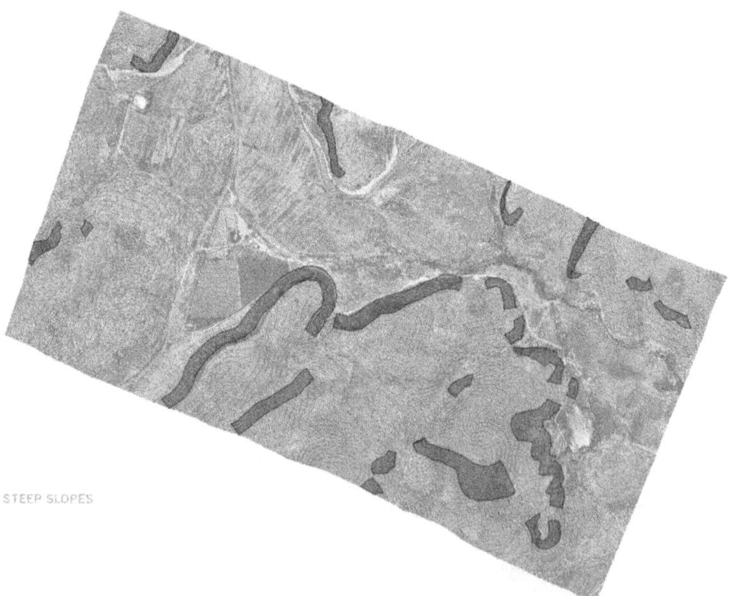

Fig. 11.10 Steep Slopes: This overlay corresponds to the land where the slope exceeds 25 percent. This land is being protected from development because of the damage due to erosion caused by building on steep slopes. Illustration by Anthony Anella.

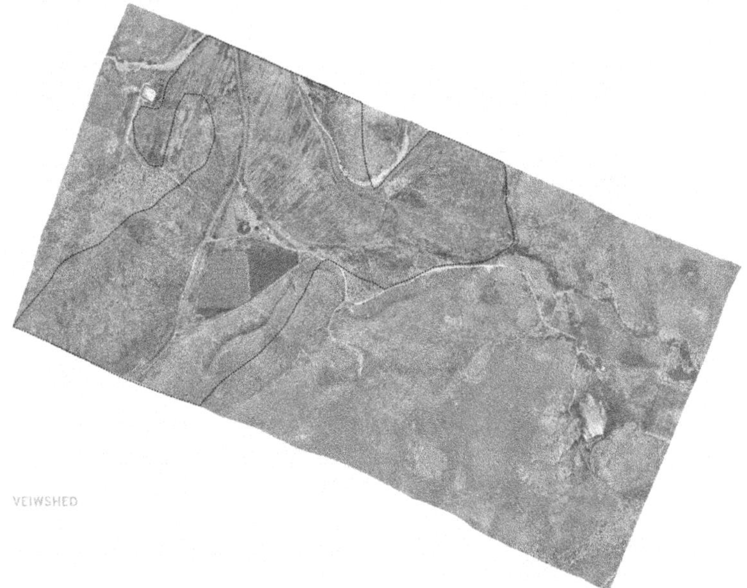

Fig. 11.11 Public Viewshed: The public viewshed is identified as that part of the study area that is visible from the public roadway. To protect this area it is mapped as being off-limits to development. By protecting the viewshed, the experience of driving through the rural landscape leading up to the house sites is preserved for both the homeowners and the public. Illustration by Anthony Anella.

sites, and the relationship of each site to the landscape (topography, vegetation, water) and the cycle of the seasons (wind, sun, precipitation) (figure 11.14). Of the house sites shown in the Conservation Development (figure 11.15), all but three are concealed from view of the other house sites by taking advantage of the topography. To prove the credibility of each house site, photographs are taken to document the relationship of the site to the landscape. Further, an analytical diagram of each site relative to the features in the landscape is created. These diagrams have the potential to serve as a tool for better understanding the land, marketing it for site-sensitive development, and helping to ensure that the individual houses complement the site-sensitive quality of the overall development.

Step Five: Lay Out the Roads

Laying out the roads is based on the following principles:

1. Avoid crossing areas prioritized for conservation.
2. Make the roads as inconspicuous from the house sites as possible by following the contours and by avoiding long straight stretches.
3. Minimize the length and cost of new roads.
4. Use existing roads where possible.

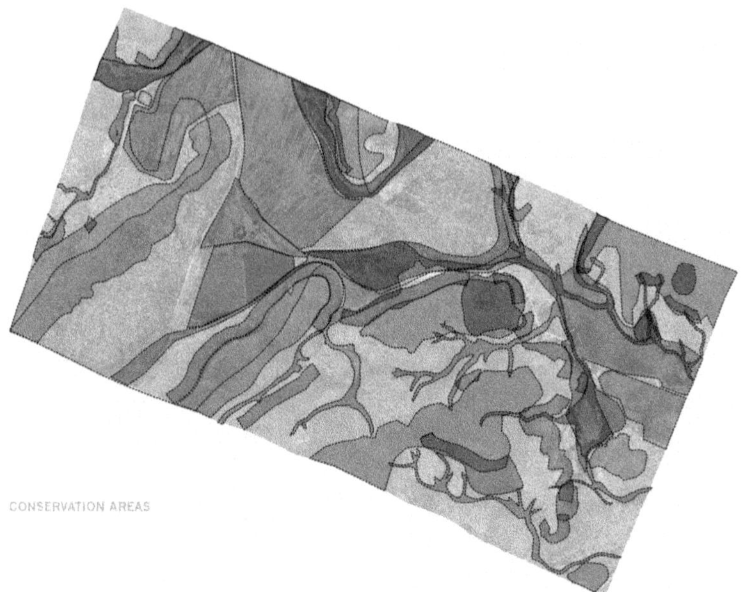

Fig. 11.12 Conservation Areas: This is a composite of the preceding maps. What is revealed is a pattern of conservation priorities. It is an organic pattern based on what is perceived to be important for protection. The land that falls through the "sieve" of conservation priorities is the land that is most appropriate for development. It is also the land whose value is most enhanced by the protection of what is not developed. The gray area on this composite map of the conservation areas becomes the red area on the following map of buildable land. Illustration by Anthony Anella.

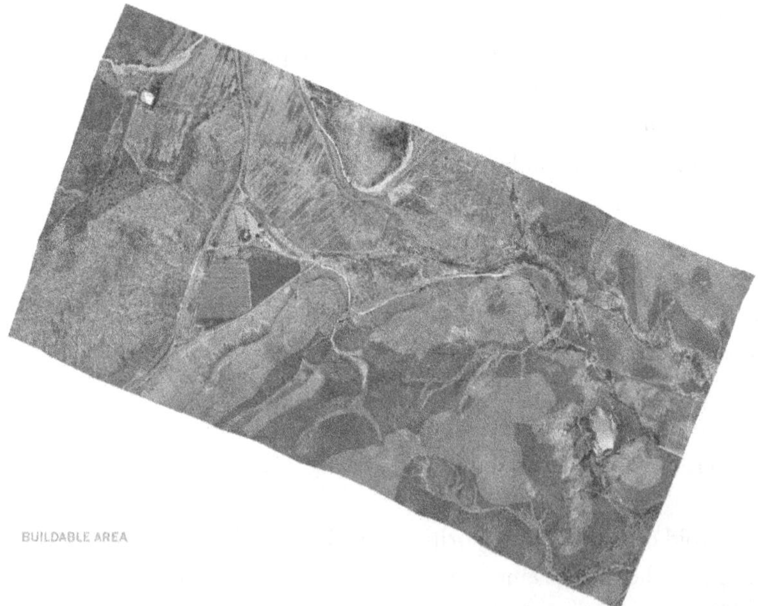

Fig. 11.13 Buildable Land: The red area on this map corresponds to the gray area of the preceding map of conservation areas. It is the land that has fallen through the "sieve" of conservation priorities. Illustration by Anthony Anella.

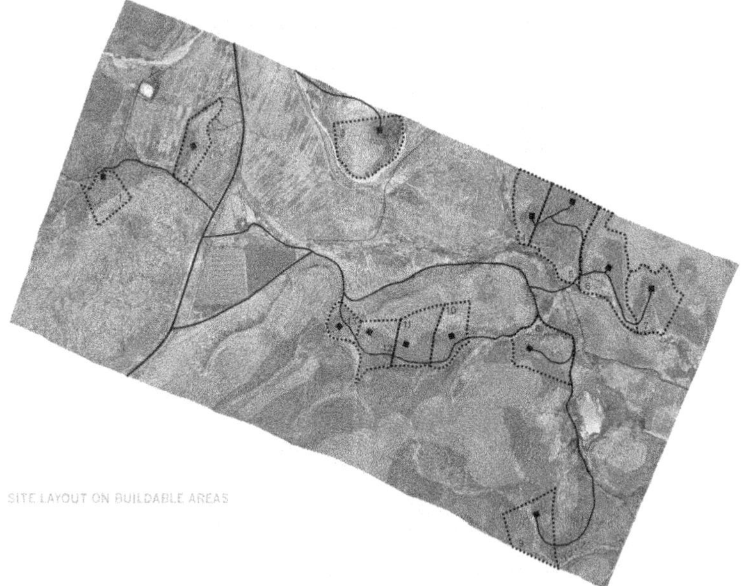

Fig. 11.14 House Sites Relative to Buildable Land: Designating the house sites within the areas identified as being appropriate for development is best accomplished by walking the land and field-verifying the optimal sites based on views to the surrounding landscape, views to the other house sites, and the relationship of each site to the landscape (topography, vegetation, water) and the cycle of the seasons (wind, sun, precipitation). Illustration by Anthony Anella.

Designing roads based on these conservation principles may add to the initial cost, but these costs are offset by the enhanced value of the house sites. This contrasts with the road design criterion in conventional development that is exclusively quantitative: minimize costs by keeping roads short and avoiding steep slopes.

Step Six: Draw the Lot Lines

Once the conservation areas have been identified, the house sites designated, and the road alignments determined, drawing the lot lines is a mere formality. However, there are at least two possible legal frameworks for ownership to accomplish this formality. One is to subdivide all the land into plats of fee-simple ownership. The other is to create an open space development with smaller platted areas of fee-simple property and the owners sharing an undivided interest in the remaining open space. The remaining land—whether individually or jointly owned—is protected from development through conservation easements.

Figure 11.15 depicts a conservation development with the owners sharing an undivided interest in the open space. This approach offers several advantages. By only allowing the smaller lots to be fenced, the jointly owned areas are left

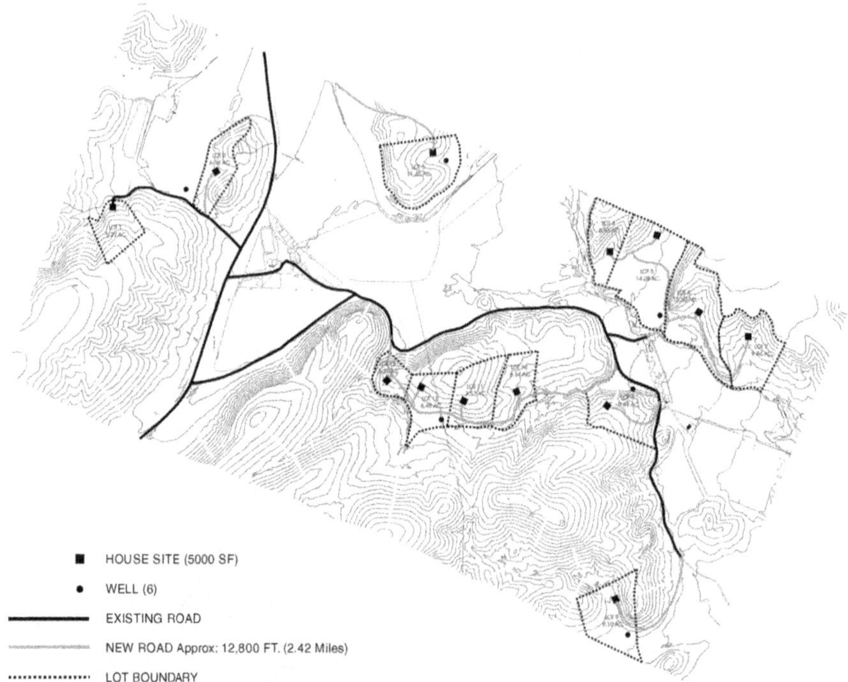

Fig. 11.15 Conservation Development: Once the conservation areas have been identified, the house sites designated, and the road alignments determined, drawing the lot lines is a mere formality. However there are at least two possible legal frameworks for accomplishing this formality. One is to subdivide all the land into plats of fee-simple ownership. The other is to create an open-space development with smaller platted areas of fee-simple property and the owners sharing an undivided interest in the remaining open space. In either case, houses may only be built on the designated house sites. The remaining land—whether individually or jointly owned—is protected from development by a conservation easement. This figure depicts an open-space development. Illustration by Anthony Anella.

completely open for shared uses such as horseback riding. The smaller lot sizes also minimize the maintenance responsibilities for the individual owner. The cost to maintain the common open space is shared by the other homeowners. The main advantage to the buyer is that of owning a house site that is surrounded by open space. Figure 11.16 depicts a conventional development. It is important to note that even though the lot sizes are smaller in the conservation development than the lot sizes in the conventional development, the number of lots remains the same. For purposes of comparison, the density of development is neutral. Keeping the number of lots constant allows the comparison to emphasize the qualitative advantages of the conservation development and its impact on lot prices. What would the buyer be willing to pay more for—a lot surrounded by protected land or a lot surrounded by private land with unknown future development possibilities?

Fig. 11.16 Conventional Development: It is important to note that even though the lot sizes are smaller in the conservation development compared with the lot sizes in this conventional development, the number of lots remains the same. For purposes of comparison, the density of the development is neutral. Keeping the number of lots constant allows the comparison to emphasize the qualitative advantages of the conservation development and its impact on lot prices. What would the buyer be willing to pay more for—a lot surrounded by protected land or a lot surrounded by unprotected land with unknown future development possibilities? Illustration by Anthony Anella.

Conclusion

Unlike the Ancestral Puebloans we are buffered from the elements by central heating and air conditioning. We have lost much of our vulnerability and therefore our sensitivity to the environment. This is evidenced by the prevailing land settlement pattern we see today in contrast to the prehistoric Ancestral Puebloan settlement pattern of the same landscape. We have also lost our sense of belonging to a larger natural whole. The contemporary land ethic is motivated by short-term profit. It tends to destroy long-term value by ignoring the visual and environmental impacts of new development on the very resources that make the land attractive for development in the first place. This is our modern dilemma and the predicament of conventional development. It would be futile to try to ignore the dilemma posed by the modern world by retreating into simpler agrarian existences. But we can learn to revere again the basic premise that sustained the Ancestral Puebloans: that man is a part of nature, not separate from it. We can learn again to build with the land and not merely on it. As a design process, "sieve mapping" identifies the conservation value of the land and demonstrates how to capitalize on this value. It works within the conceptual framework of economic self-interest as a way of convincing both the landowner and the developer to adopt conservation as a profit-making principle of enlightened development. However, in so doing, it seeks to change the way the land and man's relationship to it are viewed. It seeks to shift the contemporary ethic of extracting immediate value from the land as an individual privilege to a new ethic of creating long-term value through ecologically based design and planning. It seeks to provide the contemporary practice of land development with a systematic process for protecting the integrity of the land for future generations in a way that is economically expedient as well as environmentally ethical.

Notes

1. Based on information from the Southwest Multiple Listing Service Inc. provided to me on August 28, 2001, by Gary L. Wells, the qualifying broker at the Rio Rancho office of Coldwell Banker Legacy.
2. See note 1 supra.
3. See note 1 supra.
4. Based on information provided to me on August 23, 2001, by Nancy Rose, a resident of La Luz since 1973 and a former Hertzmark Parnegg realtor with over twenty years' experience selling La Luz townhouses, and by Robert Peters, FAIA, a resident of La Luz since 1974.
5. Conversation with Gary L. Wells, the qualifying broker at the Rio Rancho office of Coldwell Banker Legacy on August 28, 2001.
6. This six-step design process and the accompanying illustrations are from *The Open Lands Demonstration Project* by Anthony Anella with photographs by Edward Ranney. This project was funded by grants from the Graham Foundation for Advanced Studies in the Fine Arts, the Ucross Foundation, and the Koldyke Family Foundation.

References Cited

Arendt, Randall G.

1996 *Conservation Design for Subdivisions: A Practical Guide to Creating Open Space Networks*. Washington, DC: Island Press.

Erdman, James A., Charles L. Douglas, and John W. Marr

1969 *Wetherhill Mesa Studies: Environment of Mesa Verde, Colorado.* Washington, DC: National Park Service.

Fausold, Charles J., and Robert Lilieholm

1996 *The Economic Value of Open Space: A Review and Synthesis*. Phoenix, AZ: Lincoln Publications Institute.

McHarg, Ian
1992 *Design with Nature*. New York: Wiley.
Sofaer, Anna
1997 The Primary Architecture of the Chacoan Culture: A Cosmological Expression. In *Anasazi Architecture and American Design*, ed. Baker H. Morrow and V. B. Price, 88–132. Albuquerque: University of New Mexico Press.

Chapter Twelve

Landscape and Survival

Thoughts on New Urbanism and Ancestral Puebloan/Pueblo Strategies for Designing Pragmatic Desert Built Environments

by V. B. Price

While American architecture and landscape planning have reoriented themselves in the last twenty-five years to focus on site locations and the specifics of place, gaining insights from the environmental movement, ecological science, and the concept of sustainability, designers in the arid American Southwest have largely failed to make use of the pragmatic expertise in landscape management and horticulture developed by Ancestral Puebloan and Pueblo peoples. V. B. Price links the goals of contemporary architectural and landscape theories, such as New Urbanism, with the deep understanding of microclimates and microecologies that allowed indigenous people in the Southwest to sustain themselves, and often flourish, for more than two thousand years. In his comprehensive "Eight Points," he lays out a challenging series of precepts for an intelligent design of the Southwestern landscape in the twenty-first century.

Like all conservationists, I'm troubled by waste. I'm especially annoyed by wasted information and know-how that's no longer privileged because of its association with antiquated technologies. In a world moving too fast for any new technique to become, as the old saying has it, both "tried and true," I'm distressed that traditional building technologies with staying power aren't employed in modern design and construction techniques. This seems a particular shame in desert climates like the American Southwest's where ancient and traditional builders have mastered the requirements of survival.

My dismay is tempered somewhat, however, by recalling an incident in the history of architecture in Italy. When Brunelleschi was overseeing the construction of his design for additions to the Cathedral of Florence in the mid-1400s, he had to reinvent ancient Roman construction machinery and practices to build the massive dome, considered now perhaps the most graceful in the world. In the American Southwest, however, most developers and designers act as if they didn't know an ancient architectural and landscape tradition even exists for them to adapt to modern needs, despite virtually endless archaeological and contemporary cultural examples.

So when I first read the preamble to the "Charter of the New Urbanism" published in 2000, I was happily struck by its deep similarities to what I know about the pragmatic principles of the creation of form and space in Ancestral Puebloan/Pueblo built environments, using technologies and principles deeply grounded in tradition (figure 12.1). But I also felt a kind of despair, understanding as I do that American culture values "the new" above all else, even in poetry, as Ezra Pound's modernist dictum of the 1920s,"make it new," attests.

The New Urbanist preamble states, in part, "We recognize that physical solutions by themselves will not solve social and economic problems, but neither can economic vitality, community stability, and environmental health be sustained without a coherent and supportive physical framework." One can see that sentiment still at work in the physical arrangement of virtually every pueblo still extant and in the ruins of most ancient town sites. I have grave doubts about the modern world's ability to find a synergy, a hybrid vigor, between these two worldviews in the service of creating cost-effective conservationist strategies for living successfully in the resource-poor, hostile environments of the arid Southwest. But it's certainly worth a try.

Recently, when I was reading *Natural Capitalism* by Paul Hawken and Amory and L. Hunter Lovins (1999), I was struck again by the similarity of their attitudes to what I've sensed about Ancestral Puebloan and Pueblo views of the built environment. When they speak of "radical resource productivity," "eco-efficiency," and "capital as if living systems mattered," I think they're talking the language of the Ancestral Puebloan and Pueblo philosophy, if not the local dialect. This seems to me to be a philosophy of survival rather than "sustainability" or any other such phrase that connotes forcing the environment to conform to human needs rather than humans adapting successfully in a natural context to which they intimately belong. If this means, as environmental educator Steve Van Matre observes, "going back," then "the only question is how far, how fast, and what do we take with us." Of course, I'm not advocating that we go back and imitate Ancestral Puebloan

Fig. 12.1 Ritual played a key role in Ancestral Puebloan life east of the Rio Grande. Photo by Baker H. Morrow.

builders. I am saying, however, that our survival here in the desert mountain West may depend on how seriously we study their successes and failures to survive in an environment as harsh as the one we both inhabit over time. I have to admit that though I feel sensibly hopeful from time to time because of the sound logic of learning from the past, I am not optimistic that we will.

As the familiar phrase "time out of mind" tells us, time isolates as much as culture and geography. And what can be surmised of the Ancestral Puebloan view of landscape and economics one thousand years ago is not in our minds at all today. That's the sense I've gotten over the years of advocating the study of indigenous built environments in the Southwest and meeting resistance as I attempted to explore how their technological solutions and philosophy of place might contribute to modern planning and building practices. It's become clear to me, however, that if one could strip away the idiosyncrasies of history and culture, one would find general principles common to both ancient and modern needs.

But even at the beginning of the new millennium, as dramatic climate changes and drought conditions threaten the desert and intermountain West once again, as El Paso faces the alarming predicament of running out of groundwater in fifteen years, and as water wars from Denver to Los Angeles loom expensively in the courts, mainstream developers, planners, bankers, and even radical thinkers still cannot conceive of a more effective and site-specific way to design the built environment to suit arid conditions. And, I imagine, most don't even think they

Fig. 12.2 Swallows' nests with pictographs, Tompiro country. Photo by Baker H. Morrow.

should bother. Yet, as Southwestern archaeologist David Stuart has pointed out in his groundbreaking book *Anasazi America* (2000), the high desert civilization here a millennium ago in Chaco Canyon succumbed to climate change, water shortages, and social pressures for what appear to be very modern reasons: they overdeveloped and overpopulated the landscape, extending themselves well beyond their capacities to remain organized and flexible enough to survive prolonged hard times.

But post-Chaco Ancestral Puebloan builders, and their Pueblo descendants in Arizona and New Mexico, did struggle successfully to learn the lessons of wasteful overdevelopment. They apparently never overextended themselves again in the grand mode of politically grandiose and sprawling Chaco. Yes, over the next 250 years they built huge pueblos but, from what we can tell, never, as Stuart says, "complex systems" like Chaco. Ironically, he observes, as their built environment and social structure became less complex and more egalitarian, their farming strategies became ever more complicated, site specific, risk averse, and waste resistant and came to mirror their newfound, or rediscovered, survival know-how (Stuart, pers. comm. 2001). It could be said, in general terms, that Pueblo descendants of the Ancestral Puebloans tended to return to and refine traditional building and landscape strategies that have allowed them to survive and flourish culturally intact in this harsh environment, with its cycles of drought and unstable weather patterns, right to the present moment (figure 12.2).

Fundamental to their success was the recognition that landscape architecture, the creation of outdoor spaces, and the site location and construction of buildings are not discrete entities. We can see this sense of unity not only implied in archaeological sites, but also conveyed by modern Pueblo thinkers. There apparently is not the kind of strict divorce of the built environment from the "natural" environment in indigenous thinking as there is in our own. Humans are part of the natural flow of the world. And so it is the norm for Pueblo people, not the exception, to consider their surroundings as part of themselves. Their survival has depended on it. There's no doubt that Ancestral Puebloan/Pueblo people made costly miscalculations and fell prey to excess and various forms of greed. They were not protoecologists as some might label them. And "sustainability," whatever that might mean in the jargon of utopianists, cannot be pinned on them either.

Still, the irrefutable fact is that their know-how, and sensitivity to what the land could afford them, allowed them to endure.

The long history of their cultural flourishing bears out the pragmatic validity of their view of the world. And yet, in many architectural, planning, and engineering circles, as well as business networks, just to mention the lessons to be learned from the ancients arouses a dismissive response. I don't believe it's a response of prejudice or even of modernist superiority, though I could well be wrong. I chalk it up to a sense of technological closed-mindedness and understandable, though regrettable, cultural blind spots. If homogenization, standardization, and interchangeability are the hallmarks of the millennial world economy, why would any company or its hired political operatives pay attention to local and venerable solutions to specific environmental challenges? The development business in America traditionally does not establish long-range commitments to a community. It is committed to change, not to continuity.

While modern development in Denver and Albuquerque, Tucson and Las Vegas, still dribbles tract houses helter-skelter over the landscape, while New Urbanist designers still import progressive design programs from Midwestern and East Coast climates and cultures to colonize Western environments, while desert aquifers dangerously diminish and rivers are bled dry by exploding populations, and while scholars draw parallels between the collapse of ancient civilizations and the ecological threats to our own, obvious solutions to misplaced development in the arid West—indigenous and ancient solutions—simply go unanalyzed.

Yet thinkers like the New Urbanists would agree, I believe, with the following minimum list of implicit admonitions drawn from observations of Ancestral Puebloan/Pueblo landscape and site planning (figure 12.3), observations I'll try to expand on later in this chapter:

1. Never miss an opportunity for the benefits of any solar energy and heating.

Fig. 12.3 Southwest juniper woodland—classic Ancestral Puebloan settlement area. Photo by Baker H. Morrow.

II. Minimize exposure to cold and wind.
III. Make sure the most vulnerable connections and weakest links are overbuilt or redundantly reinforced.
IV. Encircle.
V. Allow the landscape to tell you where and what to build.
VI. Adopt a survival view of water and adapt yourself to it.

This Ancestral Puebloan–based pattern would also make sense to contemporary thinkers like Wes Jackson, author of *Becoming Native to This Place* (1996); to Santa Clara Pueblo art historian Rina Swentzell; and to ecologist and educator Gregory Cajete, also from Santa Clara, author of *A People's Ecology* (1999) and *Native Science* (2000). This language of design embraces concepts such as viewing the "landscape as mentor," described by Donlyn Lyndon of *Places* magazine; cultural and landscape ecology outlined in a book edited by Joan Iverson Nassauer entitled *Placing Nature* (1997); and ethnoecology described in a book by the same name edited by Virginia D. Nazarea (1999), which deals with "situated knowledge" and "located lives."

So far, these intelligent and avant-garde spokespeople for a new way of looking at land use and development in America remain almost relegated to the role of cult figures on the progressive fringe, and public awareness of the Native

American thinkers is painfully but not surprisingly all but nonexistent, as prophets often are in their own homeland.

I believe many design professionals in the West dismiss ancient building traditions on aesthetic grounds, considering the mimicking of their appearance to be "regional" and passé. So, there is an important distinction to be made between matters of style and symbol and pragmatic landscape sensitivity. My thoughts here generally deal with the latter.

There's little question, in my mind, that development in the West is digging its own grave. Societies, even technologically sophisticated ones, cannot grow and build against basic conditions of climate and landscape forever. Sooner or later the character of the land will catch up with them. Ancestral Puebloan migrations from Chacoan sites, forced usually by climate change as well as factional disputes and design miscalculations, make that clear.

Both before and after the decline of Chaco and other monumental sites, the Pueblos and Ancestral Puebloans embraced insights that remain the hallmark of indigenous builders in the arid West. They can be summed like this: Submit to the local conditions of specific landscapes. Know your place. Don't force the land to be what it's not. For example, don't put generic tract developments in the desert far away from natural resources. The weakest link controls everything. And the unpredictability of water is our greatest weakness. When water is short, distance determines cost which determines availability. When you submit to local conditions you won't try constructing landscapes in the desert that require the kind of moisture naturally occurring in, say, Georgia. And when you modify the landscape to make it fit your needs, do so in ways that don't obstruct its major patterns and movements of energy. Modify where you can, but do so mimicking natural conditions. And be ready to change your modifications when natural forces overwhelm or circumvent them (figure 12.4). For instance, don't build in arroyos or drive in paved-over water paths during flash floods.

Any culture that survives in arid circumstances, especially city-builders like the Ancestral Puebloan/Pueblo peoples, understands that the desert cannot be tamed to accommodate an unlimited number of people; that urban built environments do not create their own conditions independent of local weather and resources; and that technological fixes cannot override natural conditions in both the short run and the long run.

Such fallacies arise from an economic view of nature as a free resource to be exploited that is in diametric opposition to what we know of the Ancestral Puebloan/Pueblo worldview.

Santa Clara architectural historian and theorist Rina Swentzell gives an eloquently clear picture of how Pueblo peoples see the world. "At the center of the Pueblo belief system is the conviction that people are not separate from nature and natural forces. This insoluble connection with nature has existed from the

Fig. 12.4 Franciscan priests created a cloistered environment of their own in the desert within the *conventos* of the seventeenth century. Photo by Baker H. Morrow.

beginning of time. The goal of human existence is to maintain wholeness or oneness with the natural universe" (quoted in Morrow and Price 1997:186). The parallels between this Native American view and the Euro-American conservation ethic are useful and intriguing (figure 12.5).

Aldo Leopold summed it up when he wrote, "We abuse land because we regard it as a commodity belonging to us. When we see land as a community to which we belong, we may begin to use it with love and respect. There is no other way for land to survive the impact of mechanized man, nor for us to reap from it the esthetic harvest it is capable, under science, of contributing to culture" (Leopold 1987:viii).

These views have an unexpected convergence in a central concept in Hawken and the Lovins' *Natural Capitalism*. One of the four basic strategies of "radical resource productivity," or "capital as if living systems mattered" (Hawken, Lovins, and Lovins 1999:9), which is at the heart of their economic concept, is what the authors call "biomimicry" (14). Looking to nature as a force to emulate rather than as an obstacle to overcome has to do with replicating the efficiency of natural systems when it comes to waste reuse. "Smart designers," the authors assert, are "apprenticing themselves to nature" both when it comes to learning the "benign chemistry of its processes" and the unimpeded flow of its energies and modulating conditions (16). This would seem to be directly in

Fig. 12.5 Ancient Puebloan stone masonry was adapted in the early seventeenth century for use in Franciscan mission complexes. Photo by Baker H. Morrow.

keeping with both a Ancestral Puebloan/Pueblo and conservationist respect for the necessary processes of animate and inanimate nature upon which human life depends. It's the difference between understanding that natural processes are absolute givens, capable only of temporary modification, and the view that human ingenuity can subvert and overcome such limitations permanently and at will. There is no question, of course, that massive short-term modifications of the environment such as hydroelectric dams can subvert natural processes in ways that seem comparable to nature's own power itself. But Ancestral Puebloan/Pueblo builders, contemporary conservationists, and natural capitalists would contend that our tendency to descend to grandiosity smacks of the kind of hubris that nature loves to overturn and undermine. And this seems to happen regularly commensurate with the outrageousness of our pretensions and heedlessness.

The lesson modern builders and planners in the arid West can learn from Ancestral Puebloan and Pueblo tradition is that it is ultimately pragmatic to pay attention to where you are. Anything short of complete attention is potentially calamitous. As historian William deBuys wrote of the hard life in northern New Mexico in his book *Enchantment and Exploitation*, "In an unforgiving environment, small errors yield large consequences.... This minor yet muscular truth characterizes every pioneer experience, and it is one of history's themes in New Mexico. Centuries of human experience afford abundant examples of small miscalculations leading to large-scale misfortunes" (deBuys 1985:xix).

One of those miscalculations in New Mexico was the wishful thinking fantasy that there was a body of water the size of Lake Superior under Albuquerque. The city draws fifty-five to seventy thousand acre-feet a year from the aquifer, which city officials started analyzing only in the late 1980s. The U.S. Geological Survey has sobered city officials by demonstrating that a Lake Superior–sized body of water never existed. A couple of relatively deep ponds, perhaps, but no lake. The city's future growth is now in jeopardy, having already outgrown its water budget, mining more than can be annually replaced by natural processes.

That surely would not have happened, given contemporary technology after World War II, if Albuquerque business and political leaders had paid attention to where they are and employed the scientific acumen of Albuquerque's national laboratories, instead of importing pipe dreams. Like so many places in the West, Albuquerque was alienated from the life of its surroundings. Its leaders considered it their possession, not our habitat. "Indeed, to know any kind of physical landscape," Gregory Cajete wrote, "you have to experience it directly; that is, to truly know any place you have to live in it and be part of its life process" (2000:181). Instead of imposing a template of commercial and fantasy design fads on a landscape, trying to smooth out its flaws and inconveniences so advertising can create a demand for products that are the cheapest and fastest to produce, an Ancestral Puebloan/Pueblo view of the built environment was that it took place in a landscape that was "in a perfect state," Cajete wrote. "The real test of living was to be able to establish a harmonious relationship with that perfect nature—to understand it, to see it as the source of one's life and livelihood, and the source of one's essential spiritual being" (179).

The work of harmonizing personal and social activity with the "perfect nature" of a place that changes seasonally and randomly at its own pace is so utterly different from the contemporary notion of "sustainable development" that it gives rise to an alternative goal—which I'll call survivability—something I believe all people who are not destroyed by difficult environments understand almost intuitively. Terms like "sustainability" imply a negative stasis or finding ways to make the natural world conform to a static pattern of human action that is, itself, not adaptable. Survivability stresses agility, mutability, and a flexible response to the demands of necessity dictated by natural conditions.

Another version of such thinking that bears striking resemblance to Cajete's and Swentzell's views is called "landscape as mentor." The editor of *Places* magazine, Donlyn Lyndon, wrote recently about seeing the natural world as a wise guide and tutor:

> The fundamental premise is that we can and do learn from the landscapes we experience. We can be tutored by consideration of places that are dominantly formed by, or evidently conditioned and changed by, the forces of nature—by sun, wind, rain and the cycles of weather, by the vegetation that roots in the soil and seeks to reach its own place in the sun, by the shape of the land and the flow of water across it, and by the shapes that result from the colossal geological forces of uplift, compression and erosion over unthinkably long periods of time. We need to learn from the landscape its lessons of interconnectedness, growth, decay, and steady, subtle endurance. (2000:9)

If there's any key ingredient to achieving the "subtle endurance" of survival when it comes to creating human landscapes and built environments it's summed up in the title of a book by Wes Jackson, *Becoming Native to This Place.* An advocate of organic agriculture and the founder of the Land Institute in Salina, Kansas, Jackson believes that "at some level, most of us want to live within our means, to become native to this place at the very time the target appears to be receding faster than the shot we aim at it" (1996:104). He continues that "in this world now dominated by economic thought, we have discovered that comfort and security are not solutions to the human condition and that affluence has not solved the economic problem.... Furthermore, economic development has led to enormous ecological destruction" (105). Jackson, like Lyndon, Swentzell, and Cajete, sees nature "as the standard," as "measure," and quotes not only Milton's warning about not offending nature's "sober laws / And holy dictate of spare Temperance," but also Alexander Pope's admonition to "let Nature never be forgot," and to "Consult the Genius of the place in all" (quoted in Jackson 1996:74).

Though Ancestral Puebloan and Pueblo thinkers made no distinction between human and nature, Jackson's, Pope's, and Milton's common-sense knowledge about adjusting one's ambitions and intentions to the "genius of the place" would make complete sense to any builder or gardener in the desert who hadn't deluded himself or herself into believing that engineering and technology could override the inherent risks in living in marginal and largely inhospitable natural environments. Knowing where you are, and what it requires of you, and dealing with it on its own terms is the essential quality of long-term survival (figure 12.6).

What we know and can surmise of the Ancestral Puebloan and Pueblo worldview as it relates to the built environment supports this survival vision of understanding and working with the deep and changing realities of a specific place. Baker Morrow, in his chapter entitled "The Berry Gardens of Quarai and the Pocket

Fig. 12.6 Gardens in the ancient Southwest often follow the flow of nearby water. Photo by Baker H. Morrow.

Terraces of Abó" in this volume, uses the metaphor of a garden to describe both the agricultural and landscape practices of the early Puebloan peoples, practices that ultimately allowed them to survive and culturally flourish.

It is intellectually improvident to think we know anything more than snippets about the big picture of the Ancestral Puebloan and Pueblo past. But when it came to growing food it's safe to say, at the moment, that Ancestral Puebloans and their Pueblo descendants did not practice what one might call big field farming (Baker Morrow, pers. comm. 2003). They engaged in a massive farming enterprise, with as many as ten thousand acres under cultivation at ancestral Zuni (Beath, this volume), but all on a small scale, with multitudes of crop types, vast numbers of small plots, waffle gardens, flood fields and arroyo bench farming, sand orchards, wild plant cultivation, and multiple kinds of mulching, with growing areas situated everywhere water was. The Hopi, for instance, made use of 134 of the 150 plant types in their surrounding landscape (Bol 1998:46), intensively cultivating and harvesting not only domesticated foodstuffs, but wild plants for both food and other material uses. They couldn't have survived doing it any other way. Their method was to plant redundantly in as many microclimates and microenvironments as possible to minimize risk of complete crop failure. Hopi farmers even planted four to five seeds in a single hole so they'd get what amounted to many oases of multiple cornstalks that were growing so densely together that they provided shade and wind protection for one another. Ancestral Puebloan and Pueblo farmers could have, I suppose, actually moved water around to irrigate large leveled tracts of land, had there been enough water available. They had the human ingenuity and labor to do it. But they apparently chose not to, deeming it too risky.

The point to be made here is that Ancestral Puebloan and Pueblo farmers were so native to their place, they knew it so well, that they could make its harshness work for them, rather than against them. The garden image, I think, is apt here, in the sense that cultivating a garden landscape causes us to pay particular attention to the tiniest details of the microclimates and variable conditions in our own backyards. It doesn't seem all that far-fetched, and there is some evidence for it, that much of Chaco Canyon was under cultivation with corn and other crops at various times of the year. In addition to the Chaco breadbasket in the Red Mesa Valley some thirty miles south, Chaco Canyon itself had several hundred farmsteads that shared the same space with the great houses and great kivas (David Stuart, pers. comm. 2001). Those farmer/gardeners could have created a discrete garden environment that was even still, perhaps, too large and requiring too complex a social organization to maintain.

If a culture makes no distinction between buildings and landscapes and if its worldview sees no fundamental distinction between humans and the rest of nature, then the total built environment tends to be adapted to what the land and weather and celestial forces will give it. There's really no other choice. The total place has to be considered. When distinctions are made between buildings and landscape, and when humans are seen as something inherently different from or superior to the land around them, the basic conditions of the landscape and its weather patterns tend to be ignored, at least in the industrial West.

While it may seem impossible for modern American designers, planners, and financiers to assimilate the practical building solutions of a worldview so utterly different from our own, it must be stressed that practical solutions are not stylistic ones, or "aesthetic" ones, but, indeed, are pragmatic in the American sense of doing something that works. By that I mean something much more than short-term economic success. Of course, a culture that conceives environmental practicality in terms of building lots with obsolescent houses on them that can be "turned over" multiple times for multiple profits before they are turned under and the same lots sold again at higher prices with bigger houses on them has nothing at all to do with Ancestral Puebloan/Pueblo building practices or worldview. Nor does selling houses and landscape configurations based on a universally marketed design type that exists in a number of standard models as much for the convenience of the home repair and building supply industry as it does for the heavily marketed satisfactions of the "American dream."

But in ecologically troubled times, such as our own, the market for housing in desert environments will probably start demanding something different from what mainstream advertising sells so vociferously. Chances are that as gasoline becomes more expensive, as heating and electricity prices skyrocket, and as water scarcity becomes a determining factor in urban planning, so-called market forces in the built environment will move toward more community-structured, resource-efficient development, much like New Urbanist proposals. And that means, ultimately, design strategies based on local knowledge rather than generic patterns placed anywhere on the landscape.

Successful models for such strategies exist in New Mexico, for instance at La Luz on Coors Boulevard on the West Mesa in Albuquerque. Designed by Antoine Predock from 1968 to 1974, La Luz is a cluster development of ninety-six town houses on some forty-two acres of developed land on the edge of a five-hundred-acre parcel of open space. Each dwelling has complete privacy, protected outdoor space, and connections to small patios and *placitas*. Although Predock chose not to design La Luz as a regional-style New Mexico adobe, he blended modernist forms with the kind of Ancestral Puebloan/Pueblo desert design principles described in this chapter. La Luz has been financially successful for over thirty years. But it has never been used as a prototype for clustered infill development in Albuquerque. Perhaps in times of scarcity ahead, La Luz will make more sense to bankers and New Urbanist designers.

What follows is a briefly described, and certainly incomplete, program for a New Urbanist design agenda in the desert mountain West, based on a preliminary assessment of Ancestral Puebloan and Pueblo principles expressed earlier in this chapter. These principles do not address New Urbanist macroplanning issues, but they are suitable for some retrofitting of neighborhoods, and for all new neighborhood developments. They are not "sustainable" in the sense of perpetuating nonadaptive building forms and strategies. They all arise from a pragmatic survival interpretation of human activity, which emphasizes paying close attention to the opportunities and limitations imposed by a harsh climate, highly varied topography, and a generally arid habitat.

1. Sunlight. In keeping with the Charter of the New Urbanism's dictum that "architecture and landscape design should grow from local climate, topography, history, and building practice," making the most of sunlight and its warmth, and the shade it can occasion, is an art form that on-site observations by even nonspecialists can affirm Ancestral Puebloan builders mastered almost from the start. This respect for sunlight has little to do with design motifs or building materials and technologies, though stone and mud construction does both retain heat and insulate against cold. Over and above various passive solar technologies, along with solar cells, which certainly are an advantage in the arid West, Ancestral Puebloan/Pueblo builders can teach us never to miss an opportunity to orient structures, and even landscapes, to the southeast to make the most of morning sun and minimize afternoon heat. Something as simple as site location, so often ignored by contemporary builders, can make an enormous difference in comfort and energy efficiency.

2. Site protection. Because of often rapid temperature fluctuations in the deserts, Ancestral Puebloan/Pueblo builders seem to have located their structures and their gardens not only to maximize solar efficiency, but to protect against cold and wind. Evidence suggests that the Ancestral Puebloans liked to build near the walls and rims of canyons and other landscape features, rather than in the middle of them, seeking natural shelter where they could. Their understanding of wind and rain helped them to avoid making their structures vulnerable to direct assaults from prevailing weather patterns in their area. They would have found it hilarious and stupid, for instance, to build exposed living structures on the tops of vulnerable promontories just for the view, or in cold sinks for short-term economic expediency. They tempted the fate of the weather as little as possible.

3. Redundancy. What I admire most about Ancestral Puebloan/Pueblo builders and farmers is that they left as little as possible to chance. In Chaco Canyon, major sites reveal a tendency to overbuild and to overprepare for negative eventualities at the weakest points in both structures and agricultural practices. Supporting walls are much thicker than they need to be, making structures secure and adding levels of insulation a more skimpy building practice would have missed. Ancestral Puebloan/Pueblo farmers could not afford a single season of total crop failure. Although their diet was augmented by hunting and harvesting wild fruit and seed plants, Ancestral Puebloan farmers planted selected crops near virtually every conceivable water source. If one set of conditions failed, chances are some of the others would not. Just as engineers today tend to overbuild the connections that attach, say, bridge spans to cables, so Ancestral Puebloan builders and site planners seemed to position their structures in ways that overwhelmingly reinforced their weakest links. Climate and water sources were always mixed blessings, as they are still in the desert West. Building sites were not far from water sources, for instance, nor were they precariously positioned to be vulnerable to a variety of climatic conditions. As much as possible, buildings constructed tall blockages to wind and cold and openness to sunlight, and they were dug into the earth to provide ultimate protection from the elements. Theirs was always a defensive but cooperative building strategy, one that sought to maximize positive conditions, and rarely if ever displayed the kind of arrogance and overconfidence that might openly defy weather patterns with poorly sited structures.

4. Encircle. Site plans and aerial views of Chacoan and post-Chacoan Ancestral Puebloan ruins all send the same message: a positive social and survival strategy for building in the arid Southwest inevitably leads to clustering and encircling. Site after site shows relatively compact built environments that enclose a central and communal plaza, sometimes numbers of them. These built environments are inward looking, protective, providing their own shade and weather protection, and, placed in such a way as to minimize climate damage, making the most of the sun and lessening demand for other energy sources. The encircling quality of Ancestral Puebloan forms could be adapted commercially today for both condominiums and apartments, and even small shopping centers, too. The inner plaza, if kept at a human scale, could provide families with a space for the same kind of conviviality and community oversight of children that Jane Jacobs wrote so warmly about in older East Coast neighborhoods. It's not difficult to see a New Urbanist infill development, let's say, composed of a number of encircling cluster neighborhoods, placed selectively in an open space field planted to maintain privacy, refresh the spirit, and recycle water.

5. Landscape as guide. Ancestral Puebloan/Pueblo builders rarely, if ever, placed built environments on land that they needed for agriculture. They let topography and its relationship to the sun, the patterns of the seasons, water, and places of religious power determine where they placed their buildings and laid out their fields. Much like what's known as sieve, or overlay, mapping today, which sifts out land appropriate for development, ancient builders were alert to every advantage the land could give them. They must have analyzed a site by identifying all the land they didn't want to build on, and then made use of the rest in whatever way sustained their survival. Ancestral Puebloan site planners would not place buildings in the middle of fruitful land, nor in places susceptible to flooding or in places where they would have to bear the full brunt of the wind. The land and weather informed them. And they were predisposed to pay attention because they understood that to go against what their surroundings offered, a high price would have to be paid.

6. Waste not water. That frugality and conservation were survival skills well honed by even the relatively extravagant Chaco Ancestral Puebloans is more than a powerful possibility. In the desert there simply aren't enough resources to squander. Marginal environments require minimum waste and maximum reuse. Combining Ancestral Puebloan/Pueblo traditional thriftiness with what the authors of *Natural Capitalism* would call "biomimicry," water was recycled and dampness mulched in countless different ways. Rain was channeled, fields flooded, dammed, and preserved. New Urbanist desert enclaves with cluster housing, enclosed plaza and patio spaces, and surrounding open space could both adapt to and shape topography just enough to divert rainwater and recycle it into tree ponds, flower beds, and irrigation canals that could form linear gardens throughout a complex of buildings. By making the recycling of water the determining design criteria, New Urbanist enclaves in desert Southwestern cities could become models for innovation in not only water management and integrated garden environments, but also in the conservation and self-sustaining activities of permaculture and gray water management.

7. Don't create blockages. Just as the body's energies, electrochemical messages, and liquids must keep flowing or eventually cause the body to become fatally sick, so must the built environment not be allowed to impede the flow of natural forces at work on the land, or exacerbate their damaging effects, especially those of water and wind. In recent sprawl developments in the desert landscape outside Albuquerque in the booming town of Rio Rancho, developers cleared a large parcel of land of its scrub and grasses. The denuded landscape was left thus "prepared" and waiting for construction crews for more than a year. The sand and dust storms that were whipped up from that site could be seen and felt all over the city and, though no measurements could be made, contributed considerably to Albuquerque's dust-polluted air. Perhaps the most amazing fact about the builders and lenders in the desert West is how little anyone understands about aquifers and how they are recharged. In Albuquerque, again, it's thought that the Rio Grande charges only a small portion of the aquifer beneath the city and that large arroyos out of the mountains have been feeding and topping off the aquifer in the eastern part of the city for millennia. Many of those arroyos now are concrete chutes that not only speed up the flow of runoff down to the river, but completely block its reabsorption back into the water table. Obviously, New Urbanist enclaves based on Ancestral Puebloan principles would neither leave land barren, ready for erosion, nor prevent the draining, pooling, and slow moving of water through its precincts. The trick with water is always to minimize its damage and keep it moving, while at the same time retaining and recycling it.

8. Culture and landscape. Ancestral Puebloan/Pueblo built environments can be described as a seamless integration between the built, the tended, and the "natural" environment. Baker Morrow's garden metaphor helps us understand how the ancient built landscape in the Southwest not only reflected but reinforced the Pueblo worldview of humanity's synonymity with nature. Euro-American built environments in the desert reflect industrial culture with its emphasis on intervention and radical alteration of landscapes rather than cooperation with them. Survival and conservation-oriented New Urbanist cluster neighborhoods in the desert would serve symbolically to signify and reinforce "alternative" and highly adaptive tendencies in Euro-American culture: our pragmatism and willingness to do whatever works, even if it might entail looking "backward" in time to technologically simpler and more elegant solutions to common environmental challenges; our intellectual and problem solving omnivorousness, which might allow us to respect and make use of knowledge from other cultures to help us cope with increasingly harsh situations; and, finally, our indomitable optimism, arising from a "can do" subculture of science and engineering, despite the hopelessness their often ham-fisted approach can cause.

These alternative tendencies in our culture, which mitigate, to some extent, our fascination with force in all its forms, from bulldozers to atom bombs to colonialism, could help us come to understand that our current building practices in the Southwest are not survivable in a period of high energy costs, drought, overused rivers, and depleting aquifers. We have a model of survivability right under our noses in the effectiveness and efficiencies of our cultural neighbors who have survived here in one form or another for more than two thousand years.

References Cited

Bol, Marsha C.

1998 *North, South, East, West: American Indians and the Natural World.* Pittsburgh: Carnegie Museum of Natural History.

Cajete, Gregory

1999 *A People's Ecology: Explorations in Sustainable Living.* Santa Fe, NM: Clear Light Publishers.

2000 *Native Science: Natural Laws of Interdependence.* Santa Fe, NM: Clear Light Publishers.

deBuys, William

1985 *Enchantment and Exploitation: The Life and Hard Times of a New Mexico Mountain Range.* Albuquerque: University of New Mexico Press.

Hall, G. Emlen

2002 *High and Dry: The Texas–New Mexico Struggle for the Pecos River.* Albuquerque: University of New Mexico Press.

Hawken, Paul, Amory Lovins, and L. Hunter Lovins

1999 *Natural Capitalism: Creating the Next Industrial Revolution.* Boston: Little, Brown.

Jackson, Wes

1996 *Becoming Native to This Place.* Washington, DC: Counterpoint.

Lekson, Stephen H.

1999 *The Chaco Meridian: Centers of Political Power in the Ancient Southwest.* Walnut Creek, CA: AltaMira Press.

Leopold, Aldo

1987 *A Sand County Almanac.* Introduction by Robert Finch. New York: Oxford University Press.

Lyndon, Donlyn

2000 Landscape as Mentor. *Places* 13 (3): 4–11.

Morrow, Baker H., and V. B. Price, eds.

1997 *Anasazi Architecture and American Design.* Albuquerque: University of New Mexico Press.

Nassauer, Joan Iverson

1997 *Placing Nature: Culture and Landscape Ecology.* Washington, DC: Island Press.

Nazarea, Virginia D., ed.

1999 *Ethnoecology: Situated Knowledge/Located Lives.* Tucson: University of Arizona Press.

Ortiz, Alfonso, ed.
1979 *Handbook of North American Indians*. Vol. 9, *Southwest*. Washington, DC: Smithsonian Institute.

Reisner, Marc
1993 *Cadillac Desert: The American West and Its Disappearing Water*. New York: Penguin.

Sabini, Meredith, ed.
2001 *The Nature Writings of C. G. Jung*. Berkeley, CA: North Atlantic Books.

Scurlock, Dan
1998 *From the Rio to the Sierra: An Environmental History of the Middle Rio Grande Basin*. Fort Collins, CO: Rocky Mountain Research Station, Forest Service, U.S. Department of Agriculture.

Stuart, David E.
2000 *Anasazi America: Seventeen Centuries on the Road from Center Place*. Albuquerque: University of New Mexico Press.

Chapter Thirteen

The Chaco Ancestral Puebloans

Lessons Learned

by David E. Stuart

The collapse of Chaco Canyon as the "capital" of Ancestral Puebloan high culture in the A.D. 1150s was brought about not only by a drastic change in weather patterns, but also, perhaps, by the trap of uncontrolled growth, social hierarchy, political rigidity, and agricultural insensitivity to landscape. Pueblo peoples worked strenuously and successfully never to find themselves in such a position again. Archaeologist David Stuart draws a startling and compelling parallel between the inefficient power dynamics at Chaco and what he sees as a similar situation in modern America, one in which farmland is ultimately neglected in favor of sprawl development and in which community harmony is sacrificed by a growing split between haves and have-nots.

What is now New Mexico has been inhabited for more than ten thousand years. Its Native peoples celebrated at least eight millennia as hunters and gathers before corn, beans, and squash were introduced from Mexico. Once introduced, small plots of casually tended crops supplemented the ancient hunting-gathering economy for centuries. Knowledge of agricultural techniques gradually advanced and the Southwest's population grew, due primarily to modest increases in food production. Eventually the enormous space needed for foraging became scarce. So, shortly after the birth of Christ, some people settled into modest seasonal villages of two or three dug-out pit houses to farm and forage, largely abandoning the dramatic nomadism of the older hunting-gathering way of life. This represented a significant shift in use of the vast, varied Four Corners landscape.

Farming, Foraging, and Trading, A.D. 300-800

From among these Native farmers arose the distinctive village culture in northwestern New Mexico that archaeologists a century ago labeled "the Anasazi." The ecological and logistic challenges to this lifestyle were dominated by spotty irregular rainfall, variable growing seasons (especially in the uplands above 6,000 feet), and a limited repertoire of cultigens to plant in a wide variety of farming situations.

The greatest risks to a given family were overdependence on one crop and lack of midsummer rain when the corn was tasseling, which was needed to ensure full cob development. The worst scenario would have been a winter season of scarcity when a family's seed corn was actually eaten, leaving nothing to plant in the spring. It should come as no surprise that archaeologists now find traces of food remains in these farming hamlets that provide hard evidence of a mixed food economy—foraging, farming, and hunting.

Farming by itself was simply too risky. As a consequence, these farmers took another eight centuries to refine the agricultural, technological, and social foundations of what was to become the fabulous society that created Pueblo Bonito at Chaco Canyon (figure 13.1). Those foundations included both imports and local development of new varieties of larger-cobbed corn, improved farming techniques and implements, the production of pottery, and a more complex social order. Over time, that complex social order came to depend increasingly on trade among isolated, far-flung villages. The trade between scattered villages in slightly different environments reduced the risks of hunger. When one was fortunate, the rains came and some of the small harvest surplus could be traded for lovely black-on-white bowls made twenty or thirty miles away. In a bad year, one made pottery for trade to others. In a good year, corn was traded out for bowls from other districts. It should come as no surprise that both trade and successive changes in pottery styles increased dramatically between A.D. 500 and 800.

The larger-cobbed corn produced more food for the same investment of labor, making occasional surpluses available to trade. For example, long-rooted varieties of corn could be planted in sandy soil. Other varieties were probably drought resistant or fast-maturing. Better farming techniques also enhanced food production relative to labor invested. Corn, beans, and squash were sometimes planted together in little hillocks. Each hillock became a microenvironment. The beans climbed the cornstalks and the large squash leaves shaded the soil from parching midsummer sun. Larger, flatter grinding surfaces on the stone manos and metates (specialized forms of mortar and pestle) used to grind corn into flour made that work more efficient, and pottery quite dramatically revolutionized the

Fig. 13.1 Pueblo Bonito, Chaco Canyon. Photo by Baker H. Morrow.

ancient stone-boiling method of cooking that had previously required large quantities of fuel and many tedious steps. By the eighth century community houses and religious chambers, called kivas, had been added to many small villages—clear signs that religious and social ties were beginning to bind individual families together into well-organized communities.

During these eight centuries Ancestral Puebloan farmers relied on many clever incremental technological and logistical efficiencies and myriad local trading arrangements to manage risk, sustain their farming communities, and permit modest growth. This attention to efficiency was a direct cultural legacy of their hunter-gatherer ancestors. Hunter-gatherers have the most efficient societies on earth—they are typically small, waste little, and resist growth. But Ancestral Puebloan farmers had grown substantially in numbers by about A.D. 800. They therefore faced new challenges unknown to their foraging ancestors.

Growth, Surplus, and "Market Diversification," A.D. 800-1000

By the ninth century, Ancestral Puebloan society faced a problem that simple efficiencies could not solve. As farmers, these people depended on midsummer rainfall to nurture their corn during its critical tasseling phase. Yet, in the Southwest, rainfall is not only spotty and variable from year to year, but the period around A.D. 750–850 was one of dramatically variable precipitation. To complicate matters even more, the annual patterns of precipitation north and west of Chaco Canyon were different from those to the south and east, which were (and are) shaped by the late June and July summer monsoons from the Gulf of Mexico (Cordell 1997:385–87). This meant that optimal varieties of corn, farming techniques, and agricultural risks/successes in any given year varied as one moved from the Ancestral Puebloans' northwestern (Utah) to their southeastern (Albuquerque) frontier.

By the A.D. 800s, people in several of Chaco Canyon's small villages already realized that harvests were more abundant to the northwest in some years, while in others, the southeast prospered. To take advantage of this phenomenon, those villages, among them Pueblo Bonito, dramatically expanded the number of their storage rooms (Vivian 1990:157), becoming "great houses," and acted as intermediaries—trading surplus corn from a district that had prospered for dried meat, pottery, or other handcrafts from one that had not (Stuart 2000:63). Thus Chaco Canyon society was born, creating an ancient trading center that gained enormous political and religious influence by joining once isolated farming communities scattered across the vast San Juan Basin into *one* vast economic system.

By establishing a system that regularly moved surplus corn from the fortunate to the unfortunate in exchange for other goods, the Chacoans lowered the risk that any one farm family would be left to starve or lack the necessary seed corn to plant again in spring. At this time more organized district-wide trading patterns emerged and Chaco Canyon no longer needed to manufacture much of its own pottery. Over the next several centuries, Chaco Canyon became powerful because it introduced a new level of security to the farming enterprise—much as investing in a mutual fund of many stocks is less risky than investing in only one stock.

Almost exactly a millennium after these events at Chaco, an emerging American nation sensing its own "manifest destiny" pushed westward and swallowed up an entire continent to create an even larger economic system that muted risk by virtue of diverse geography, weather, and a huge, interconnected economy. In this sense we are all like the Chacoans.

Chacoan society's classic logistical response to spotty rainfall introduced enough security to unleash an explosive wave of growth during the A.D. 800s and 900s. Thousands of new farmsteads, called "unit pueblos," were founded. In fact, almost half of all the archaeological sites ever created during the San Juan Basin's ten thousand years of prehistory were built in just the two hundred years between roughly A.D. 850 and 1050 (Stuart and Gauthier [1981] 1988:70). In today's terms, "housing starts" were at an all-time high. This worked, so long as farmers in outlying districts expanded their agricultural base more rapidly than population increased. To do this they founded new farms with a vengeance and planted many more fields than could ever be expected to produce a harvest, given the spotty rains.

By the late A.D. 900s, the dramatic expansion slowed and Chacoan society paused. Population had grown too rapidly. The richest soils had already been farmed and the best sources of permanent water were already overtaxed. So new farms were established on more marginal soils (Cordell 1997:280). Malnutrition began to plague the farmers in some outlying districts. There is also clear osteological evidence of this at Chaco Canyon's own farmsteads (Akins 1986). In a century and a half, raw growth had simply used up the initial benefits of Chaco Canyon's economic and geographic solution to spotty, variable rainfall.

The Chaco Ancestral Puebloans: Complexity, Growth, and Infrastructure, A.D. 1000-1140

Chacoan society might have withered after this first blooming had climatic patterns not become more favorable, just in the nick of time, at about A.D. 1000. Thus began the Chacoan Millennium. For nearly 130 years, the crucial midsummer rains fell more reliably than they had ever fallen before—or have fallen since. Now more tasseling cornfields in more localities received the gift of rain each summer than ever before. Chacoan society could have used this reprieve to improve the lot of individual farmers and create new incremental efficiencies, but it did not. Instead it chose growth and power.

This second blooming was different from the first. Farmsteads did expand into many previously unfavorable localities. Archaeologist W. James Judge said it best twenty years ago when he argued in a now-classic paper that it was almost as if Chaco had expanded to use every shred of available ecological diversity in the San Juan Basin, then could grow no more (Judge 1979). After A.D. 1000, Chacoan society didn't just diversify ecologically. It became far more complex, instead of merely larger. More great houses were built in Chaco Canyon, so that by the A.D. 1070s there were a dozen immense structures in the canyon itself (figure 13.2). Pueblo Bonito had six hundred rooms and stood four stories tall. Though the Chacoans had neither horses nor wheeled vehicles, well-made roadways were built outward from Chaco Canyon and great houses were exported to many of the outlying farming districts.

Eventually there were more than a hundred Bonito-style great houses spread across the southern San Juan Basin, nearly all connected to the canyon by hundreds of miles of roadway. The great houses combined vast storage capacity with residential rooms and large kivas for religious ceremony (figure 13.3). Clearly, religion had become part of the "glue" that made Chacoan society function and grow. Eventually, religion was so important to Chacoan logistics that John Stein currently speaks of "religious landscapes" in Chacoan times (Stein 2000).

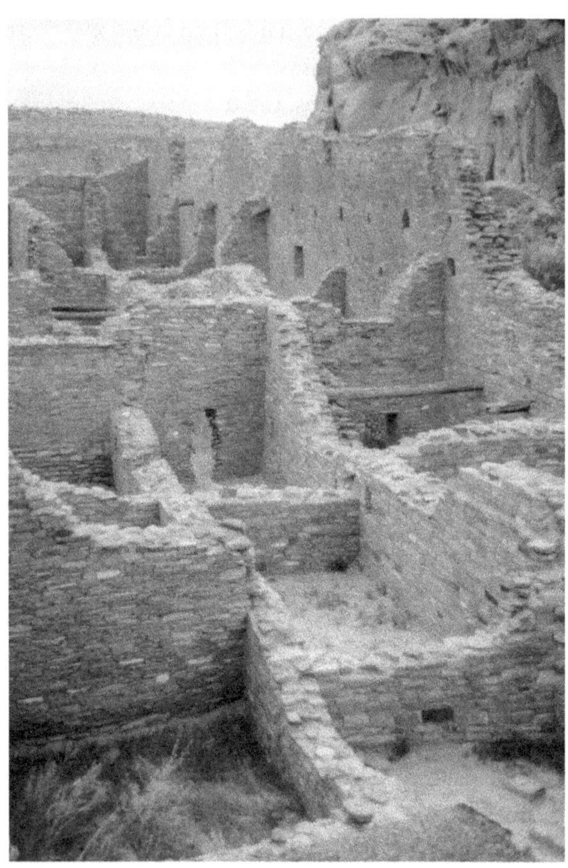

Fig. 13.2 Chetro Ketl great house, Chaco Canyon. Photo by Baker H. Morrow.

Archaeologist Steve Lekson estimated that it took *two million* man-hours to build the dozen or so great houses in Chaco Canyon (Lekson 1986). I estimate it took another sixteen to twenty-four million hours to build the outlying great houses. And how much labor did it take to build an estimated four hundred miles of surveyor-straight roadways averaging fifteen to thirty feet in width—a prepared sand/dirt road surface of more than forty million square feet? No one knows. Archaeologists call this period (ca. A.D. 900–1100) the Chaco Phenomenon, and it was phenomenal.

Chacoan society had become huge, complex, and powerful. Macaws, copper bells, and shell for *heishi* came from Mexico. Its trade network extended from southern Canada to the Gulf of Mexico, and southwest to the Sea of Cortés. But it also had become socially and economically stratified in the process. There were Chaco Canyon's great house elites, the outlier elites, and the farmers. The evidence from burials of the time—both the human bones and the grave offerings—are eloquent and irrefutable testimony to this stratification (Akins and Schelberg 1984).

Fig. 13.3 Pueblo Bonito plaza and great house, Chaco Canyon. Photo by Baker H. Morrow.

This complexity imposed great costs on Chacoan Society, and some of those costs eventually led to Chaco's undoing. At the height of its power in the A.D. 1070s, Chaco's great house inhabitants averaged 1.8 inches taller than those living in the farmsteads nearby (Akins 1986:135). At Pueblo Bonito, 9.5 percent of children died by age five. In the canyon's farmsteads 26 percent were dead by the same age, while 45 percent died in the outlying farming districts (61). A baby born at Pueblo Bonito was three or four times more likely to survive than was one born at a farmstead!

By the A.D. 1070s, farmers in the overused Red Mesa Valley, which straddles Interstate 40 between McCartys and Gallup, New Mexico, were in desperate circumstances. Malnutrition and infant mortality were endemic. Estimates suggest that infant mortality was about 50 percent, and the local farming population may have actually begun to decline at this time (Tainter and Gilleo 1980:86). Some long-established and overworked farms were abandoned during this era and displaced farmers may have provided labor to build the roads.

Then at about A.D. 1090, nature temporarily withdrew its gift of reliable summer rains. A drought lasting about five years ensued. Desperation spread beyond the Red Mesa Valley to other farming communities. Chacoan society appears to have been temporarily immobilized, shocked by widespread crop failures that created hardship even among the elites. More farms were abandoned and seed corn undoubtedly became scarce. Finally the elites responded—building even more roads, ritual kivas, and great houses! Rather than adapt, they merely repeated the formula that had worked before. That formula dictated that they construct more roads, more kivas to host more ritual, and more great houses with their immense, unneeded storage capacity.

From the mid-1090s to about A.D. 1120, the canyon's great houses expanded to their final size and numerous kivas were built. Huge great houses and more roads were also built in newly developed districts to the north of Chaco Canyon. This strategy temporarily held much of elite Chacoan society together, but small farmers in the southern districts continued to walk away from failed farms, further reducing regional harvests. True, these last large construction projects may have again temporarily absorbed displaced surviving farmers, just as did the Civilian Conservation Corps (CCC) and Works Progress Administration (WPA) during the Great Depression, but they could not be supported for long as the great house storerooms emptied.

Then came the second major drought about A.D. 1130. Like "Okies" portrayed in John Steinbeck's *The Grapes of Wrath*, most remaining farmers walked away to start over in the uplands at ancestral places like Mesa Verde. Abandoned by the desperate farmers whose surpluses had once made it so powerful, Chacoan society collapsed. Raiding and warfare replaced the previous period of tranquility, and chaos prevailed. Some elites hung on, hungry and impoverished, in their great houses. Others established new, smaller Chaco-style communities near Colorado's Montezuma Valley and near Zuni. But within a generation the vestiges of pure Chacoan society had faded away.

The Fall of Chaco, A.D. 1090-1140, and the 1997 Nobel Prize in Economics

Chaco Canyon society was the grandest and most complex in ancient North America. At its peak, larger than any one European principality of the same era, it covered an expanse of more than fifty thousand square miles and included as many as twenty thousand farmsteads. How could a powerful society that had cleverly interconnected so many farms across its vast landscape to reduce economic risks have come undone so easily?

Since much of modern America still functions economically in close accord with the same general principles established by the Chacoans, we need to reflect on recent parallels. In 1997, Robert Merton and Myron Scholes won the Nobel Prize in Economics for their analytical model of market values and risk management in international investment strategies. They proposed that if one invested continually so as to maximize diversification of investments at a rate somewhat faster than the overall growth in international markets, financial risks could be reduced to negligible levels. They relied, in part, on the mathematics of the Japanese scholar Itoh to operationalize their theory into a working investment model. After winning the prize, Merton and several associates formed their own investment house, Long-term Capital Management.

Having won the coveted prize named after Alfred Nobel, the gentleman whose initial fame and fortune derived from putting real horsepower into high explosives for military applications, they then sought investors to help them do their version of the same thing—put real horsepower into international investing for high rollers. It all went swimmingly for about two years. They and their investors rapidly infused great sums into ever more diversified international stock holdings and even more rapidly increased their young corporation's wealth as a consequence. All this while remaining seemingly immune to the vicissitudes of mere mortals' daily economic reality. Cool theory. Cool prize. Cool megabucks. Life was good. If only it had gone on forever.

But it didn't.

Two fundamental problems emerged as Merton and company approached maximum diversification in international markets. First, it got harder and harder to stay ahead of the overall market. (Now go back and reread Jim Judge's brilliant characterization of Ancestral Puebloan ecological expansion!) Second, the unexpected happened. A currency crisis hit hard in Singapore, seriously injuring the value of Long-term Capital's Southeast Asia holdings, followed closely by the collapse of the ruble in Russia. (Now reread the short passages on the Chacoan droughts of A.D. 1090 and 1130!)

Long-term Capital lost money after these bubbles burst even more rapidly than it had made money on the way up. Such is the chimera of a growth model gone bad. Growth models are sweet on the front end but brutal when they abruptly come undone. As any seasoned administrator or business person knows, it is far easier to expand/grow from a small base than it is to sustain the monster after you have grown it to full size. Merton and colleagues discovered this the hard way just several years ago. The Chacoans had already been there and done that by A.D. 1140.

Chacoan behavior and the Nobel Prize investment strategy were virtually identical. Chaco had expanded its farming enterprise in a frenzy of growth during the A.D. 800–900s and again throughout the first half of the eleventh century. Chacoan "market holdings" consisted of decorated pottery and stored corn. Its "international market" was the greater San Juan Basin. When Chaco had nearly maximized its farming enterprise, its natural growth slowed down and it became more vulnerable. Then two unexpected droughts about thirty years apart destroyed it utterly. True, the Chacoans attempted to impose an artificial growth cycle in the late 1000s, but it had begun to fail even before the droughts of the A.D. 1130s. The Chacoans were as brilliant as the most brilliant economic strategists of our modern age. But both made the same fundamental mistake. They focused primarily on growth instead of sustainability. And the growth, of course, had been based on the continually expanding productivity of their garden plots and farms.

The Uplands, Once Again Farming, Foraging, and Trading, A.D. 1140-1300

Descendants of Chaco's farmers who fled to the uplands after its fall (Mesa Verde, Bandelier, Gila Cliff, El Morro, Zuni, and Canyon de Chelly) eventually became today's Puebloan peoples. Like modern America, Chacoan society had incorporated linguistically and culturally diverse peoples at its height. By A.D. 1500, their descendants formed many separate and self-sufficient pueblos, focused not on growth and power, but on efficiency, equality, and stability as core values. But before that came about, hard lessons in land use were learned in the uplands.

Upland life in the late A.D. 1100s was fraught with conflict, hunger, and tragedy. Chacoan society had come to depend disproportionately on surplus crops of large-cobbed corn that grew well in the warmer, longer growing seasons of the central and southern San Juan Basin between 5,500 and 6,500 feet in elevation. But the flight into the uplands took survivors to elevations of between 6,500 and 8,000 feet above sea level.

The move to higher elevations, particularly for those who went north toward the Mesa Verde, brought them more rain and winter snows to offset remembrances of the two Chacoan droughts of the 1090s and 1130s. As we noted, the first farmers to leave Chaco also escaped from the hungry and increasingly desperate mass of population in the Chacoan core. Sadly, their respite was short lived, for they simply could not grow the customary quantities of large-cobbed corn in the uplands due to shorter growing seasons and cool nighttime temperature. This created an ecological and demographic disaster that quickly degenerated into appalling conflict during the mid-1100s. Fighting and raiding seemed to have been at their worst in the Gallina Highlands along the west face of the Jemez Mountains, where one estimate puts nearly 40 percent of adults dying through violence during this time (Dick 1976). Clearly, the Ancestral Puebloan population was reduced during the twelfth century.

In short, the uplands forced the Ancestral Puebloans into yet another, different use of the landscape. As the worst of the violence raged, families in isolated pit-house settlements reverted to the mixed economy of growing smaller-cobbed corn, supplemented by the aggressive hunting and foraging that their Basketmaker ancestors had relied upon five centuries earlier. Trade networks broke down almost completely for a time.

When the worst of the violence had passed, new pottery styles like St. John's Polychrome were developed (ca. A.D. 1175), numerous larger (ten to twenty rooms) aboveground pueblos were constructed throughout the northern Southwest at elevations from 6,500 to 7,500 feet, and an upland trade network in polychrome bowls emerged. This trade connected distant but ecologically similar localities. This strategy did not completely solve the need for ecological diversity but lowered local community risks to a degree, evening out latitudinal variations in upland precipitation by trading from south (St. John's and Springerville, Arizona; Zuni and Cebolleta Mesa, New Mexico) to north (southeastern Utah, southwestern Colorado, Mesa Verde, Taos) and vice versa.

The upland method of risk management worked well enough that it ushered in the era of "Cliff Palace" construction that characterized the early to mid-1200s A.D. In contrast to Chacoan great houses, the cliff palaces primarily served surrounding local farmers who withdrew to their safety from mesa-top farmsteads in late fall and winter. This protected their harvests from raiding. No roads were built in the uplands and the huge kivas and religious gatherings that anthropologists believe once helped Chacoan society to maintain its regional integration ceased as Chaco faded away (Sebastian 1992).

By the mid-1200s, a number of large (fifty to five hundred rooms) mesa-top pueblos were being built at roughly 7,200 feet in elevation and larger-cobbed corn was again being grown. Whether the climate warmed up temporarily and/or new varieties of fast-growing larger-cobbed corn were developed is not currently known. Just as post-Chacoan upland society seemed to have gotten on a solid footing about a century after the awful exodus from the San Juan Basin, upland precipitation began to fluctuate dramatically. It deepened into serious, spotty droughts as the A.D. 1270s wore on.

Still, upland society was much more fragile at this point than Chaco had been. The mixed subsistence economy of corn, beans, squash, and gathered wild resources in the uplands, coupled with cool nighttime temperatures, had reduced the Ancestral Puebloan farmer's capacity to generate crop surpluses large enough to provide critical multiyear storage. The ecological similarity between one upland district and another simply provided less risk buffering than had the larger, more diverse Chacoan trade system. Finally, judging from human skeletal remains of the period, nutritional stress seems to have haunted upland communities. Infant mortality remained dangerously high.

As a consequence, evidence suggests that regional population loss characterized the late A.D. 1200s (Hunter-Anderson 1979:181; Stuart and Gauthier [1981] 1988:53), and entire upland districts were depopulated—never again to be farmed by the Ancestral Puebloans. The districts most completely abandoned primarily faced west (like Mesa Verde), so they did not benefit as greatly from those diminished summer monsoons that did reach the Four Corners during these droughts.

East-facing districts, like the Pajarito Plateau (Bandelier National Monument) fared the best.

In the east-facing districts, survivors of the droughts came down from their mesa tops in the late 1200s, built pueblos on the canyon floors below, then systematically followed the more reliable canyon-bottom streams (most flowed in an easterly direction) until they came to the larger streams and rivers at lower elevations (the Rio Grande, Taos Creek, the Chama, and the Rios San Jose, Zuni, Pescado, and Nutria, for example [Stuart 1989]). This drought-induced shift in settlement forced yet another major experiment in use of the landscape.

Rivers and the Search for Sustainable Communities, A.D. 1300-1500

Two centuries of trial and error followed. Life at river's edge presented its own problems. The major rivers were not dammed then as they are now and many ran dry some years but flood-wild in others. As a consequence, some communities sought out lower-elevation environments similar to upland ones, like Arroyo Hondo near Santa Fe. But clinging to the past simply did not work well. The lower ecological diversity made most of these communities as fragile as those in the true uplands had been. After struggling for about two centuries, they faded away, victims of poor risk management and infant mortality as high as that suffered by the Chacoan farmers three hundred years before (Palkovich 1980:23).

Nearly all those pueblo communities that survived the 1400s had several elements in common (Stuart 2000:163–68). They were adjacent to permanent streams and rivers. Each surviving individual pueblo reduced its *own* agricultural risks by holding diverse lands from rivers to the mountains, not by re-creating another regional economy. They expanded the diversity of their crops and their planting techniques. They also invested labor and ingenuity in infrastructure that produced food efficiently, such as irrigation systems, reservoirs, and grid gardens. They never again built roads and monuments to power, or permitted a community that let some starve while others prospered. They had become more egalitarian than the Chacoans. They were also quite homogeneous compared to Chaco and a community member's role and rights were balanced by very specific obligations to the pueblo.

Trade moved primarily along the narrow riverine corridors and was not used to manage ecological/economic risk in the way it had been by the Chacoans. As just noted, those risks were managed by obsessively holding diverse lands from the mountains to the rivers, crosscutting all of the regional lifezones. How well did this model of risk management work? Well enough that by A.D. 1500 infant mortality in the surviving Pueblos was as low as it had been for Pueblo Bonito's great house elites nearly five hundred years before. Finally, the later Ancestral

Puebloans had brought the benefits once enjoyed by the mighty to virtually every family in the community.

Survival: Then, A.D. 1500, and Now

The arrival of the Spanish in the late 1500s, and the new diseases they brought, tested Chaco's descendants again, as did raiding by Apache, Navajo, Comanche, and Ute tribes. The introduced diseases took a demographic toll that makes any other historical interaction pale by comparison. By 1706, the year Albuquerque was founded, just eighteen pueblos (excluding Hopi) survived with a total population of only 6,440 people (Schroeder 1979:254). This was all that remained of the once fabulous Chacoan society. Twenty thousand communities now cut down to fewer than twenty! Yet, against all demographic and social odds, each of these pueblos, save one (Pecos), have survived intact to this day. How? By applying the lessons learned from the 1300s to the 1500s and working actively at sustaining their communities. As of this writing, there are over sixty thousand Pueblo people in New Mexico.

And what has Chaco Canyon and the Pueblo experience to do with "our" modern American society? Well, like the Chacoans, we seem to have forgotten to care for the landscape, focusing instead on uncontrolled growth and political power. As America has grown larger, more heterogeneous, and more complex, our sense of community seems to have weakened. Indeed, some among us are hungry, even as others prosper. We, too, build roads and monuments as "make-work projects" but neglect farmland. Our best soils and our most reliable sources of water are already at risk. There are recurring shortages of fuel and electricity.

And what about America's children? Did you know that a baby born (1990) in Marin County, California, north of San Francisco, was four times more likely to live to age one than a child born (1990) in the delta country of Jefferson County, Mississippi? That California child was born to a household four times richer and four times more likely to have a college-educated parent than the Mississippi child (Stuart 2000:192–93). While we all live better nowadays than Chaco's desperate farmers, there were actually *greater* disparities in life's possibilities between children born in those California and Mississippi counties in 1990 than there were between Chaco's farmhands and great house elites in A.D. 1100. Given the risks that America is currently taking, can we really be certain that American society will survive for another millennium, as have the Puebloan descendants since Chaco's fall?

If we truly intend to maintain "modern" American society for any substantial length of time, we, too, will have to work at community. Further, we must treat not just our own landscape with much more respect, but also the earth's—now economically globalizing. In every hour of peril, the Ancestral Puebloans were forced to restrategize their basic relationships to the land. One day, so shall we.

In twenty years or less, the world's economy will have completely globalized. Our national version of the Nobel Prize growth model will again fail. There will be no way to continue recent economic growth and diversification at a rate faster than overall growth in the world economy. Given our size, complexity, and appetite for energy and resources, something will go wrong—it's a matter of when, not if. In short, America's version of industrial society desperately needs to develop new economic, political, and social strategies to reduce our long-term risks. Moreover, those strategies had better be based on sustainability rather than raw, uncontrolled growth. That lesson, rather than their magnificent buildings and pottery, is the Chacoans' real gift to all of us.

The full story of the Chaco Ancestral Puebloans and their descendants, on which this article is based, appears in Dr. Stuart's *Anasazi America*, published by the University of New Mexico Press (2000).

References Cited

Akins, Nancy J.

1986 *A Biocultural Approach to Human Burials from Chaco Canyon, New Mexico.* Reports of the Chaco Center, no. 9. Santa Fe, NM: Division of Cultural Research, National Park Service.

———, and John D. Schelberg

1984 Evidence for Organizational Complexity as Seen from the Mortuary Practices at Chaco Canyon. In *Recent Research on Chacoan Prehistory*, ed. W. James Judge and John D. Schelberg, 89–102. Reports of the Chaco Center, no. 8. Santa Fe, NM: Division of Cultural Research, National Park Service.

Cordell, Linda S.

1997 *Archaeology of the Southwest.* 2nd ed. San Diego: Academic Press.

Dick, Herbert W.

1976 *Archeological Excavations in the Llaves Area, Santa Fe National Forest, New Mexico, 1972–1974.* Archeological Report, no. 13. Albuquerque, NM: USDA Forest Service, Southwest Region.

Hunter-Anderson, R. L.

1979 LA 133. Explaining Residential Aggregation in the Northern Rio Grande: A Competition Reduction Model. In *Archeological Investigations in Cochiti Reservoir, New Mexico*, Vol. 4, ed. J. V. Biella and R. C. Chapman, 169–75. Albuquerque: Office of Contract Archeology, University of New Mexico.

Judge, W. James

1979 The Development of a Complex Cultural Ecosystem in the Chaco Basin, New Mexico. In *Scientific Research in the National Parks*, Vol. 2, ed. Robert M. Linn, 901–5. Washington, DC: National Park Service.

Lekson, Stephen H.

1986 *Great Pueblo Architecture of Chaco Canyon, New Mexico.* Albuquerque: University of New Mexico Press.

Palkovich, Ann M.

1980 *The Arroyo Hondo Skeletal and Mortuary Remains.* Santa Fe, NM: School

of American Research Press.
Schroeder, Albert H.
1979 Pueblos Abandoned in Historic Times. In *Handbook of North American Indians*. Vol. 9, *Southwest*, ed. Alfonso Ortiz, 236–54. Washington, DC: Smithsonian Institution.
Sebastian, Lynne
1992 *The Chaco Anasazi: Sociopolitical Evolution in the Prehistoric Southwest.* Cambridge: Cambridge University Press.
Stein, John R.
2000 Comments Made during a Computer Presentation of Chacoan Landscapes to UNM Class "Anasazi, Pueblo and Modern America." Albuquerque, New Mexico, November.
Stuart, David E.
1989 *The Magic of Bandelier*. Santa Fe, NM: Ancient City Press.
2000 *Anasazi America: Seventeen Centuries on the Road from Center Place.* Albuquerque: University of New Mexico Press.
———, and Rory P. Gauthier.
[1981] 1988 *Prehistoric New Mexico: Background for Survey*. Albuquerque: University of New Mexico Press.
Tainter, Joseph A., and D. A. Gilleo
1980 *Cultural Resources Overview Mount Taylor Area, New Mexico*. Albuquerque, NM: USDA Forest Service and Bureau of Land Management.
Vivian, R. Gwinn
1990 *The Chacoan Prehistory of the San Juan Basin*. San Diego: Academic Press.

Suggested Readings

Cordell, Linda S.
Archaeology of the Southwest. 2nd ed. San Diego: Academic Press.
Morrow, Baker H., and V. B. Price, eds.
1997 *Anasazi Architecture and American Design*. Albuquerque: University of New Mexico Press.
Ortiz, Alfonso
1969 *The Tewa World*. Chicago: University of Chicago Press.
Stuart, David E.
1989 *The Magic of Bandelier*. Santa Fe, NM: Ancient City Press.
2000 *Anasazi America: Seventeen Centuries on the Road from Center Place.* Albuquerque: University of New Mexico Press.
Vivian, R. Gwinn
1990 *The Chacoan Prehistory of the San Juan Basin*. San Diego: Academic Press.

Epilogue

by Baker H. Morrow

At Wupatki in Arizona there is a blowhole—a curious natural geological feature—just a few steps away from the ball court. Blowholes spew cold streams of air straight into the sky from the bowels of the earth, and they are as rare an occurrence as any of us is ever likely to see in North America. Powered by a deep cavern complex that no one quite understands, the blowhole at Wupatki, only six inches square, is the breath of the god of the winds according to local Pueblo lore. A mysterious and singular landscape feature, we can stand by it and imagine how it cooled the sweating faces of the players after a hard game some seven hundred years ago in this most northerly of all Southwestern ball court sites.

Religion or recreation?

Social event for the local townsfolk or simply a curious imported ritual from the far south?

The ball court and the blowhole are good examples of the remarkable way in which the ancient Puebloan landscape is slowly beginning to reveal itself to us as we learn to recognize its component parts.

"We don't understand how they farmed these dunes," says renowned archaeologist Michael P. Marshall as he talks about a ridgetop pueblo in the Chupadera Mesa country of central New Mexico. The Chupadera people, who built a large complex of towns south of Mountainair in the thirteenth and fourteenth centuries, are often called the Tompiros or Humanos. First described by Fray Alonso de Benavides and other early Spaniards about A.D. 1630, their town complexes, consisting of two or more related pueblos plus outlying or associated villages and field houses, are constructed in the local limestone and sometimes of puddled adobe. They are scattered profusely around the fringes of the Chupadera country.

One of the great questions hanging over these poorly known people, the builders of improbable towns in this very wild and remote country, is this: where did they drink? Modern expeditions to the old Tompiro settlements find town after town on hilltops or along ridges windswept and bleaching in the sun, without a seep or a pool or a spring to be seen.

Walk-in wells?

Probably. But there is only the barest hint of these on the surface now. And the Tompiros built check-dams (today they would look to us like cattle tanks) in the bottoms of dusty arroyos and hollows. These we can sometimes make out.

Was the climate wetter those six or seven centuries ago? Possibly, in some places. Certainly colder, with all the Northern Hemisphere in the grip of the Little Ice Age. Perhaps colder equaled wetter.

These towns and hamlets are sometimes ringed with long terraces planted in wolfberry, or by ancient plantings of cholla, fourwing saltbush, or algerita. Singleseed juniper is everywhere, producing its nourishing berries, modest roof and wall timbers, and tough bark strips with a dozen uses for a Tompiro town.

These plants all look wild to modern eyes. But in the Tompiro country they were probably as hard used, as widely planted, as commonly understood, and as beloved as any landscape plants of the thirteenth century, as manipulated by and useful to people in their everyday lives as crabapple trees and red raspberries would be today.

These durable tree and shrub species flourish in the cold. They resist droughts. And they often grow just fine in sand, silt, clay, or rocky soil. They are just the ticket for the harshness of central New Mexico—or almost anywhere else in Arizona or New Mexico, for that matter—if you're thinking of good landscape plantings.

Food, shade, shelter from the wind, medicine, beauty. Clothing, town construction, handicrafts, firewood, weaponry. And religion. The Ancestral Puebloans and the Pueblos, their modern descendants, have utilized the flora they have known in the Southwest for all the same purposes that people everywhere have used plants for thousands of years.

And they have combined plants with the systematic development of open space (and often roadways or paths) in their towns and villages to fashion several kinds of distinct landscape forms. Their patios and courtyards, plazas and terraces, are the most obvious of these. We recognize these landscape features, and we have names for them. But the Puebloan grid and mulch gardens, the ability of Ancestral Puebloans to utilize what seems to European eyes to be hot and barren wasteland as they create one ingenious series of planting plots after another, and their subtle religious works, developed in these cultivated landscapes as key elements of Puebloan social systems, will all bear much further study.

What shall we call these landscape elements, and what do they say about the people who made them?

Where one person sees a cliff face punctuated with random markings, another smiles and nods and leaves pinches of cornmeal in appreciation for clear notes on proper conduct and religious observance. A casual visitor to a red Southwestern mesa notices a scatter of schist in the midst of some sandstone rubble and walks on; the next person to pass by sees in the same stone pieces a stack of hoes and digging-stick tips along a dry stream at the edge of a hollow that is a still-functioning fourteenth-century garden.

Subtlety is the hallmark of the traditional Ancestral Puebloan landscape.

Out in the hilly countryside around an old pueblo we will also find many edible and otherwise useful plants that were "encouraged" by the ancient Southwesterners and used regularly in their diets or handicrafts or trade. Among these are prickly pear, Gambel oak, currants, cotton, tobacco, chokecherries, sand plums, buffalo berries, and a number of other favorites. Yucca and agave, sand dropseed and Indian ricegrass, and juniper and piñon were much appreciated for their shade, fiber, flowers, seeds, and fruit, and for their cheerful ability to survive droughts and the endless ravages of the wind.

Are these plants truly domestic? Are they garden species?

Sort of, and sometimes.

It is perhaps best to think of them as growing in woodland gardens—or in stretches of shrubby desert upland—without walls or fences. As is true of many other elements of Ancestral Puebloan landscape architecture, they may not fit comfortably into modern concepts of how people should systematically develop the open spaces of their cities and towns. Contemporary people, using European languages and ideas to describe them, frequently don't know what they are. We moderns barely see them at all, and when we do they are out of focus. We cannot imagine them at the height of their beauty and usefulness. More's the pity, we cannot know what the people who built these handsome landscape features actually called them.

They are parts of the Ancestral Puebloan landscape that we don't quite understand, as are the gardens that we know once flourished in the sand, green and shimmering in the bright sunshine of May and June. How might they have done so?

By working to better understand the planning and design that went into the creation of the open spaces in and around the venerable Ancestral Puebloan towns, we may gain a little insight into the real relationship of our own vast and blunt civilization with this dry country of mesas and plains. The simple truth of the matter, of course, is that in this sunswept place we all live in the midst of an ancient landscape of unusual garden-farms and small stone settlements, and it will tell us its story if we can sit quietly and listen.

Contributors

ANTHONY ANELLA is an architect, teacher, and writer working in Albuquerque, New Mexico. He is the author of *Saving the Ranch*, with John B. Wright.

KURT ANSCHUETZ is an archaeologist and specialist in ancient Tewa and Tiwa settlements and farming practices who works with the Rio Grande Foundation in Santa Fe, New Mexico.

MARY BEATH is a writer and award-winning poet and artist who has worked in Zuni, New Mexico. She is the author of *Refuge of Whirling Light.*

BRUCE BRADLEY is an archaeologist, author, and expert flintknapper currently teaching at the University of Exeter, England. His latest book is *The Fenn Cache*, with George Frison.

CAROL BRANDT is an ethnobotanist and the former program manager for the New Mexico Alliance for Graduate Education and the Professoriate at the University of New Mexico.

LOUIS A. HIEB is an author and professor at the University of Washington.

JAMES E. "JAKE" IVEY is a historian with the National Park Service in Santa Fe, New Mexico. He is the author of *In the Midst of a Loneliness.*

STEPHEN H. LEKSON has been an archaeologist with the Museum of New Mexico and the National Park Service. Currently curator of anthropology at the University of Colorado Museum, he is the author of *The Chaco Meridian.*

BAKER H. MORROW, FASLA, is the founding director of the Master's Program in Landscape Architecture at the University of New Mexico. He is the author of *Best Plants for New Mexico Gardens and Landscapes.*

V. B. PRICE, a poet and columnist, is the recipient of the Erna Fergusson Award for Outstanding Achievement of the Alumni Association of the University of New Mexico. He is the author of *Albuquerque: A City at the End of the World.*

KENNETH A. ROMIG is a landscape historian and landscape architect in Albuquerque, New Mexico.

DAVID E. STUART, former associate provost and vice president of the University of New Mexico, is a Southwest archaeologist with special interests in settlement development and decline. He is the author of *Anasazi America* and *The Guaymas Chronicles.*

RINA SWENTZELL, a member of Santa Clara Pueblo, is a writer and an art and architectural historian living in Santa Fe, New Mexico. She is the author of *To Touch the Past: The Painted Pottery of the Mimbres People*, with J. J. Brody.

Index

Page numbers in italic text indicate illustrations.

Abó, xix; dances of, 20–21; Espinoso Creek and, 20; irrigation ditch of, 23; jacal structures of, *19*; kivas of, 22; map of, *18*; Mute Stone Bench case of, 20–23; petroglyphs at, 20, *21*; pocket gardens of, 20–23; ritual landscape of, 22; sandstone of, 19; shrine at, *28*; Tompiro people of, 17, 18; trade of, 21; water at, *23*
Acer negundo (boxelder), 25
Acer saccharum (eastern sugar maple), 25
Acoma (Keres) people, 20
Acoma Pueblo, 2
Albright, Horace, 143
algerita, 25
amaranth. *See Amaranthus*
Amaranthus (amaranth), 22, 25, 26, 37, 66
AMREP Southwest Inc.: lawsuit against, 149; negligence of, 149–51; Rio Rancho city and, 149–50; River's Edge I housing development by, 146
Anasazi America (Stuart), 172
Ancestral Puebloan architecture: of Chaco Canyon, 152–53; of Mesa Verde, 151–52; Prudden on, 46; Rohn on, 47; stone masonry of, *177*
Ancestral Puebloan communities, 68; movement/relocation of, 40–41
Ancestral Puebloan landscape, 5; Bohrer on, 41; Colter on, 137–38; New Urbanism and, 169; reading of, 33–44; site planning of, 173–74; Varien on, 40, 41–42
Anderson, David, 11
Apocynum (dogbane), 37
archaeology: intraregional movements and, 4; transcontinental migration and, 4
Arendt, Randall G., 156
Arthur, Chester A., 119
Arts and Crafts movement: Colter architecture and, 134
ash. *See Fraxinus*
Atriplex (saltbush), 38
Aztec, 1, 10, 11

Bandelier, Adolph, 9–10
barley grass, 66
Basketmaker III, 39, 40; burned structures in, 35; landscape of, 36–37
bean, domestic. *See Phaseolus vulgaris*
Becoming Native to This Place (Jackson), 174, 179
beeweed. *See Cleome serrulata*
Benavides, Alonso de (Fray), 26
Bender, Barbara, 113–14
Benedict, Ruth, 2, 6
Bering Strait theory, 4
Berry, Michael, mobility study by, 5
BIA. *See* Bureau of Indian Affairs
Black Rock Dam, 91–92, 104
blazingstar. *See Mentzelia*
Bohrer, Vorsila, 41

boxelder. *See Acer negundo*
bugseed. *See Corispermum*
Bureau of American Ethnology, 114
Bureau of Indian Affairs (BIA), xviii, 90, 91; Santa Clara Day School and, 125
Bureau of Reclamation, 91

Cactaceae, 34
Cajete, Gregory, 174, 178
Casas Grandes (Paquimé), 2, *3*, 11, 20
Center for Southwest Research: of University of New Mexico, 83
Chaco Canyon, xvii, 1, 2, *9*, 10, 11, 14, 138, 183; Albuquerque in, 201; architecture of, 152–53; Chetro Ketl great house of, *9*, *194*; complexity/growth/infrastructure (A.D. 1000–1140) in, 193–96; fall of (A.D. 1090–1140), 172, 196–98; farming/foraging/trading (A.D. 300–800) in, 181, 190–91; great houses of, 9, 88, 193–94; growth/surplus/market diversification (A.D. 800–1000) in, 191–93; lessons learned from, 175, 189–202; malnutrition in, 195; 1997 Nobel Prize of Economics comparison and, 197; Pueblo Bonito at, *153*; rivers/sustainable communities search (A.D. 1300–1500) and, 200–201; survival (A.D. 1500, now) of, 201–2; Toll on, 35; Uplands (A.D. 1140–1300) and, 198–200
chapalote (Mexican corn), 26
"Charter of the New Urbanism," 170, 182
Chenopodium (goosefoot), 38, 39
Chetro Ketl great house, of Chaco Canyon, *9*, *194*
Chihuahua, xx, 11, *12*, 20, 42
Chililí, 18, 83
chokecherries, 25
cholla cactus, 25
Chrysothamnus (rabbitbrush), 38
Chuska Mountains: Great Pit Structure at, 35
Clematis ligusticifolia (virgin's bower), 27
Cleome serrulata (beeweed), 37
Cliff Palace Community, *54*, 138, 151–52, *152*, 199; Sand Canyon Pueblo *vs.*, 52–53
cliffrose. *See Cowania neomexicana*
Colorado Plateau, 5, 8; Chaco/Aztec in, 13; pueblo ruins of, 8–9
Colter, Mary Jane, xviii; on Ancestral Puebloan landscape, 137–38; Arts and Crafts architecture and, 134; Desert View Watchtower by, 138–41; El Navajo hotel by, 142; Hermit's Rest by, 136; Hopi House by, 136; Hull and, 142; Indian Building at Alvarado Hotel design by, 135; Lookout Studio by, 136–37; Maier and, 142; as National Park Service architect, 133; Native American imagery and, 135; Schweizer and, 137
common reedgrass. *See Phragmites communis*
Concepción mission, 82
Conservation Design for Subdivisions (Arendt), 156
conservation land planning, 156–65; conservation area identification, 156–57; house sites designation in, 159, 161, *163*, *164*; information maps in, 157–59, *158*, *159*, *160*, *161*; information synthesis in, 159, *162*; lot line drawing in, 163–64, *164*, *165*; road layouts in, 161
Continental Divide, 89
Corispermum (bugseed), 37, 39
corn: adaptability of, 101; in Chaco Canyon, 190–91; cooking with, 96–97; Galinet on, 97; herbicide/insecticide use on, 99; hybridization of, 99–100; National Corn Growers Association on, 96; palaces of, 96, *97*; Pioneer Hi-Bred seed company for, 99; pollination of, 101–2; products of, 96. *See also Zea mays* (maize)
Cowania neomexicana (cliffrose), 37
Cowboy Wash, 41
Crow Canyon Archaeological Center, 6
Cucurbita pepo (squash, domestic), 37
cultural landscape: Morrow on, xvi; Pueblo roads in, 12; of Tewa people, 61
cultural relativism, 2

currants, 25, *25*
Cushing, Frank, 89
Cycloloma atriplicifolium (winged pigweed), 38, 39

Datura meteloides (Jimsonweed), 38
Dawes Act, 119
deBuys, William, 178
Dellenbaugh, Frederick S., *116*; on Hopi landscape, 114–17, *117*; Powell expedition and, 115
Desert View Watchtower, at Grand Canyon, *141*; Colter design of, 138–41; kiva of, 138, 140
Design with Nature (McHarg), 156
devil's claw, 66
A Dictionary of Landscape Architecture (Morrow), xvi
dogbane. *See Apocynum*
dropseed grass. *See Sporobolus*

Eagle Cage (Dellenbaugh), *116*
Echinocereus, 35
El Navajo hotel: Colter design of, 142
Enchantment and Exploitation (deBuys), 178
Espada mission, 82
Española Basin, 67, 68; of Tewa people, 61
Espinoso (Spiny) Creek, 18–19; Abó and, 20
Estancia (New Mexican Hacienda), 75–85; Acomilla, 77; at Las Majadas site, 77; of Pecos Mission, 77–78, *79*; as ranching/farming grant, 76; of San Antonio area, 82; at Sanchez site, 77, *78*; of Sandia Mission, 81–82; Texas recording of, 82, 83; trade connections of, 83; Velasco on, 76; von Wobeser on, 76
Estancia Acomilla (LA 286), 77
Estancia Zalazar, 26

Fausold, Charles, 155
Ferguson, T. J., 5
Fewkes, Jesse Walter, 118, 121
Final Report of Investigations among the Indians of the Southwestern United States (Bandelier), 9–10
5MT765. *See* Sand Canyon Pueblo
5MT10206, 41
5MT10207, 41
Four Corners tower forms, 138, 139
Fraxinus (ash), 37
Fred Harvey Company: Colter and, 133, 135; concessionaire architecture of, 141–42; Native American crafts and, 135

Galinet, Walton, 97
gardens: Abó pocket, 20–23; LA 503 size of, 22; Pecos Mission priests', *80*, *81*; of Quarai, *24*, 24–29; shrub-hollow, 27; of Tenabó, 22; of Tewa people, 65; vegetables of, 26; of Zuni, 180–81
Gaura, 38
globemallow. *See Sphaeralcea*
Good, Albert, 142
goosefoot. *See Chenopodium; quelites*
Graham, Ray, 155; as La Luz condominium developer, 146, 154
Grand Canyon: Desert View Watchtower at, 138–40, *141*; Hermit's Rest at, 136; Hopi House at, 136, *137*; Lookout Studio, 136–37, *138*
grape. *See Vitis arizonica*
The Grapes of Wrath (Steinbeck), 196
grass: *Muhlenbergia*, 19
The Great Drought, 13–14
Great North Road, 1, 12
Great Pit Structure, *36*, 40, 43; communal use for, 36; fire at, 36; at LA 61955 site, 35–40, *36*; plant species of, 37–38; roofing timbers of, *37*
groundcherry. *See Physalis*

hacienda: Offut on, 76; Taylor on, 76. *See also* Estancia (New Mexican Hacienda)
Hart, E. Richard, 5
A Harvest of Reluctant Souls (Benavides), 26
Harvey Company. *See* Fred Harvey Company
Hawken, Paul, 170, 176, 184
Hawkes, C. F., 58
Helianthus (sunflower), 38, 66, 88

Hemenway Southwestern Archaeological Expedition, 114; Fewkes and, 118; Stephen and, 118

Hermit's Rest, at Grand Canyon: Colter design of, 136

Hohokam, 5, 13

Hopi: akchin fields of, 100, *101*; Arthur and, 119; clan migration of, 117–18; Dawes Act for land division of, 119; as modern Pueblo people, 88; plant types of, 180–81; Stephen on, 118–22

Hopi House, at Grand Canyon, *137*; Colter design of, 136

Hopi landscape, narrative construction of, 113–23; Bender on, 113–14; Dellenbaugh on, 114–17, *117*; Johnson on, 113; Namingha on, 114; Stephen on, 114, 118–22; Wiki on, 114, 117–18

Hopitutsqua, as Hopi sacred land, 118

Hovenweep National Monument, 138, *139*

Hull, Daniel, 142

Indian Building, at Alvarado Hotel: Colter design of, 135

Indian ricegrass. *See Oryzopsis hymenoides*

Iowa State University: ZSAP of, 87

jacal structures, of Espinoso Creek, 19

Jackson, J. B.: of *Landscape* magazine, xv, xviii–xix

Jackson, Wes, 174, 179

Jemez River, 24

Jimsonweed. *See Datura meteloides*

Johnson, Hildegard Binder, 113

Jornada Mogollon irrigation ditch, 23

Juncaceae (rush family), 38

Juniper. *See Juniperus*

Juniperus (Juniper), 25, 38, 88, 105; woodland of, *174*

kiva: of Abó, 22; accesses in, 50; construction sequence of, 48–52, *49*, *51*; of Desert View Watchtower, 138, 140; functional space of, 51–52; of Sand Canyon Pueblo, 47–49, *48*, *49*; of Tenabo, 22

knotweed. *See Polygonum*

LA 286. *See* Estancia Acomilla

LA 503 garden size, 22

LA 591. *See* Las Majadas site

LA 20,000. *See* Sanchez site

LA 61955 site: Great Pit Structure at, 35–40, *36*; Sant as field director of, 35

"Ladder of Reference" (Hawkes), 58, 59, 60

Lake Estancia, 18; salt beds of, 24

La Luz condominiums, xviii, *148*, 182; emulation of, 154–55; Graham and, 154; Olmsted and, 155; by Predock, 146, 154; property value of, 146–47

Lamiaceae (mint family), 38

landscape: Abó ritual and, 22; cultural, xvi, 12; engineering, xix–xx, 173; as formula, xvi; Hopi narrative construction of, 113–23; Jackson on, xvi, xviii–xix; New Urbanism and, 169; Tewa agricultural, 57–61, *62*, 65–68. *See also* Ancestral Puebloan landscape

Landscape, xv

Landscape magazine, xv, xviii–xix

La Purísima Concepción de Quarai, 28

Las Majadas site (LA 591), 77, *77*

LeBlanc, Steven, 7

Lilieholm, Robert J., 155

Lincoln Institute of Land Policy Research Paper (Fausold/Lilieholm), 155

Long-term Capital Management, 197

Lookout Studio, at Grand Canyon, *138*; Colter design by, 136–37

Lovins, Armory, 170, 176, 184

Lovins, L. Hunter, 170, 176, 184

Lycium/wolfberry, 34

Lyndon, Donlyn, 174, 179

macaws, 27, 194; of Casas Grandes, 20

Maier, Ed, 142

maize. *See Zea mays*

The Man Who Killed the Deer (Waters), 139

Manzano Peak, 21

McElmo Dome, 46

McHarg, Ian, xvii, 156

Mentzelia (blazingstar), 37
Merton, Robert, 196
Mesa Verde, 2, 14, 138, *140*, 198; architecture of, 151–52; cliff dwellings of, 8; community centers in, 41. *See also* Sand Canyon Pueblo
Mesa Verde National Park: Nusbaum and, 142
Mesoamerica, 11, 14
Mexican corn. *See chapalote*
migration, 4, 117–18; Reid on, 6
Mina-Coya: Old Salt Woman of Jemez country legend, 24
mint family. *See* Lamiaceae
Mississippian chiefdoms, 14; Anderson on, 11
mobility: Berry on, 5; long term, 5; seasonal, 4–5
Moki Indian (Dellenbaugh), *117*
Montezuma Valley, of Colorado, 18, 46, 151, 156
Morrow, Baker, xvi
Muenchrath, Deb: as corn physiologist, 88; Zuni project of, 94–95
Muhlenbergia grasses, 19
Mute Stone Bench case: of Abó, 20

Namingha, Dan, 114
Nassauer, Joan Iverson, 174
National Corn Growers Association, 96
National Park Service, 142; Albright on planning process for, 143; Good and, 142; Hull and, 142; Maier and, 142; New Deal and, 143
National Science Foundation: on Zuni, 88
Native Science (Cajete), 174
Natural Capitalism (Hawken/Lovins/Lovins), 170, 176, 184
New Mexico: ranches of, 75
New Mexico Organic Commodities Commission, 95
New Urbanism, 182; Ancestral Puebloan landscapes and, 169; charter of, 170
New Urbanism design agenda: blockages creation and, 185; culture/landscape and, 185; encircling and, 183–84; landscape as guide in, 184; redundancy in, 183; site protection in, 183; sunlight and, 182–83; water conservation and, 184–85
New World: archaeology/native history of, 4
Nicotiana attenuata (tobacco), 38, 66
1997 Nobel Prize in Economics, 196
Nuestra Señora de los Ángeles de Pecos (Pecos Mission), 77–78, *79*; buildings of, 80; priests' garden of, *80*, *81*
Nusbaum, Jesse, 142

oak. *See Quercus*
Offut, Leslie, 76
Olmsted, Frederick Law, Jr., 135, 155
Opuntia (prickly pear cactus), 38, 41, 66, 105
Oraibi Pueblo, 2, 8, 9
orchards, 26; Zuni peach, *105*, 105–6, *106*
Oryzopsis hymenoides (Indian ricegrass), 22, 25, 26, 136

paleoethnobotanist, 33
Paquimé. *See* Casas Grandes
Park and Recreation Structures (Good), 142
parrots, 12; of Casas Grandes, 20
Parthenocissus inserta (woodbine), 27
Patterns of Culture (Benedict), 2, 6
Pecos Mission. *See* Nuestra Señora de los Ángeles de Pecos
A People's Ecology (Cajete), 174
Perea, Estévan de (Fray), 83
Phaseolus vulgaris (bean, domestic), 37, 42
Phragmites communis (common reedgrass), 37, 38
Physalis (groundcherry), 25, 38
piñon nuts. *See Pinus edulis*
Pinus edulis (piñon nuts), 25, 38, 88, 104–5
Pinus ponderosa (ponderosa pine), 36, 38
Pioneer Hi-Bred seed company, 99
Places magazine: Lyndon and, 174, 179
Placing Nature (Nassauer), 174
Pleistocene Era, 18
pocket gardens: of Abó, 20–23
Polygonum (knotweed), 38
ponderosa pine. *See Pinus ponderosa*
Portulaca (purslane), 38

Powell, John Wesley: Dellenbaugh and, 115
Predock, Antoine, xviii, 155, 182; La Luz condominium design by, 146, 154
prickly pear cactus. *See Opuntia*
"The Primary Architecture of the Chacoan Culture" (Sofaer), 152
Prudden, T. Mitchell, 46
Puebloan architecture: impermanence of, 8; permanence of, 2, 8–9
Pueblo Bonito, 9, *10*, *191*, 192, *195*, 200; at Chaco Canyon, *153*
Pueblo I, 35
Pueblo II, 39, 41, 46
Pueblo III, 39, 40, 41, 46, 55
Pueblo Pardo, 18
Pueblo Revolt of 1680, xx, 83
Pueblos: mobility of, 3; violence at, 7, 13
Pueblo Seco, 18
purslane. *See Portulaca*

Quarai, 83; berry gardens of, *24*, 24–29; corn/beans/squash of, 22, 28–29; currant/sand plums of, *25*; implements/tools of, *27*; map of, *18*; orchards of, 26; Perea of, 83; plants of, 25; priest's garden of, *26*; red sandstone of, *27*; terrace gardens of, *27*; Tiwa people of, 17, 19; Zapato Creek of, 18
quelites (goosefoot), 22, 25
Quercus (oak), 38

rabbitbrush. *See Chrysothamnus*
Red Mesa Valley, 195–96
Reid, Jefferson, 6
Rio Grande valley, 59; estancias of, 81
Rio Rancho city, 149–50, 155, 185; AMREP and, 149–50; deficient flood control at, 149–50
River's Edge I housing development, *147*; in Albuquerque, NM, 147; by AMREP Southwest Inc., 146; open space of, 155–56; property value of, 146–47
Rohn, Arthur, 47
rush family. *See* Juncaceae
Ruskin, John, 135

Salinas Pueblo Missions National Monument, xix, 17, 80
Salix (willow), 38
saltbush. *See Atriplex*
San Antonio area: estancias of, 82
Sanchez site (LA 20,000), 77, *78*
Sand Canyon Pueblo (5MT765), 45–56; Cliff Palace Community *vs.*, 52–53; kiva suite of, 47–49, *48*, *49*; location of, *46*; plan map of, *47*
sand dropseed, 22, 26, 146
Sandia Mission, 81–82
sand plums, 25, *25*
San Gregorio, church of, 20
San Juan Basin, 59, 192–93, 193, 198
San Juan mission, 82
Santa Clara Day School, 125–32; atmosphere of, 129; of BIA, 125; location of, 128–29; Pueblo *vs.*, 130–32; western education influence on, 128–31
Santa Clara Pueblo, xviii, *129*; life at, 126–27; location of, 126
Sant, Mark: La 61955 field director, 35
"Sayataca's Night Chant," 42
Scholes, Myron, 196
Schweizer, Herman, *140*; Colter and, 137
Serrano, Luis Martín (don), 83
serviceberry, 25
Sha'lak'o celebration, of Zuni, 98
Sleeping Ute Mountain: archaeological sites of, 41
Smithsonian Bureau of Ethnology, 106
snakeweed, 105
Sofaer, Anna, 152
Spanish Mission architecture, 134, 135
Sphaeralcea (globemallow), 38
Sporobolus (dropseed grass), 38
squash, domestic. *See Cucurbita pepo*
Steinbeck, John, 196
Stephen, A. M., 114; as Hopi advocate, 119–21; on Hopi political landscape, 114, 118–22
Stuart, David, xvii, 172
sugar maple. *See Acer saccharum*
sunflower. *See Helianthus*
Swentzell, Rina, 174, 175–76, 178–79

Tabirá, 18

Tajique, 83
Taylor, Walter, 76
Tedlock, Dennis, 89
Tenabó: garden size of, 22; kivas of, 22; Manzano Peak, 21
Tewa people, 57–73; as agrarian communities, 58; agricultural landscapes of, 57–61, *62*, 65–68; agricultural tools/stone implements of, 62, *63*; cultural landscape of, 61; Española Basin and, 61; grid gardens of, *65*; paleoclimatic studies of, 61; religious beliefs of, 64–65; Santa Clara Pueblo of, 126; water conservation of, 63–64, *64*, 66
Thoreau, Henry David, 134
Tiwa people, 17, 18; corn/squash/bean crops of, 26–27
tobacco. *See Nicotiana attenuata*
Tohono O'odham: Muenchrath on, 99
Toll, Mollie, 35, 37
tomatillos, 25
Tompiro people, 18
Tonto Basin of Arizona: archaeological project of, 6
tropical birds: at Aztec/Chaco Canyon/Paquimé, 11

United States: Pueblo architecture in, 2; Zuni lawsuit against, 5–6, 89–92
University of New Mexico: Center for Southwest Research of, 83

Varien, Mark, 40
Velasco, Luis de (Viceroy), 76
Vergara, Gabriel de (Fray), 82
Villa de Santa Fe, 75
Vint, Thomas, 143
virgin's bower. *See Clematis ligusticifolia*
Vitis arizonica (grape), 27
volcanic eruption, 13
von Wobeser, Gisela, 76

water conservation: New Urbanism design agenda and, 184–85; of Tewa people, 63–64, *64*, 66; of Zuni, 100–101
Waters, Frank, 139
wheat, 27
White House, 12; mass execution at, 13
Wiki: as chief priest of Hopi Antelope Society, 117; on Hopi moral landscape, 117–18; as Hopi religious leader, 114
willow. *See Salix*
winged pigweed. *See Cycloloma atriplicifolium*
wolfberries, 25
woodbine. *See Parthenocissus inserta*
Woods' rose, 25
Wupatki, 13

Yucca, 38

Zalazar, Catharina de (doña), 83
Zapato "Shoe" Creek, 19, 26–27; of Quarai, 18
ZCP. *See* Zuni Conservation Project
Zea mays (maize), 38, 41, 65; of Zuni, 87–111; Zuni evolution and, 102–3
ZSAP. *See* Zuni Sustainable Agriculture Project
Zuni: aboriginal land of, 89–90; Benedict on, 2; Black People battle with, 7; Black Rock Dam and, 91–92; Cushing and, 89; egalitarianism of, 8; garden cultivation by, 180–81; government dam/irrigation projects and, 91; land erosion of, 90; lawsuit against U.S. government, 5–6, 89–92; maize, 87–111, *93*, *96*, 102–3; migration of, 6; as modern Pueblo people, 88; Muenchrath on, 94–95; National Science Foundation on, 88; peach orchard of, *105*, 105–6, *106*; political structure of, 8; prayer of, 107; ritual poetry of, 42; Sha'lak'o celebration of, 98; Tedlock and, 89; water conservation by, 100–101
The Zuni Atlas (Ferguson/Hart), 5
Zuni Ceremonialism, 107
Zuni Conservation Project (ZCP), 91
Zuni Sustainable Agriculture Project (ZSAP), xix, 87, 92, 95, 103–4, 106

www.ingramcontent.com/pod-product-compliance
Lightning Source LLC
Chambersburg PA
CBHW020702270326
41928CB00005B/225